T0340053

Value-creation in Middle Market
Private Equity

To my girls for being awesome, inspirational, and supportive.
You are the joy of my life!

To Mama Pate and Hud for being the grandparents who made the difference
for this kid. I'm doing alright!

Value-creation in Middle Market Private Equity

JOHN A. LANIER

Routledge
Taylor & Francis Group

LONDON AND NEW YORK

First published 2015 by Gower Publishing

2 Park Square, Milton Park, Abingdon, Oxfordshire OX14 4RN
52 Vanderbilt Avenue, New York, NY 10017

Routledge is an imprint of the Taylor & Francis Group, an informa business

First issued in paperback 2019

British Library Cataloguing in Publication Data
A catalogue record for this book is available from the British Library

ISBN 978-1-4724-4445-5 (hbk)
ISBN 978-0-367-87979-2 (pbk)

Library of Congress Cataloging-in-Publication Data
Lanier, John A.
  Value creation in middle market private equity / by John A. Lanier.
    pages cm
  Includes bibliographical references and index.
  ISBN 978-1-4724-4445-5 (hardback)
  1. Private equity funds. 2. Small business--Finance. I. Title.
  HG4751.L36 2015
  332.63'2044--dc23

                                                          2014029595

Contents

List of Figures

List of Tables

Foreword

My perspective on private equity is multifaceted. I am a managing director in a private equity firm, Patriot Capital in Dallas. Additionally, I am also an adjunct lecturer for the MBA program at Southern Methodist University's Cox School of Business. Moreover, I am a member of the entrepreneurial fraternity, including multiple responsibilities for Heelys, the innovative children's skate shoe company: founding Chairman, start-up financing, and initial public offering.

Private equity is a significant contributor to a healthy economy in at least two respects. First, private equity is a source of capital for entrepreneurs to accelerate the growth and sustainability of their businesses. Of course, this comes with a multiplier effect that includes ever improving products and services for customers, job creation and career advancement for employees of such businesses, and taxes paid to support society. Second, private equity provides an attractive return on capital to investors, many of whom are pension funds—busily managing the retirement assets of working class Americans. This second point is particularly relevant given the surge in Baby Boomer retirement.

Just as any business, private equity develops and refines its processes to accomplish efficiencies and differentiation. Additionally, the better private equity firms encourage the same among their portfolio companies. The rhetorical question is how this may be best done. The better firms accomplish this by practicing what they preach, and providing a roadmap for their portfolio companies that makes sense—from the portfolio companies' perspective. This latter point is all too easily underestimated, yet is the essence of a healthy working relationship between private equity firms and their portfolio companies, whose objective is mutually gratifying results.

The private equity business model creates value in three ways: (1) financial engineering, i.e., deleveraging the portfolio company post-acquisition; (2) employing multiple arbitrage, i.e., exiting the investment at a multiple of cash flow higher than was paid at inception; and (3) enhancing the performance, i.e., cash flow, of the business during the investment hold period. I met the author of this book providentially at a Dallas/Ft. Worth Private Equity Forum event whose focus was private equity operating partners' change agency role for the all-important third leg of value-creation. John Lanier was one of the panelists. The subsequent cultivation of our acquaintance included my discovery of the alignment between his professional focus and academic endeavors. At the time, he was in the homestretch of a doctoral program. I invited him to lecture to my MBA class on customer service.

The upshot of our encounter is that he understands entrepreneurial value-creation in the private equity dynamic. Additionally, if my students are any indication, he possesses the ability to captivate the curiosity of those who may learn from his experiences. The fact that he could relate to my students as a fellow adult learner who had trod a similar path positioned him as an empathetic protagonist.

Before joining Excellere Partners, a private equity firm in Denver and former consulting client, John supported several private equity firms over an eight year period through a consultancy he founded called Middle Market Methods. This was an extension of six previous years in similar operational excellence endeavors in private equity. John's objective as a consultant was developing the 80/20 toolbox for chronic private equity value-creation challenges.

The evolution of the Middle Market toolbox resulted in a loyal following of clients, proselytized by results rooted in his advocated methodologies. The beauty of the methodology is rooted in two criteria: simplicity and universality. Whereas there are bookshelves full of intriguing topics for a myriad of value-creation topics, this book pulls together the holistic framework for how private equity firms and their portfolio companies may accentuate value-creation. There is only one catch: it takes commitment by all stakeholders to realize the full potential, but such is the case with all change.

You may rightly ask why I would endorse a book that our competitors may read. There are three simple reasons. First, we want the private equity industry, and in particular those businesses supported by them, to prosper because it is good for the economy and society. Second, we want to help entrepreneurs ask good questions in vetting their investment partners. And third, it is far more economical to share his book with my portfolio company managers than to hire John to implement the book's secret sauce!

Enjoy these pages as you follow John's insightful and entertaining demystification of private equity's value-creation principles, strategies, and tactics.

Patrick F. Hamner
Managing Director, Patriot Capital
Adjunct Lecturer, Cox School of Business, Southern Methodist University
Dallas, Texas

Preface

Career milestones and points of inflection sometimes appear in interesting packages at unexpected moments. My first professional job was in selling. I was mentored by some great sales people, but did not experience formal training in a sales technique until long after selling ceased as my primary focus. I was pretty good at sales (thanks to my mentors). Even so, upon exposure to sales technique training, I reflectively speculated how much better I could have been with the additional edge inherent in formal training. I encountered an analogous epiphany for the power of professional marketing. Along the way I also enjoyed some excellent credit and financial analysis training.

My next career phase entailed process improvement. There was a symbiotic relationship between the bean counting and process flow that I discovered quite valuable. Part of the change-management strategy of process improvement is demonstrating the cost-benefit tangibles. I had the opportunity to develop process improvement skills first in the reengineering era, and later with Six Sigma at GE. Lean manufacturing principles followed. I mix and mingle from all three.

I owe GE a great debt of gratitude. It was through their "At the Customer, For the Customer" initiative called *Access GE* that I first encountered private equity. Indeed, when I was in *Access GE*, a majority of the engagements were in support of private equity portfolio companies. All total, the private equity trek covers the last 12 years as both an outside consultant and inside-the-firm value-creation resource.

During my private equity career (third) phase, I discovered a latent teaching gene, perhaps honestly inherited through my mother, a retired college professor. Coaching portfolio companies is a fulfilling outlet. My passion is helping entrepreneurial Davids of free enterprise slay all manner of Goliaths. Indeed, the small guys have to do so in order for our economy to thrive. Unfortunately, they do not get the credit due them, but true to their character, they do not mope about it. Rather, they more productively resolve to slay another Goliath—and thankfully so.

To punctuate my credentials during the private equity phase, I earned an MBA and a Doctorate in Strategic Leadership. Both were beneficial to the genesis of this book—indeed a bucket list aspirations all. The best practices covered in the book reflect a personal odyssey of lessons learned, both from mistakes and successes. The successes not substantiated by research were culled, as luck is not a basis for recommendations.

Perhaps the single most valuable thing I have learned in my career is that those who embrace change as an opportunity have an inherent edge on the world. My fondest desire is for portfolio company teams and their private equity sponsors to find something accretive in these pages worthy of assimilation to bolster their individually tailored brands of value-creation. By the way, the best practices also work for independent small businesses. Indeed, by adopting them for their own purposes, they not only improve their enterprise value, but also enhance their succession and estate planning options.

Reviews for
Value-creation in Middle Market Private Equity

John has taken stock of the lessons learned in his many years of real world experience and distilled them into a useful and pragmatic synthesis in this book. It is refreshing to see the attention paid to many topics often overlooked and underappreciated as value levers in investing.

Ric Andersen, Milestone Partners, USA

When I first met John, I suggested that we were separated at birth. In working with John several times thereafter, I realized he is the smarter twin. This book needs to be open on every PE firm's deal team desks. IT diligence, hiring the right people, viewpoint gaps between the firm's financial and operating members… I could go on and on. Read this book. It will change how you create value.

Lloyd Rogers, Riverside Partners, USA

Building best-in-class companies in the middle market, while creating greater shareholder value, is both challenging and rewarding. This book contains many of the principles that Excellere Partners embraces in its own value-creation partnership model, and for good reason. We worked with John Lanier for a dozen years—seven as his client before asking him to become our partner. Creating value requires a tremendous amount of strategic thinking, coupled with a disciplined process to execute strategic initiatives—this is done to strengthen the company's foundation that will support significant future growth. This book is a gift for framing a value-creation model to both private equity firms and the companies in which they invest.

Robert A. Martin, Excellere Partners, USA

Chapter 1

Introduction

The only true wisdom is in knowing you know nothing.[1]

Small business is the job creating engine in the US economy. Private equity investment is a significant source of small business capital. Both the small businesses in which private equity firms invest, and the private equity firms making the investments, face intra-company leadership challenges as they grow. Moreover, there are inter-company leadership challenges. The fiduciary responsibilities of the private equity firm necessitate an activist board role. This posture carries over into the portfolio company's daily operations.

The complexities continue. Individual private equity professionals are typically members of multiple investment teams for the firm. The teams may be characterized by mixed membership, as the investment teams may not be identical across the portfolio companies they support. Not only may each investment team have its own unique leadership style, but its diverse members have to assimilate styles for each team they support relative to a specific portfolio company.

Finally, acquisitions are high probability scenarios for portfolio companies during the investment hold period. Acquisition integration poses yet another leadership challenge as the acquiree must be integrated into the acquiring company. Cultural integration ranks among the most chronic acquisition obstacles. Given the leveraged (debt-heavy) capital structure of portfolio companies, the cost of a misstep is painful. Accordingly, the stakeholders of private equity transactions do well to embrace leadership best practices in their value-creation toolbox, especially with regard to the more chronic challenges of value-creation in the middle market.

The objective of this book is imparting holistic value-creation best practices gleaned from working with both private equity investment professionals and their portfolio companies. Each stakeholder encampment possesses accretive core competencies. However, both have room for improvement in how they: (i) perceive each other; and (ii) collaborate with each other to realize the shared objective of value-creation. As with many solutions to puzzles, the essence of a challenge must be distilled to its fundamental elements before root causes are clear and viable solutions are embraced by constituents. This odyssey fares better when complexity is displaced with simplicity. Such is the aim of this book.

What is Private Equity?

The most important single about a free market is that no exchange takes place unless both parties benefit.[2]

The objective of this section is to provide a basic explanation of private equity to non-investment professionals. Beginning in the Clinton administration, the term "investor class" was brandished to explain that the majority of households own public equities. This tends to be in the form of their workplace 401k or some similar vehicle. These 401K investment options include a menu of various mutual funds. For example, Fidelity Magellan is one of the most renowned mutual funds. Individuals and corporations may contribute to the fund. Professional investors manage the fund. Funds have different investment personalities. For example, Morningstar, a popular fund rating medium, classifies funds as domestic stock, international stock, municipal bond, and taxable bond.[3]

Private equity mirrors a similar model to mutual funds—but predominantly "privately," that is to say, not on a traded exchange. This means that access to this option is not open to the general public. Private equity and venture capital investors are different. Whereas private equity investments tend to be with established companies with appetizing growth prospects, venture capital investors pursue start-ups or early-stage businesses.[4]

Private equity firm organizational structure may be more easily defined in legal terms than in managerial terms.[5] The mechanics are as follows:[6]

- A private equity firm tends to have a legal status as general partner of a limited partnership that manages a fund on behalf of investors.

- "Fund raising" entails a targeted amount of money for a specific fund, e.g., $400 million. The private equity firm solicits potential limited partners whose individual commitments total the size of the fund. The commitment lasts upwards of 10 years, i.e., the life of the fund. The typical private equity portfolio company investment lasts about five years.

- Private equity firms typically manage several funds whose lives overlap.

- The limited partners tend to be institutional investors and wealthy individuals.

- The private equity general partner, on behalf of the fund limited partnership, pursues investments in attractive opportunities. The investments may be controlling or minority.

- Size of prospect and industry vertical are other common distinguishing characteristics. The term "industry vertical" regards the preferred industry in which a particular private equity firm specializes and prefers for investment. Private equity firms tend to invest in more than one industry vertical.

- The true focus for investment professionals is EBITDA (earnings before interest, taxes, depreciation, and amortization) as a measure of cash flow.[7] Private equity transactions are sometimes described as leveraged buyouts (LBOs) because of the substantial amount of associated indebtedness. Free cash flow is a key variable in determining the amount of debt the company can support in the capital structure. Accordingly, the private equity firm would much prefer a smaller sales volume with a strong EBITDA margin than a large sales volume with a modest EBITDA margin.

- Firms earn a modest maintenance fee on the fund; however, this is not how the firm makes the bulk of their income. Rather, the firm participates in the gain—when the investment is sold—after the limited partners experience a minimum return threshold. The maintenance fee is reimbursed to the limited partners from the firm's share of capital gains.

- An "investment thesis" encapsulates the private equity firm's objective for the portfolio company investment.[8] "Investment thesis" and "strategy" are functionally interchangeable terms.

Private equity may be considered among the poster children of agency theory. The firm investment professionals may accomplish significant economic rewards for producing attractive financial returns for the fund limited partners. These returns commonly eclipse the returns of blue chip stocks traded on the New York Stock Exchange. However, the investment professionals' agency may be considered holistically beyond financial engineering. Keen focus is applied to fiduciary responsibilities. Private equity firms manage investments by proxy through their portfolio company leadership teams. This is one of the things that make private equity so fascinating. Not only does the firm have to execute its business model functions effectively, but the firm's ultimate success is predominantly reliant on its influence over the leadership of the portfolio companies creating the enterprise value for the fund's (and its limited partners') benefit. Therefore, a Sword of Damocles scenario looms omnipresent. Private equity firms are only as good as their last fund's performance. Thus, the pressure to produce results never subsides.

A sample of salient statistics substantiate the economic impact of private equity:

- Private equity firms manage an estimated global asset value of $2 trillion.[9] Prequin defines "assets under management" as "the uncalled capital commitments (dry powder) plus the unrealized value of portfolio assets."[10]

- In 2013, private equity firms consummated 2410 transactions. Fifty three percent of these were add-on acquisitions to existing private equity portfolio companies.[11] Using the "middle market" definition of $5–$25 million of EBITDA rationalized later in this chapter, and applying Bain & Company's average transaction valuation EBITDA multiple of 4.7,[12] this corresponds to approximately half of all 2013 private equity investment transactions.

- At the end of 2013, 2797 US private equity firms comprised $426 billion in equity investment across 17,744 companies employing 7.5 million people.[13]

- The 2797 firms referenced above are in excess of half the 5200 estimated active global private equity investors.[14]

- Private equity portfolio companies employ approximately 6.5 percent of the 115.5 million 2013 year-ending private sector workforce.[15]

- "Through 2012, private equity funds worldwide have distributed more than $1.4 trillion to limited partner investors."[16]

- "As of September 2013, private equity outperformed the S&P 500 Index by 1.0 percentage points and 6.6 percentage points for the five- and ten-year periods."[17]

- In 2011, approximately 150 public employee pension funds invested about $220 billion, or 11 percent of their assets in private equity. The pension funds actually *increased* their relative holdings from 8.6 percent.[18]

- "The biggest investors in private equity include public and private pension funds, endowments and foundations, which account for 64 percent of all investment in private equity in 2012."[19] The rationale is pretty simple. The pension funds have to achieve a minimum threshold in anticipation of cash outflows. The higher yielding private equity investments have to be in the mix to make up for the lower yields common to highly liquid, lower risk securities.

- The Private Equity Growth Council cites a 2011 Prequin Ltd. Report to state that "the 20 largest public pension funds for which data are available (including the California Public Employees' Retirement System, the California State Teachers' Retirement System, the New York State Common Retirement Fund, and the Florida State Board of Administration) allocated approximately $224 billion to private equity investment, delivering strong investment returns to their 10.5 million beneficiaries."[20]

- "A review of 146 public pension funds across the US found that private equity delivered a 10.0 percent median 10-year annualized return to pension funds, outperforming the returns of other asset classes (fixed income, listed equity and real estate)."[21]

Even the federal government is a private equity player through the Small Business Administration's (SBA) Small Business Investment Company (SBIC) program:

- SBICs are a type of private equity firm that is licensed by the SBA.

- The SBIC program raises capital by issuing SBA guaranteed, publicly offered, ten-year debentures.

- The debentures may comprise up to three times the SBIC's fund base.

- SBICs are limited to specifically-defined small businesses.

- "At the end of FY 2011, the SBA had over $8.2 billion invested in 299 funds. Together with private capital of approximately $8.8 billion, the program totals over $17 billion in capital resources dedicated to America's entrepreneurs."[22]

The World Economic Forum offers the following descriptors for private equity controlled investments (portfolio companies):

- A majority of private equity transactions are now outside of the United States.

- Innovation and intellectual property is more prevalent in private equity investments.

- Governance is flexible.

- Management is better, particularly from an operational perspective. Consequently, year over year efficiencies outpace industry peers. The gains tend to result in higher wages without reducing profitability.

- Job reductions tend to be proximal to post-close (probably to reduce extraneous costs). Thereafter, greenfield hires, or new hires from growth, tend to be more robust than industry peers. There is less employment disruption in private equity investments than industry vertical peers. This may be at least partially due to private equity investment emphasis in healthy industries.

- Acquisition and divestiture is more active (probably to accomplish a more refined strategic focus for the business model).

- Private equity firms are economic catalysts, or change agents, for their investment verticals. Target market industry verticals also tend to grow quicker in terms of production, employment, and value-creation.[23]

The story is compelling. Small business leaders pursued by private equity investors are receiving a genuine complement. Not only does such interest attest to achievements to date, but also prospects for the future. The private equity-portfolio company tandem accelerates value-creation and buoys employment. Accordingly, private equity is a valuable contributor to the global economy.

What is the "Middle Market?"

It's not the size of the dog in the fight, it's the size of the fight in the dog.[24]

The middle market lacks an academic definition. "By general consensus, the middle market comprises businesses with revenue between $5 million and $1 billion."[25] This cuts a wide swath through the economy. Consequently, the middle market is sub-segmented into lower, middle, and upper. Active investors in the middle market may offer different definitions, perhaps in deference to their particular investment perspective and branding strategy. Contrary to a layman's use of revenue as a criterion for market segmentation, private equity investors tend to regard revenue as a secondary gauge. The preferred criterion is EBITDA—a measure of cash flow. As argued above, the EBITDA benchmark pertains to the ability to service the debt in a leveraged capital structure. The amount of debt in the capital structure varies relative to the general health of the economy. However, this is but one material variable affecting capital structure. Debt for a middle market private equity portfolio company approximates two-thirds of the capital structure during stable economic cycles and may dip to about half during recessionary periods.[26]

EBITDA is not a Generally Accepted Accounting Practice (GAAP) line item in the standard income statement presentation of an audit. An analyst has to derive EBITDA from the income statement, sources and uses of fund statements, and footnotes in an audit. Audits themselves may be problematic to the lower middle market prospects. Some businesses may be auditing the books for the first time as a condition of the private equity investment. Up to that point, these entrepreneurs may have eschewed the audit expense in favor of compilations or reviews. Compilations merely compile the numbers in a standardized format without any opinion as to their veracity. Reviews have a bit more rigor, but typically stop short of inventory scrutiny and other more strenuous financial tests.

The lower middle market is defined by EBITDA of $500 thousand to $15 million. The middle range of the middle market is defined by EBITDA from $15–$50 million.[27] For purposes of this book, we will stick between the lower and middle sub-segments of the middle market for a relative sweet spot of $5–$25 million in EBITDA. The impact of the middle market on the economy may be more clearly comprehended using the Small Business Administration's (SBA) statistics for "small businesses" (firm's with fewer than 500 employees):

- There are 22.9 million small businesses.

- These businesses constitute 99.7 percent (by number of entities) of US employer firms.

- Small businesses create 64 percent of net new private-sector jobs.

- Small entities constitute 49.2 percent of private-sector employment and cover 42.9 percent of private-sector payroll.

- Small organizations account for 46 percent of private-sector output, 43 percent of high-tech employment, 98 percent of exported goods, and 33 percent of exported value.

- Half of small business startups survive at least five years. One-third of them survive at least 10 years.[28]

Entrepreneurism and Value-creation

What is not started will never get finished.[29]

Both the leaders of private equity portfolio companies and the investment professionals of the private equity firm fit the entrepreneurial profile. Accordingly, the foundational common denominator should be vetted. As will be made clear in the course of the book, both groups of stakeholders apply entrepreneurism through different prisms. Even so, the convergence of these interests is necessary to enhance value-creation.

Peter Drucker imparted great wisdom encapsulated in these three points:

- the purpose of a business is to create and keep a customer,

- the customer rarely buys what the business thinks it is selling to them, and

- the best way to predict the future is to create it.[30]

Small business entrepreneurs are an integral subset of value-creation protagonists.

> *An entrepreneur is an individual who takes agency and initiative; who assumes responsibility and ownership for making things happen; is both open to and able to create novelty; who manages risk attached to the process; and who has the persistence to see things through to some identified end-point, even when faced with obstacles and difficulty.*[31]

Entrepreneurial actions are often instinctual. Making a sale is an entrepreneur's preferred personal validation in lieu of exhaustive research.[32] Entrepreneurs learn by doing. Mistakes may be corrected and overcome by speed and agility. Entrepreneurs:

- "connect different markets," e.g., build supply chains across geographical regions;

- exploit "market deficiencies," e.g., delivering product to an underserved segment;

- create, and are responsible for, "time-binding" through implicit or explicit contractual arrangements; and/or

- complete components, or inputs through an organizational structure, i.e., combine raw materials in a differentiable configuration.[33]

"An entrepreneur is one who creates a new business in the face of risk and uncertainty for the purpose of achieving profit and growth opportunities, and assembles the necessary resources to capitalize on those opportunities."[34] Entrepreneurial traits include:

- desire for responsibility,

- preference for moderate risk,

- confidence in the ability to succeed,

- appetite for immediate feedback,

- stamina and high energy level,

- futuristic vision,

- organizational skills,

- achievement over economic rewards,

- passionate commitment,

- tolerance of ambiguity,

- resolve for accomplishment,

- flexibility, and

- tenacity.[35]

Essentially, entrepreneurs are calculated risk takers. Collectively, entrepreneurs comprise the special forces warrior-class of capitalists. Two-thirds of all jobs are created by small business.[36] From the spectator seats, small business entrepreneurs seemingly defy gravity, that is to say entrepreneurs seem unaware that their feats of ingenuity are beyond the realm of possibilities. Their modus operandi may entail repeating a proven business model, such as a franchise, or commencing a startup. "A startup is a new business venture in its earliest stage of development."[37] The stakes are steeper for startups. One third of startups fail in their first two years; by year four the number is four-fifths.[38]

Small business entrepreneurs are lovable economic mutants. If a perceived market is not served—or is under-served, the value-creating process is sparked. Such perceptions of opportunity may be catalyzed by an economic "externality." An externality occurs "when the actions of one party affect the well-being or production possibilities of another party outside an exchange relationship. Externalities can prevent a free market from being efficient."[39] Governments are frequently the wellsprings of externalities. However well-intentioned legislation (and consequent regulation) may be, the results have predictably unintended consequences, exacerbated by politicos' inability to admit and correct their mistakes.

The prevailing United States healthcare architecture is a prime example of the unintended consequences of externalities whose roots are arguably traceable to wage and price controls imposed on the World War II economy. Producers competed amid labor shortages by offering "free" healthcare. This established a precedent for consumers to misinterpret healthcare as different from any other good or service of finite quantity—especially in terms of its cost. Progressive policy wonks, civil servants, and elected officials exacerbated this perspective by positioning healthcare as a rightful entitlement, mysteriously paid by someone else. The "someone else" is now the unborn who will inherit swelling national debt resulting from costs exceeding tax revenues. The trajectory of US healthcare is toward socialized medicine. Former British Prime Minister Margaret Thatcher encapsulated the conundrum succinctly: "The problem with socialism is that you eventually run out of other people's money."[40]

The Affordable Care Act (ACA) is likely to follow tradition as another salvo of government induced externality. Externality analysts may be amused that the same government that "manages" Fannie Mae, Freddie Mac, Amtrak, and the Post Office now controls one sixth of the US economy. Although ACA is amid implementation transition as of this writing, the Congressional Budget Office is already reporting that the legislation does not bend the cost curve and will be more—not less—expensive than what the bill purported to fix. ACA will likely catalyze unforeseen market mutations.[41] For example, smaller companies are already tinkering with part-time employment status and the 50 headcount workforce threshold to avoid the costs of ACA.

Comparing small business entrepreneurs to the Fortune 500 is like comparing a speed boat in the ocean to a battleship in a bathtub. For numerous reasons (that this book will explore), one brandishes agile and quick actions that the other finds difficult to fathom, much less execute. The larger companies employ lobbyists to influence the economic externalities to their favor. In some instances they have to do so. Large companies face a mathematical leviathan. A new product has to be nearly gigantic to make a difference to its profitability.

Consider the pharmaceutical giant Merck, number 58 on the 2013 Fortune 500. Figures from Merck's 2013 10-K annual report filed with the US Securities and Exchange Commission (SEC) will be used.[42] Merck's 2013 net profits were $4.5 billion on sales of $44.0 billion. In order for a growth initiative, for example, a new drug and/or new market, to impress analysts, the results have to make a material influence on earnings. Suppose this figure is a 10 percent increase in earnings, or $450 million for Merck. At Merck's 2013 level of after tax profitability of 10.3 percent, that constitutes approximately $4.4 billion in sales. This is a tall order. Comparatively, Januvia, a diabetic drug, is Merck's top selling product at slightly over $4 billion in revenue, or 9.1 percent of total revenue.

Merck has another problem. It takes a long time to usher a new drug through clinical trials for Food and Drug Administration approval—and that is just the US regulatory labyrinth. Presently, patent protection for this type of intellectual property lasts 20 years from its invention. However, the prerequisite clinical trials time eats into those 20 years. Clinical trials prior to final approval for sale may literally take up to 15 of those 20 years[43] at an average cost of $1.2 billion.[44]

Merck's challenges continue. The US tax code is generally progressive (higher tax rates apply to incremental income levels), but very complicated with numerous mitigating provisions. Accordingly, the highest Federal marginal tax rate of 35 percent does not necessarily match the company's effective tax rate—even after considering the addition of applicable state income taxes. To wit, Merck's 2013 10-K SEC filing reflects the effective tax corporate income tax rate was 12.8 percent in 2011, 27.9 percent in 2012, and 18.5 percent in 2013.

For the sake of argument, worst case—or highest marginal rate—numbers will be used in a simple example. This means 35 percent at the Federal level. State marginal rates range from zero in states like Texas, to 12.3 in California. Adding the Federal highest marginal rate to California's highest marginal rate produces a combined income tax rate of 47.3 percent. Indeed, analytical purists may criticize such assumptions. However, the attempted point is directional and relative—not precise.

What would Merck have to do to: (i) recover the "average" benchmark above of $1.2 billion in the five years remaining on the patent protection period of five years (20 years net of the 15 consumed by development and clinical trials); AND (ii) average across the remaining five years its 2013 8.4 percent return on equity? The answer is that Merck would have to average $570 million in after tax profits in 2013 numbers. This compares with average annual revenues over those five years of over $1 billion [$570 million / (1−47.3 percent tax rate)]. Such a performance would approach Merck's top 10 products. Alternatively, the math may be applied to Merck's average tax rate of the last three years of 19.7 percent. The result is approximately $710 billion [$570 million / (1−47.3 percent tax rate)]. This remains a sizeable figure. Recapping the major point, big companies have to make big numbers to move the needle—and this amid the bureaucracies of their ecosystem, inclusive of self and stakeholders.

Small companies lack the purse and K Street (the prime residence of major lobbyists in Washington, D.C.) connections. They also avoid the potential for corruption inherent in concentrated power that Lord Acton warned us about in his axiomatic assertion that "power corrupts and absolute power corrupts absolutely."[45] Small business entrepreneurs lack the individual heft to play "the game." Rather, these business people tend to sniff exploitable opportunities, be they catalyzed by externalities or not, that would be lost in rounding error to a gargantuan enterprise. Small businesses can establish a foundation from which to scale a platform on a relatively Spartan budget. When a small company's earnings are only five million dollars, tripling them to $15 million in three years is a stretch, but plausible goal. Compare this to the 2013 Fortune 500 top dog Walmart tripling its $17 billion earnings to $51 billion in three years.

Actually, the relativity argument is one of the alluring enticements for private equity investment in small businesses. Using a baseball metaphor, the Fortune 1000 represents "the show," or the major leagues. Private equity activities approximate the farm club system by identifying and developing talent. A, AA, and AAA baseball is roughly analogous to the size of lower, middle, and upper middle market private equity firm target markets.

Another interesting contrast between large and small companies is the intra-company political theatrics. Jockeying for position inside a bureaucratic behemoth may resemble the city-state warfare of the Renaissance. If a power-hungry person within a bureaucracy is as good as they think they are, then why would they not strike out on their own to prove it? The truth may reside in knowing that seizing power is a path of less resistance compared to creating power. Signing a personal guarantee and mortgaging one's home occupied by their family is a sobering moment of truth for would be Caesars.

Entrepreneurial value-creation may be accomplished absent creativity or innovation, per se. None-the-less, private equity lionizes all architects of value-creation. Private equity firms in the lower to middle markets are particularly fond of the disruptively innovative small business entrepreneurs. Such innovation may come in three forms: product (including services), process, or a combination thereof. In the context of forming, storming, norming, performing, and adjourning (see Figure 1.1),[46] middle market private equity firms tend to pursue investments in the norming and performing range of the entrepreneur's business life cycle. The portfolio company traits are nearly

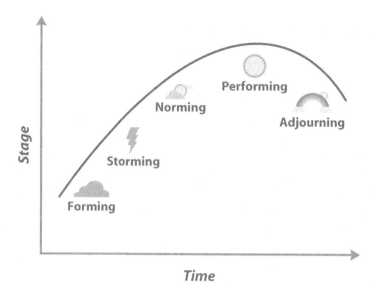

Figure 1.1   The evolution of organizational teams

paradoxical. On the one hand, these companies embody relatively higher value-creation opportunities. On the other hand, a plethora of execution scalability impediments await resolution. These points will be explored in this book.

The People, Processes, and Tools of Value-creation

> *You don't get paid for the hour. You get paid for the value you bring to the hour.*[47]

A business model embodies the articulation of people, processes, and tools to create value relative to its strategy. (See Figure 1.2.) Both private equity firms and the portfolio companies in which they invest face challenges—some common to both, and some unique to each. Whereas the workforce is approximately split equally between men and women, private equity firms tend to be a fraternal order of Caucasian men. The C-levels among portfolio companies are also predominantly male. No studies are available to substantiate this, but a horizon scan of websites and press clippings produce a statistically reliable sample attesting to the phenomenon. There is little evidence of overt discrimination, however. In recent years, private equity has made a deliberate effort to address the issue. Moreover, the private equity firm's influence on portfolio company hiring practices reflects progress, albeit anecdotal.

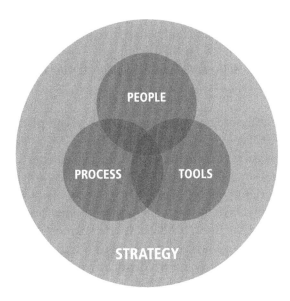

Figure 1.2   People, processes, and tools relative to strategy

The private equity firm has unique challenges. A firm is typically comprised of highly educated financial engineers. Half have at least a masters' degree.[48] The degrees tend to come from some of the finest B-schools in the world. For example, over one-fifth of Harvard's 2012 graduating class headed for private equity jobs.[49] Despite enviable academic credentials, operating experience is limited. Moreover, the professionals tend to be relatively young compared to the C-levels within their portfolio companies. Contrast this with the typical portfolio company executives who are not necessarily Ivy Leaguers. Their seasoning comes from the school of experience—hard knocks. Consequently, there is an inherent communications problem that tends to rear its head when results do not meet expectations. This is a form of Murphy's Law: "anything that can go wrong, will go wrong."[50]

Both parties have something else in common—even though it comes in different forms. Not only may each party *not* know something, they may *not know* that they do not know it. This phenomenon is described as unconscious ignorance.[51] From the firm professionals' perspective, the hazard is typically rooted in operations. For example, a precision manufacturing quality problem does not jibe with efficient capital structuring credentials. From the portfolio company professionals' perspective, leadership issues tend to emerge as the company scales. Unless the portfolio company C-levels came from a Fortune 1000, they may not recognize the challenge. A common example has to do with human resource compliance once Federal law thresholds are reached. Both the private equity firm and portfolio company have distinct, differentiable leadership traits. At best, the traits of the two constituencies may only partially overlap. (See Figure 1.3.)

The laws of nature are not new. They merely await discovery. Physics is an example. The facts have always existed. Mankind's intellect had to catch up to comprehend them and creatively mix the ingredients for manufactured outcomes. Germs, atoms, DNA, and Higgs boson particle are examples. Timing is one of the material variables of comedy. Is it not also true of leadership? Future President Lincoln delivered a Senatorial nomination acceptance speech in 1858 that included the line: "A house divided against itself cannot stand." The statement was a prophetic message about the imminent US Civil War. Lincoln lost the race, but became President two years hence and successfully ushered the country through one of its darkest periods. Lincoln was not using original material. He borrowed (without attribution) the words from the New Testament: Mark 3:25. If one exegetically examines the scriptural verse, several Old Testament connections await discovery. Jesus used the passage to summarize Torah history for application to Roman occupied Palestine. Lincoln mimicked the model 19 centuries later. The point was equally applicable. These are leadership principles. Facts, cultural truths, and research discoveries may be conflated by manufacture to stimulate thought about new value whose recipe includes vintage ingredients. Accordingly, this book endeavors to repeat this model to affect outcomes by applying known material in a novel configuration.

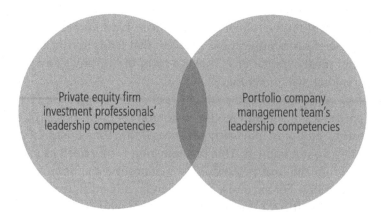

Figure 1.3   **Leadership competency comparisons between private equity firms and portfolio companies**

Values and Value-creation

When your values are clear to you, making decisions becomes easier.[52]

Values are an integral part of societies, yet their origins are elusively mysterious. Individuals and organizations acknowledge values, and some brandish them. Values count when we place them above our lives and fortunes. Cassie Bernall professed her spiritual faith before being murdered in Colorado's Columbine High School massacre on April 20, 1999. Prior to his execution during the American Revolutionary War, Nathan Hale explained that "I regret that I have but one life to lose for my country." Values are core to morality. However, when governments attempt to anchor them in legislation, the outcomes are problematic. Instead of teaching people to fish, government programs tend to addict constituents to "free" fish. Milton Friedman reminds us that "there is no such thing as a free lunch."[53] A more reliable and efficient model relies on free enterprise to create value, with its beneficiaries disposing of the profits according to conscience.

US history is punctuated with noble examples of this model. For example, Andrew Carnegie made his money on steel and his philanthropy funded public libraries throughout the country. In more recent history, Bill Gates pledged to dispose of the vast majority of his wealth and is focusing on endeavors like education and healthcare. These examples are indicative of successful entrepreneurs helping individuals in society to improve their stations and develop productive independence. Even in a "worst case" scenario entailing conspicuous consumption of wealth, jobs are created. "Punishing" this wealth tends to hurt the ones targeted for benefit. For example, the luxury tax imposed during the George H.W. Bush administration destroyed industries such as yacht manufacturers whose workers were sent to unemployment lines. Alternatively, social institutions such as churches, temples, and mosques should guide the populace in charitable distributions. This model is also self-governing in terms of matching inflows and outflows. John Wesley, an 18th century Anglican pastor and progenitor of modern Methodism framed the model as:

> *Do all the good you can. By all the means you can. In all the ways you can. In all the places you can. At all the times you can. To all the people you can. As long as ever you can.*[54]

Knowing nothing is called ignorance. Ignorance can be corrected. Stupidity is eschewing the opportunity for enlightenment. Prima facie evidence indicts tax policy as stupid. Swimming against the current of "externality" stupidity is the intrepid entrepreneur and the shrewd investors that inject their value-creating machine with the requisite growth fuel: cash. Accordingly, this book is an ode to their persistence, tenacity, and guile.

Greed is a frequent criticism of capitalism. However, such arguments falsely assume that greed is limited to the capitalist model. "The problem of social organization is how to set up an arrangement under which greed will do the least harm. Capitalism is that kind of a system."[55] Left to laissez faire mechanisms, however, capitalism occasionally experiences treacherous outcomes. Reactionary socialism is not the solution, beginning with the fact that no socialist model has succeeded in world history. Nonetheless, centralized control appears the Pavlovian reaction to most crises. Even if the character of these centralized power overlords commence as passionately altruistic, they are mortal. Unfortunately, their successors are more likely to become corrupted by power as predicted by Lord Acton.[56] Machiavellianism's end justifying the means eclipses altruism. What then, is root cause? Could it be the implosion of societal value systems? Who is coaching and mentoring the next generation? Leadership deficiencies on Wall Street are encapsulated in Michael Lewis' book, *Liar's Poker*:

> *Wall Street makes its best producers into managers. The reward for being a good producer is to be made a manager. The best producers are cutthroat, competitive, and often neurotic and paranoid. You turn those people into managers, and they go after each other. They no longer have the outlet for their instincts that producing gave them. They usually aren't well suited to be managers. Half of them get thrown out because they are bad. Another quarter gets muscled out because of politics. The guys left behind are just the most ruthless of the bunch. That's why there are cycles on Wall Street ... because the ruthless people are bad for the business but can only be washed out by proven failure.[57]*

Jack Welch, retired GE CEO, asserted Wall Street is one of many industries that harbor bad bosses.[58] One could all too easily fixate on Wall Street as the poster child for narcissism and greed run amok. However, Wall Street may only be more visible because "if it bleeds, it leads" in mass media. Ample evidence exists that this phenomenon is more common throughout business than exceptional. The rhetorical question is "How does business avoid this mess?" The answer is important to society to prevent killing the goose that lays the golden eggs.

Bias Disclaimer

Fortunately for serious minds, a bias recognized is a bias sterilized.[59]

Bias cannot be eliminated[60] in the presentation of arguments about private equity activity in the middle market. Therefore, I cannot deny my own. My perspective on the subjects discussed in this book is more aligned with the "Chicago School" of free market economics, for which Milton Friedman is the spiritual standard bearer. Friedman is arguably the most intelligent economist since Adam Smith. One of Friedman's witticisms imparted that "most economic fallacies derive from this simple insight, from the tendency to assume that there is a fixed pie, that one party can gain only at the expense of another."[61] Fortunately, small business continues to bake new pies while progressive policy wonks argue over who should receive slices and in what proportion.

Friedman was not a fan of Keynesian economics, a popular, but flawed, theory promoted during the Great Depression. Keynesians believed that that government had the spine to turn off the stimulus faucet once it worked. If the first place, it did not work. In the second place, governments did not turn it off even after it failed. Friedman's critique explained the phenomenon with "nothing is so permanent as a temporary government program."[62]

Friedman was a proponent of low taxes: "I am in favor of cutting taxes under any circumstances and for any excuse, for any reason, whenever it's possible."[63] Friedman defended low tax rates as inherently stimulative to free markets. As a social model, free market capitalism has relieved more misery than any economic model in world history. Through its innovative manifestations, capitalism has improved the quality of life for generational multitudes.[64]

The taxation debate was revisited by new tools in the 1980s. The Laffer Curve (see Figure 1.4) bounded an argument that: (i) zero taxation posits no barrier to value-creation; and (ii) 100 percent taxation poses an absolute impediment to value-creation.[65] The rhetorical question was the tipping point whereby marginal taxation disincentivizes (sic) value-creation, and hence, job-creating investment. As it turns out, the tipping point is about 33 percent, that is, the apogee of disincentive.[66] Beyond that point, incremental tax rates retard tax receipts. For perspective, consider that the top federal corporate and personal rates already exceed this figure. State and, in some instances, local taxes only aggravate the ballast. Yet, policy progressives are pressing for even higher rates. Both the Laffer argument and effective taxation rates are hotly contested topics.

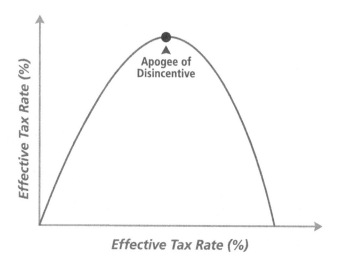

Figure 1.4   Adapted from the Laffer Curve depiction of tax optimization

Why are fiscal, economic, and social policies relevant? "The only way that has ever been discovered to have a lot of people cooperate together voluntarily is through the free market. And that's why it's so essential to preserving individual freedom."[67] Small businesses that drive the economy with their disproportionately high job formation, innovation, and intellectual property creation are presently fighting an uphill battle. Emergence from the 2008 recession remains lethargic as of this writing. Were startups occurring at the rate of 2007, the US economy would be 2.5 million jobs ahead of its present level.[68] Entrepreneurs take risks when they perceive a commensurate potential reward, that is to say the forming step depicted previously in Figure 1.1. The data suggest that "something is rotten in the state of Denmark."[69] Instead of forming value-creating engines, entrepreneurs are waiting. Since commencing in the 1990s, confidence measures for the small business community are wallowing at historic lows as this goes to press.

Applying the Points of this Book

> *Directions are instructions given to explain how. Direction is a vision offered to explain why.[70]*

This book caters to an industry whose stewardship role is finding small business investment opportunities on behalf of investors they represent. This book addresses common issues germane to middle market private equity investments—investment professionals and portfolio company leadership teams. Resolution alternatives are rooted in reputable research. The objective is that of coaching small business portfolio companies and their investment sponsors to more efficiently unleash growth and profit potential. Everything discussed in this book reconciles with culture, growth, and efficiency depicted below in Figure 1.5. First, culture is the biggest gear that provides the most torque because people steward the business model. Second, businesses must profitably grow in order to create the most value. Third, efficiency must enable growth without inflicting duress on culture. Great leaders must relentlessly consider differentiable alternatives traceable to this model. Operationalizing these best practices is a function of prioritization, planning, delegated responsibility, inclusion, and communication.[71]

The null hypothesis imparts that there should be no performance difference between the universe of middle market companies and those pursued by private equity firms for investment. However, this is not the case, as private equity tends only to invest in the top performers. For the purposes of this book, a different application of the null hypothesis is posited. In this case, the null hypothesis suggests that there is no performance difference between the universe of middle market portfolio companies and the subset of those who implement operational best practices. Unfortunately, there is little but anecdotal evidence as firms do not wish to disclose their discoveries.

Figure 1.5   The gears of value-creation

However, observations gleaned from my consulting practice strongly suggest a correlation. Additionally, we may reasonably infer that the research presented herein makes a difference for portfolio companies because it made a difference for the subjects of the original research. The points are presented with an eye toward avoiding Type 1, Type 2, and Type 3 errors:

- type 1 error is "the risk of rejecting a null hypothesis when it is true,"

- type 2 error is "the risk of failing to reject the null hypothesis when it is not true," and

- type 3 error occurs when "the 'wrong' ... problem is ... solved."[72]

Private equity firms and portfolio companies who embrace operational best practices should not be deceived that this is a single event or assimilation. On the contrary, it is a journey of continuous improvement to remain competitively differentiable. Baseball legend Satchel Paige encapsulated the maniacal need for competitive edge: "Don't look back. Something might be gaining on you"[73]

Endnotes

[1] Socrates quotes. (n.d.). *Goodreads*. Retrieved from www. http://www.goodreads.com/quotes/9431-the-only-true-wisdom-is-in-knowing-you-know-nothing

[2] Famous Friedman quotes. (n.d.). *Capitalism and Friedman*. Retrieved from http://capitalismandfriedman.wordpress.com/2010/02/22/famous-friedman-quotes/

[3] Funds. (n.d.). *Morningstar*. Retrieved from www.morningstar.com

[4] Globalization of alternative investments: Working papers: Volume 3: The global economic impact of private equity report 2010 (2009, December 1). *World Economic Forum*. Retrieved from http://www3.weforum.org/docs/WEF_IV_PrivateEquity_Report_2010.pdf. p. iii.

[5] Gilligan, J. and Wright, M. (2008). Private equity demystified. *The Institute of Chartered Accountants for England and Wales*. Retrieved from www.icaew.com/corpfinfac

[6] Gilligan, J. and Wright, M. (2012). Private equity demystified: 2012 update. *ICAEW*. London, UK: ICAEW Corporate Faculty. (ISBN: 978–0–85760–301–2). Retrieved from http://www.icaew.

com/~/media/Files/Technical/Corporate-finance/Financing%20change/privateequity-updated-2012-final.pdf

7   Gilligan and Wright (2008).

8   Barber, F. and Goold, M. (2007, September). The strategic secret of private equity. *Harvard Business Review, 85*(9), 53–61.

9   Private equity industry overview. (2013). *Street of Walls.* Retrieved from http://www.streetofwalls.com/finance-training-courses/private-equity-training/private-equity-industry-overview/; Private equity. (2012, July). *TheCityUK.* Retrieved from www.thecityuk.com. p. 2.

10   Fogarty, I. (2014). 2014 Prequin global private equity report (sample pages). *Prequin Ltd.* Retrieved from https://www.preqin.com/item/2014-preqin-global-private-equity-report/1/8194. p. 14.

11   Breakdown report: 2Q 2014 US private equity breakdown: PitchBook_2Q2014_US_pe_breakdown_spreadsheet.xlsx. (2014, March 31). *Pitchbook.* Retrieved from http://pitchbook.com/reports.html

12   Global private equity report 2014. (2014). *Bain & Company, Inc.* Boston, MA: Bain.

13   Education: PE by the numbers. (n.d.). *Private Equity Growth Council.* Retrieved from http://www.pegcc.org

14   Fogarty (2014). p. 70.

15   *Private Equity Growth Council* (n.d.).; Economic releases: Databases, tables and calculators by subject. *United States Department of Labor: Bureau of Labor Statistics.* Retrieved from http://data.bls.gov/timeseries/CES0500000001

16   Education. (n.d.). *Private Equity Growth Council.* Retrieved from http://www.pegcc.org/education/value-creation/

17   Ibid.

18   Corkery, M. (2012, January 26). Public pension funds increase private-equity investments. *Wall Street Journal.* Retrieved from http://online.wsj.com/article/SB10001424052970203806504577181272061850732.html

[19] Education: Fact and fiction. (n.d.). *Private Equity Growth Council*. Retrieved from http://www. pegcc.org/education/fact-and-fiction/

[20] Private equity creates value for millions of Americans. (n.d.). *Private Equity Growth Council*. Retrieved from http://www.pegcc.org/wordpress/wp-content/uploads/Value-Creation-Fact-Sheet.pdf

[21] Education: Value creation. (n.d.). *Private Equity Growth Council*. Retrieved from http://www. pegcc.org/education/value-creation/

[22] SBIC program: Welcome to the SBIC program: General: FAQs. (n.d.). *US Small Business Administration*. Retrieved from http://www.sba.gov/content/faqs

[23] *World Economic Forum* (2009).

[24] Mark Twain quotes. (n.d.). *Goodreads*. Retrieved from http://www.goodreads.com/quotes/14351-it-s-not-the-size-of-the-dog-in-the-fight

[25] Miller, M. (2011, March 11). Mapping the middle. *The Deal*. Retrieved from http://www.thedeal. com/magazine/ID/038645/2011/mapping-the-middle.php

[26] *Pitchbook* (2014). Retrieved from http://pitchbook.com/reports.html

[27] Miller (2011).

[28] Frequently asked questions. (2012, September). *United States Small Business Administrations, Office of Advocacy*. Retrieved from http://www.sba.gov/sites/default/files/FINAL%20FAQ%20 2012%20Sept%202012%20web.pdf

[29] Prive, T. (2013, May 2). Top 32 quotes every entrepreneur should live by: Johann Wolfgang von Goethe quote. *Forbes*. Retrieved from http://www.forbes.com/sites/tanyaprive/2013/05/02/top-32-quotes-every-entrepreneur-should-live-by/

[30] Peter. F. Drucker quotes. (n.d.). *Goodreads*. Retrieved from http://www.goodreads.com/author/quotes/12008.Peter_F_Drucker

[31] Johnson, D. (2001). What is innovation and entrepreneurship? Lessons for larger organisations. *Industrial and Commercial Training, 33*(4), 137.

[32] Heath, C. and Heath, D. (2013). *Decisive: How to make better choices in life and work*. New York: Crown.

[33] Leibenstein, H. (1968, May). Entrepreneurship and development. *American Economic Review,* *58*(2), 74–5.

[34] Zimmerer, T.W. and Scarborough, N.M. (2005). *Essentials of entrepreneurship and small business management* (6th ed.). Upper Saddle River, NJ: Pearson Education. (ISBN: 0536308411). p. 3.

[35] McClelland, D. (1961). *The achieving society.* Princeton, NJ: Van Nostrand, p. 16; Zimmerer and Scarborough (2005). pp. 3–4.

[36] Rosen, J. (2011, April 25). Economists credit small business "gazelles" with job creation. *FoxNews.com: Economy.* Retrieved from http://www.foxnews.com/us/2011/04/25/economists-credit-small-business-gazelles-job-creation/

[37] Shad, D. (2004, September). *Success analysis of start-ups in the field of microsystems and nanotechnology in the UK* (MSc microsystems engineering doctoral dissertation, Heriot-Watt University, School of Engineering and Physical Sciences, Edinburgh, United Kingdom), 11. Retrieved from http://www.tfi-ltd.co.uk/presentations/devang%20final.pdf

[38] Campbell, A. (2005, July 7). Business failure rates highest in two years. *Small Business Trends.* Retrieved from http://smallbiztrends.com/2005/07/business-failure-rates-highest-in.html

[39] Brickley, J.A., Smith, Jr., C.W. and Zimmerman, J.L. (2007). *Managerial economics and organizational architecture* (4th ed.). New York: McGraw-Hill Irwin. pp. 72–4.

[40] Margaret Thatcher quotes. (n.d.). *Goodreads.* Retrieved from http://www.goodreads.com/author/quotes/198468.Margaret_Thatcher

[41] Howard, P. and Feyman, Y. (2013, March 14). Rhetoric and reality: The ObamaCare evaluation project: Cost. *Manhattan Institute for Policy Research.* Retrieved from http://www.manhattan-institute.org/html/mpr_14.htm#.UUt3nkPD-1s

[42] Merck & Co., Inc.: 2013 Form 10-K. (2014, February 27). *Securities and Exchange Commission.* Retrieved from file:///C:/Users/JLanier/Downloads/MRK_2013_Form_10_K_FINAL_022714%20(1).pdf

[43] Drug discovery and development: Understanding the R&D process. (2007). *The Pharmaceutical Research and Manufacturers of America.* Retrieved from http://www.innovation.org/drug_discovery/objects/pdf/RD_Brochure.pdf

[44] Average cost to develop a new biotechnology product is $1.2 billion, according to the Tufts Center for the Study of Drug Development. (2006, November 9). *Tufts Center for the Study of Drug Development*. Retrieved from http://csdd.tufts.edu/NewsEvents/NewsArticle.asp?newsid=69

[45] Hill, R. (2000). *Lord Acton*. Binghamton, NY: Vail-Ballou Press. p. xi.

[46] Tuckman, B.W. (1965). Developing sequence in small groups. *Psychological Bulletin, 63*, 384–9.; Tuckman, B.W. and Jenson, M.A.C. (1977). Stages of small-group development revisited. *Group & Organization Management, 2*, 419–27.

[47] Jim Rohn quote. (n.d.). *BrainyQuote.com*. Retrieved from http://www.brainyquote.com/quotes/authors/j/jim_rohn_2.html

[48] O'Brien, T. (2012, June 11). *The private equity e-book*. Retrieved from http://www.linksme.co.in/documents/Private-Equity-E-Book.pdf. p. 9.

[49] Ibid.

[50] Murphy's laws origin. (n.d.). *Murphy's laws site: All the laws of Murphy in one place*. Retrieved from http://www.murphys-laws.com/murphy/murphy-true.html

[51] Jung, C.G. (1916). *Psychology of the unconscious: A study of the transformations and symbolisms of the libido, a contribution to the history of the evolution of thought*. New York: Moffat, Yard and Company.

[52] Roy Disney quotes. (n.d.). *BrainyQuote.com*. Retrieved from http://www.brainyquote.com/quotes/authors/r/roy_e_disney.html

[53] Friedman, M. (1977). *There is no such thing as a free lunch*. Chicago: Open Court.

[54] John Wesley quotes. (n.d.). *Goodreads*. Retrieved from http://www.goodreads.com/author/quotes/151350.John_Wesley

[55] Milton and Rose Friedman: An uncommon couple. (n.d.). *Hoover Institution Stanford University*. Retrieved from http://hoohila.stanford.edu/friedman/quotes.php

[56] Hill, R. (2000). *Lord Acton*. Binghamton, NY: Vail-Ballou Press. p. xi.

[57] Lewis, M. (1989). *Liar's poker*. New York: W.W. Norton & Company.

[58] Welch, J. (2005). *Winning*. New York: HarperCollins. p. 300.

[59] Benjamin Hayden quotes. (n.d.). *BrainyQuote.com*. Retrieved from http://www.brainyquote.com/quotes/authors/b/benjamin_haydon.html

[60] Creswell, J.W. (2003). *Research design: Qualitative, quantitative and mixed methods approaches* (2nd ed.). Thousand Oaks: CA: Sage. (ISBN: 0761924426)

[61] Friedman, M. and Friedman, R. (1990). *Free to choose*. Orlando, FL: Harcourt. p. 13.

[62] *Capitalism and Friedman* (n.d.).

[63] Presidential report card: Milton Friedman on the state of the union. (1999, February 10). *Uncommon knowledge with Peter Robinson: The Hoover Institution*. Retrieved from http://www.hoover.org/multimedia/uncommon-knowledge/26925

[64] Hamel, G. (2012). *What matters now: How to win in a world of relentless change, ferocious competition and unstoppable innovation*. San Francisco: Jossey-Bass. p. 42.

[65] Laffer, A.B. (2004, June 1). The Laffer curve: past, present and future. *Backgrounder, a publication of The Heritage Foundation, 1765*, 1–16. Retrieved from http://news.heartland.org/sites/all/modules/custom/heartland_migration/files/pdfs/15245.pdf

[66] Hsing, Y. (1996).Estimating the Laffer curve and policy implications. *Journal of Socio-Economics, 25*(3), 395–401.

[67] *Capitalism and Friedman* (n.d.).

[68] Case, S. (2012, November). Restarting the US small-business growth engine. *McKenzie Quarterly*. Retrieved from https://www.mckinseyquarterly.com/Strategy/Growth/Restarting_the_US_small_business_growth_engine_3032#footnote2up

[69] Shakespeare, W., Mowat, B.A. (Ed.) and Werstine, P. (Ed.). (2012). *Hamlet*. New York: Simon & Schuster. Act 1, scene 5, line 100, p. 55.

[70] Simon Sinek quotes. (n.d.). *BrainyQuote.com*. Retrieved from http://www.brainyquote.com/quotes/authors/s/simon_sinek.html

[71] Drucker, P. (1985). *Innovation and entrepreneurship*. New York: HarperCollins. (ISBN: 9780060851132)

[72] Breyfogle, F.W., III. (1999). *Implementing six sigma: Smart solutions using statistical methods*. Austin, TX: John Wiley & Sons. p. 36.

[73] *Satchel Paige quotes.* (n.d.). Retrieved from http://www.satchelpaige.com/quote2.html

Chapter 2
Primary Diligence Issues: The Trifecta of Oversight

An unexamined life is a life not worth living.[1]

"Diligence" is intuitively understood among private equity professionals. Even so, diligence scopes, methodologies, and priorities are not identical. Among middle market businesses, however, only a subset has directly experienced diligence. Consequently, the term "diligence" may be less understood. Therefore, we should begin with a reality check. Diligence is analogous to the physical examination used to qualify test pilots. Potential buyers and investors attempt to directly—and indirectly by proxy through various subject matter vendors—learn the business. Four critical thinking questions generally guide the diligence process:

- In what type of business is the company—really?

- How does the business make money?

- What is competitively differentiable in the way the business makes money?

- What are the ecosystem threats to the business model?

In the course of answering these questions, two practical objectives prevail:

- the validation of enterprise value, and

- risk mitigation.

Both affect purchase price.

Private equity firms diligence many things exceptionally well. First, they tend to specialize in specific industries. The industry term for this is a "vertical." Only occasionally will they stray from this focus for "opportunistic" investments. The discipline abides by the time-tested best practice of focusing on strengths. As a firm diligences its investment opportunities, it embraces another best practice: commissioning studies to refine the firm's pulse on the vertical. This acquired knowledge serves as an analytical benchmark for prospects within the investment vertical. In practice, the firm would ask, "Why is our prospect different from the norm?" The answers vary. One possibility is a best practice that enhances enterprise value. Another possibility is an oversight that constitutes heightened risk.

Certain diligence categories are common. For example, first or second tier accounting firms, or boutique consultants, are engaged to examine the quality of earnings. This means that generally accepted accounting principles and industry practices are applied to the prospect. Areas covered include revenue recognition, matching principles, depreciation, reserves, prepaid expenses, and policies.

Another area of outsourced diligence includes compliance. There is general compliance, for example, Occupational Safety and Health Administration (OSHA), and there is specific compliance, for example, the Food and Drug Administration (FDA). A third area of compliance regards customer relations. Many private equity firms validate the value proposition by asking why customers buy the prospect's products. Although the Net Promoter® score[2] is typically not the overt objective, the feedback tends to approximate the intent. Other areas (although they may not enjoy standardized definitions) include pending litigation, operational quality methodologies (e.g., Lean manufacturing), taxation across operating venues, risk management and insurance, and facility zoning. In short, if there is a material skeleton in the corporate closet, diligence is systematically designed to discover it within the confines of prevailing jurisdictional laws and regulations. Interestingly, on some of the more sensitive aspects of the prospect's leadership assessment, powerful search engines and social media are making the job much easier. For example, the errant YouTube video of the spring break excursion in Cancun may cast a pall on personal judgment. The purpose of this section is not rehashing what is done well, but rather discussing chronically overlooked items with expensive consequences.

Management Information Systems

True genius resides in the capacity for evaluation of uncertain, hazardous, and conflicting information.[3]

Not only do great companies position the right people in the seats on the bus, but they imbue them with decision-making authority and information so that they may intelligently discharge their responsibilities. Presently, information technology (IT) due diligence scope typically emphasizes security, back-up, updates, disaster recovery, standards, and application license compliance. Unfortunately, many IT diligence engagements fail to address the single most important question: "Will the existing IT system—tomorrow morning—support a company three times the prospect's present size?" In the overwhelming majority of instances, the answer is emphatically "No!" For perspective, consider that over a dozen years, Middle Market Methods™ encountered only one company in over 100 for which the answer was an unqualified "Yes!"

Ironically, the investment banking "book" that brandishes the merits of buying the prospect commonly refers to their systems as "state of the art." This claim has become a joke to investment professionals who read these "books." Perhaps the writers of such hubris are oblivious to the damage done to their credibility. Indeed, as private equity firms become more adroit in scrutinizing systems, the erroneous "state of the art" claims will cause private equity firms to wonder about other unsubstantiated exaggerations in the "book." Most private equity firms have some level of cognizance about systems deficiencies, but have yet to adopt a diligence response to frame the issue relative to cost-benefit resolution.

Middle Market Methods™ was routinely asked to evaluate systems platforms relative to the business model's workflow. I disclaim that systems are my specialty, per se. Rather, process, that is, workflow, is. I evaluate what users desire their systems to do in support of their workflow responsibilities. When applied to the diligence phase of private equity, the assessment has an additional objective: offering an opinion for the systems' ability to support 3Xn3—shorthand for tripling the size of the business in three years.

Such engagements tended to be with clients who had become weary of my relentless sermons about inadequate IT diligence. Essentially, by engaging Middle Market Methods™, these clients were saying, "Okay, big mouth. Put up or shut up!"

The results of such engagements tended to follow a "good news, bad news" summation. The following is an amalgamation of several such experiences (I don't want any single client to feel singled out.)

My opening salvo was, "The good news is that the system reliably provides workflow support. Actually, the system could support a substantially scaled operation."

The client was feeling a little smug. However, the positioning was deliberate for effect. "So, what's the bad news?" asked the client.

"Do you know what an AS 400 is?"

"No. Is that bad?"

"It was 'state of the art' during Reagan's first term."

"I see. (A long pause.) But you said it would scale, so what is the problem?"

"Fewer people know how to fix the box and the software they are using when it breaks. It's not sexy technology any more. Your risk includes custom coding by a sole person in the company who is near retirement age. And nothing is documented."

"Oh."

These engagements also encounter another common "killer" corollary: customization. "Customization" may sound differentiable. However, in IT parlance, it may be deadly. The reasons are simple. A software application has core coding that should not be changed. Periodically, software must be updated. For example, many PC users would be familiar with the routine, automatic updates to the Windows 8 operating system for PCs. Microsoft routinely pushes these out to address software bugs, enhance functionality, and address security. However, had a programming nerd "gotten under the hood" to customize the core coding software for a vendor's Enterprise Resource Planning (ERP) operating system, upgrading may be obviated. It gets worse. Some Middle Market Methods™ clients had to migrate to new operating systems because of this. After a while, the old software is no longer supported. By example, consider Microsoft's Windows XP. Major software companies espouse product lifecycle management that "sunsets" the applications. These vendors communicate well in advance when the software will no longer be supported.

Another IT diligence muff regards the scrutiny of leadership and strategy. We live in a Moore's Law world where computing power and its cost per unit have an exponentially inverse correlation. The half-life of technology is precariously short. Today's titans may be tomorrow's case study casualties. It was not that long ago that Blackberry seemed invincible—and Apple is not immune to dethronement, especially sans Steve Jobs. The long term viability of the typical middle market company depends, among other things, on being "the" low cost provider. The ability to achieve continual economies of scale rests heavily upon automating efficient processes. ERP is a concept germane to the objective. ERP espouses that a piece of data enters a holistic system *once* for the benefit of the entire company, irrespective of function.

Two megatrends prevail in contemporary information technology parlance: cloud applications and so called "big data." Both affect the middle market. Cloud applications bypass hosted systems on local servers. Users may access applications virtually provided they have access to the internet. Salesforce.com is such an application. One of the benefits of cloud applications is that they reduce the need for system administration staff resources. Application development is another matter, however. Application development differs from customization. For example, Microsoft Dynamics CRM accommodates design of this cloud application around the company's workflow, but without changing core coding.

"Big data" is a concept. In the era of micro-marketing, granular profiling of customers—business or consumer—is essential to value-creation. Big data utilizes algorithms to find statistically significant correlations between variables. Perhaps no one does this better than Google, which places advertising with search results.

The big data questions that affect the diligence perspective are:

- What should a company ideally want to know about its customers?

- What type of data would be required to statistically profile those desires?

- How many of those data elements does the company already store?

- What would it take to capture the remainder of those data elements?

While companies may not track all of the data they need to crack the big data code, they likely have data that they under-utilize. Consider the customers' reliance on predictably quick order-to-delivery cycles. Businesses may apply the same question to their vendors. Big data principles may optimize raw materials purchases to accommodate an order surge driven by a marketing promotion without compromising delivery times.

Strong IT leadership obsessively thinks ahead about effective business model support. A telltale sign of an IT leadership deficiency is the organizational chart. Instead of a strategist who reports to the Chief Executive Officer (CEO), the "IT manager" (a generic title) may be buried under the Chief Financial Officer (CFO). At best, these people may be systems administrators who keep the e-mail server and operating system maintained. Of course, these are important functions. However, they are tactical.

IT leadership should report directly to the CEO. Common functional titles include Chief Technology Officer or Chief Information Officer. Absent a strategic leader, strategic IT is unlikely. Among the most impressive IT professionals in the middle market are the nomadic types. They learn by deliberately changing venues. This includes migrating across industry verticals. The consequent cross-pollination is beneficial to the business model.

Investment banker savvy is commensurate with their private equity "customer" constituency. They probably know that their client's systems are lacking. However, improving deficient systems as a precondition to sale may be both protracted and pricey. The protracted part threatens the timing of the intermediary's fee for transaction consummation. The pricey part has both cash and opportunity cost components. Even though the fix is largely capitalized, and thus mitigates the adverse effect on EBITDA, veterans of systems overhauls are painfully familiar with the productivity "J-curve." Systems implementation, overhauls, conversions, or any other euphemistic descriptions belie reality. These instances are woefully disruptive—even the well managed ones. At a minimum, the user community must be engaged to identify the functionality need, test the prototypes, and train for the conversion. The routine is so intense as to seemingly relegate customers as nuisances during the exercise. Any negative impact on earnings—even if only short-term—likely results in a lower sales price for the company represented by the investment banker. Not only is a lower sales price unappetizing to the seller, but it may also negatively impact the investment banker's success fee.

Mysteriously, post-close the CEO may become a born-again technology disciple when the systems deficiencies are discovered and beg resolution. However, the initiative is largely on someone else's Table In private equity transactions, owners tend to sell majority interest in their companies. Consequently, the former majority owners' financial exposure to execution risk is dramatically curtailed.

From the private equity firm's perspective, the question is "How might the investment team avoid technology risk?" Some simple best practices are available. Start with a basic map of the business model that pictorially portrays the business model's primary workflow. This may be as simple as a dozen steps from product concept to receivables collections. Against the diagram, ask what systems are in place to support those functions. For example, a manufacturer might use an ERP solution such as Microsoft Dynamics, NetSuite, Oracle, or SAP.

Follow-up questions are in order. Most operating system vendors offer multiple modules for their applications. Diligence should include which modules are activated. More curiously, diligence should ask which modules were not activated and why not. Sometimes, the quest identifies surrogate modules of superior functionality that were integrated with the base operating system. Even if this made sense when initially done, future upgrade complications may lay in store. Diligence most certainly should verify whether any coding had been customized or modified such that upgrades would be problematic.

The discussion may identify some significant gaps. For example, manufacturing may lack practical real time reports. Dialogue may identify report writer issues with the software. Another gap might be the absence of barcode or radio frequency identification (RFID) scanning for inventory control. Sometimes, the practical and cost-effective solution might reside in data dumps to a data warehouse box against which SQL Server solutions are created. Essentially, management information—including metrics—aspires to put useful data in the hands of the right people.

Yet another discovery might be the absence of any customer relationship management software. This is particularly troublesome for long cycle business models, for example, airplane manufacturing. A company could literally be quite profitable up to the day it declared bankruptcy because there were no more orders for a business whose concept to first order cycle takes years.

Diligence should not fail to ask users what they wished the system did for them. Variations of this question should be tailored to the diligence environment. When answers are provided, several follow-up questions are possible, for example "Why didn't the company do it?" The answers may reveal things about the culture and company leadership that will not emerge in any other form of diligence. As in all cases, diligence should never miss an opportunity to pose a revealing question. Even the refusal to answer may be a telling signal.

Suppose a private equity firm embraced IT diligence best practices and found serious deficiencies. Now what? The firm's tolerance of these deficiencies should be tempered by whether they thought a potential buyer would find the same problems and/or care that such deficiencies existed. There is a plausible scenario whereby this could work: a strategic buyer who would integrate the acquisition into their existing systems. This posture requires excellent knowledge and prognostication of likely buyers. However, a "war story" from my archives is worth considering in refutation of this scenario. One of my career stops included an acquisition opportunity for which our company was seriously outbid by a competitor. We thought they were nuts. However, we later learned that the buyer had lousy systems. Part of their purchase price rationale was reverse-integration to the acquired company's systems to avoid the very systems upgrade challenges described above.

A scenario on the opposite extreme of the spectrum should also be scrutinized. To be clear, this scenario is that of the investment company's acquisition target having deficient system and unclear exit prospects. Further, the private equity firm's investment professionals know that they must upgrade the system. This requires some serious soul searching. First, the firm should consult with vendors active in the specific vertical to consider price tags and timelines for their options. Second, the firm should resolve to jump on the systems issue quickly post-close because it will take a long time to implement. Third, the firm should evaluate the opportunity cost of the project because it will be a distraction from the normal value-creation activities. Fourth, the firm should be convinced that despite the J-curve effect, the remainder of the hold period will be sufficiently robust to vindicate the heavy lifting. Finally, the challenge should be reflected in the purchase price. Otherwise, the firm should pass on the deal.

In summary, key IT points should steer the diligence perspective. Good companies:

- have a clear technology strategy that robustly accommodates scalability;

- enable efficient processes with user-friendly applications;

- seamlessly integrate with complementary software vendors who offer superior functional modules, e.g., accounting;

- use reputable software vendors with reliable support functions;

- avoid "customizations" that compromise necessary upgrading;

- routinely upgrade applications to the latest version;

- put real time data in the hands of people who are empowered to make decisions; and

- train their users to obtain and apply available data.

How Does the Company Make Money?

The worst crime against working people is a company which fails to operate at a profit.[4]

The title of this segment may leave private equity professionals scratching their heads. After all, finance is their "thing." However, the tease is deliberate to set up the point. An audit substantiates profitability within the generally accepted accounting principles (GAAP) convention. Moreover, quality of earnings diligence scrutinizes this further. This question, though, is aimed at customers.

The 80/20 principle has emerged as a modern management axiom.[5] It has several corollaries. Eighty percent of profits are made with 20 percent of customers. Inversely, 80 percent of losses are with 20 percent of customers. Another application is 80 percent of profits are made with 20 percent of stock keeping units (SKUs), and inversely that 80 percent of losses are concentrated in 20 percent of SKUs.

There are two misleading temptations to the profitability question—despite the generic reliability of the 80/20 principle. Diligence commonly starts with customer concentrations. This is logical. The loss of concentrated customer volume poses obvious risk. Since a private equity capital structure is typically leveraged, the question is whether the company can adjust to the loss of a huge customer and remain profitable. The more immediate reaction would be lay-offs until the volume could be replaced. However, debt default covenants would likely be triggered. Having good answers are part of bank debt negotiations. The concentration question is something private equity firms already address adequately, so this is not the focus.

While companies know who their biggest customers are, they do not tend to know how much money they are actually making on them. The same issue prevails for major SKUs. A likely retort to these points draws upon cost accounting for an explanation. The argument tends to sound something like this: "Based on standard cost we make ... ." At best, however, the cost accounting parry only merits partial concession for the point. Cost accounting tends to be an Achilles heel in the middle market.

A small detour will be taken. The CFO's job is the hardest job in private equity. The position has two bosses: the CEO and the private equity investment team. The caliber of financial leadership in small companies tends not to be commensurate with the requirements of private equity governance. Compared to private equity standards, existing financial leadership in the middle market may be more comparable to controllers, for example, junior members on the typical portfolio company's CFO staff. Investment teams know this. CEOs of prospective portfolio companies will discover this quickly. Indeed, the CFO position is susceptible to the 80/20 principle: 80 percent of portfolio companies hire a new CFO in the first year of the investment. There is a simple explanation for the disparity in CFO credentials between pre- and post-cost scenarios. The CEO's historical needs may not have required the accountancy credentials preferred by private equity. Private equity standards for portfolio company CFOs are tougher for several reasons. Two major ones will be cited here. First, the portfolio company leveraged capital structure begs reporting metrics that serve as early warning systems. These metrics alert the investment team to corrective actions to root causes to avert potential loan covenant breeches. Second, although an initial public offering (IPO) is a statistically unlikely investment exit, PE firms tend to adopt Sarbanes-Oxley caliber governance to preserve that option.

Returning to the profitability question, suppose the prospective company had a world class cost accounting system. Does this check the box? Hardly. Standard cost accounting is grossly misleading. Let's start with an example. Suppose you are the middle child of three. (I can relate to this point.) Wearing your four year older brother's hand-me-downs may have been economically appealing to your mother, but it did not endear a teenager to the fashionistas (sic). This did not even address the difference in body shape and fit. While the older brother and I were of the same sex, the younger sister was not into androgynous attire. Such is the dilemma with standard cost.

The Boston Consulting Group wrote extensively on the false positives and negatives of standard cost accounting.[6] The solution is activity-based costing. The virtues of activity-based costing entail isolating actual overhead to a product and/or the customers who buy those products. In extreme cases, activity-based costing demonstrates that the prospect's biggest customers may be hopelessly unprofitable. How could this be? Customers are pretty sharp—especially big customers who embrace activity-based costing. Moreover, not all customers are ethical. Whereas some customers want their vendors to be profitable as a sustaining characteristic of a reliable vendor, others shortsightedly squeeze their suppliers into extinction. The rationale is that if the distribution channel is big enough, another vendor is all too eager to fulfill the axiom mistakenly attributed to P.T. Barnum's authorship: "A sucker is born every minute."

Since we are talking about customer and SKU profitability relative to diligence, what should a potential suitor do? The response tends to be in deference to relativity, that is, the more the investment team suspects that standard cost is misrepresenting profitability, the more imperative drilldown becomes. The potential solution is not necessarily taking the muzzle off of the diligence accountants. Alternatively, specialty vendors might be engaged to take a look through the Lean manufacturing prism. For example, The ProAction Group of Chicago, Illinois, approaches the issue by its proprietary methodology that examines inventory in terms of quantity versus velocity. Not only would such analysis provide insights on true manufacturing cost, but it also begs questions on pricing strategies, raw materials levels, and obsolescence. Perhaps one of the appetizing outcomes is the safety of outbidding a competitor due to confidence in the ability to quickly resolve a challenge no other bidder comprehends.

Even if activity-based costing reveals a SKU to be unprofitable, the product does not necessarily need to be discontinued. The product may be essential to a major customer relationship. However, if the SKU is a loss leader, it must be positioned as part of an overall profitable relationship. Ignorance of profitability can be corrected. The stupidity of eschewing illumination may be lethal.

The odds are de minimis that a middle market prospect will be an activity-based costing disciple. A more likely scenario is implementing the rigor post-close. However, the diligence posture on the topic relates to the aforementioned IT deficiency. The investment team should make some determination about the system's ability to support activity-based costing implementation to avoid the Rumpelstiltskin scenario of unrealistic expectations given the tools at hand.

In summary, key profitability points include:

- Be wary of standard cost accounting, especially for businesses with diverse product lines and customer concentrations.

- Good IT systems are integral to the preferred alternative: activity-based costing.

Governance

The real mechanism for corporate governance is the active involvement of the owners.[7]

Governance is the trickiest of all diligence endeavors, yet it is arguably the most important diligence topic. The subset of governance in question here is who is in charge? The easiest way to make money is when the right people possess sufficient execution latitude. Appearances may be deceptive. Companies putting themselves up for sale may either know, or may be coached to know, how to "favorably" comport themselves. This may include "hiding" certain people from diligence who may disclose business model weaknesses that diminish valuation.

In extreme cases, the CEO (who may also be the majority owner) may, in reality, have sociopathic, narcissistic, megalomaniac, and/or passive-aggressive personality traits. Indeed, three percent of the population are sociopaths, that is, decision-making devoid of conscience.[8] For sociopaths, Machiavelli's *The Prince* is their operating model, that is, the end justifies the means. The "end" may be maximizing sales price; the "means" may be subterfuge. I encountered a few apparent sociopaths in my consulting practice. Sociopaths should not be confused with otherwise difficult or prickly personalities, as these may lend themselves to satisfactory outcomes, but with extra effort. If I know about sociopathic behaviors going into the engagement, the only way I will proceed is predicated upon a clear understanding with the investment team about the hazards of the assignment. If I do not know about these untoward traits going into the engagement, but discover these amid the deliverable, I promptly disengage. There is a sound clinical reason for this posture. Win-win outcomes are not possible with sociopaths. Again, by definition, they act without conscience. Hence, they cannot be trusted. Consequently, enlightened practitioners cut their losses and head to higher ground. Not all sociopaths resemble serial killers. Among the deceptive attributes of a sociopath is the ability to be quite charming in pursuit of their self-centered objective.

Potential portfolio company leaders, take heed. If you are a closet autocratic, you must be right on 100 percent of your decisions. Otherwise, you will alienate the private equity firm investment team and make yourself expendable. Of course, the same fallibility axiom holds true for private equity professionals. However, private equity professionals control the board! Caveat: No one is right 100 percent of the time. That is why despots and tyrants rarely enjoy their golden years.

In instances whereupon the CEO (or other C-Level positions, for that matter) is turned over in the course of the relationship, the investment team is typically highly involved in recruitment. Private equity investment teams should be careful about projecting their leadership preferences onto portfolio leadership teams. "Projection" is a psychological phenomenon whereby a person projects attributes they like about themselves (or actually dislike) onto a prospective hire. (Projection may also occur in assessing incumbent leaders.) Absent a rigor to prevent projection, investment teams may "hire themselves." Since "they" might not be the right fit for the portfolio company, this should be avoided.

In less extreme scenarios, but extremely common ones, the CEO, as well as other C-level leaders, may have some developmental needs that should be identified. Unless these leaders came from a Fortune 1000, he or she may not know certain management best practices. Moreover, he or she may not know that they do not know. A common conundrum is the inability to delegate. Of course, these discoveries cannot be corrected in diligence. However, the risk should be understood in the context of time. A primary measure of investment success is internal rate of return (IRR). The measure scrutinizes profitability against a timeline. Since private equity investments are relatively short-term, getting off to a good post-close start behooves compounding principles in the IRR calculation.

Platooning an industrial psychologist to "shrink" the management team may be a deal killer. The challenge, then, is how investment teams may discretely diligence these governance aspects. Some simple approaches offer practical solutions. Let's return to the high-level business process captured in the IT evaluation section. Using this as a point of reference, the diligence person may ask who is responsible for each part of the enterprise workflow. These names should be compared to the names on the organizational chart for consistency. Additionally, diligence should have access to these people. Denied access may be a red flag. While it is possible that restricted access may be rooted in secrecy to avert injecting anxiety into the workplace, this should be carefully evaluated for legitimacy. After all, there are various teams from diligence vendors who cannot be hidden. Even if the CEO does not proactively communicate a message to the organization about the "strangers," the informal communications network, "the grapevine," will fill the vacuum with something—and perhaps counterproductively.

Consider a particular limb on this decision tree. Suppose the CEO affords access to at least some "process owners." Is access chaperoned or unrestricted? Let's explore both. If chaperoned, does the CEO let the person speak, or does the person look to the CEO for a signal before answering? Scenarios speak volumes in non-verbal communication. If unrestricted, what should be asked? For starters, the diligence person should ask the interviewee what is done in their area. Follow-ups should include the "suppliers" and "customers" of their function. Another question regards the tools provided to do the work. Diligence should listen for things like the availability of information supplied by IT. In complement, diligence may ask something along the lines of "How do you know when you are doing a good job?" Finally, diligence should pursue how decisions are made. For example, "What happens if you determine that a piece of equipment has to be replaced?" The answers may shed light on autonomy (or lack thereof) and undocumented policies. A holistic approach ideally includes senior people, mid-levels, and junior people.

Measures are particularly interesting. Investment teams tend to skew their focus on output metrics, for example, revenue and profitability margins. However, input and process metrics may be leading indicators, and are particularly crucial to long cycle businesses. In some business models, input and process metrics predominate. If these metrics are within certain ranges, profitability is a fait accompli. Another measurement favorite regards quality. Edwards Deming's legacy is that quality is the price of admission. However, quality is often incorrectly measured. For example, some companies only check quality before shipment. This enjoys the virtue of only shipping "good" product to customers. However, this ignores everything that happened along the way, including reworks and scrap that dramatically increase the effective production cost per unit of output.

The "cost of quality" is a major component of untapped profitability. The benchmark of comparison is Toyota's Total Quality Management System. Toyota knows intimately that variation and defects both increase cost and compromise quality. The questions for diligence include:

- What is measured?

- When is it measured?, and

- Who has the authority to do something with it?

Again, improvements may not be addressed until post-close. The focus at this juncture is the baseline from which the value-creating scale will commence.

Board of directors' composition is yet another governance signal. Does the CEO sandbag the board with "yes" people, or use the board to challenge decisions and guide the company. Private equity firms are dramatically improving the diversity of their post-close portfolio company boards. Over time, most firms have outgrown the perfunctory status symbol of firm members dominating the board in favor of recruiting outsiders with relevant perspective who will challenge management assumptions and pronouncements with critical thinking questions. During diligence, the board composition should be scrutinized for its signals about CEO leadership behavior. In short, is the present board comprised of yes-people or independent thinkers? The answer may telescope conflict scenarios with the investment team post-close.

A final point is offered in summarizing this section. Suppose all the governance signals were acceptable. Further suppose the private equity firm successfully acquired the business. How were the employees told and by whom? Again, my archives are worth revisiting. Some owners of closely held businesses do not know how to announce the investment to their employees. This may be exacerbated by their inherent conflict avoidance proclivities. One of my engagements entailed root cause identification to problematic integration of sites into a "franchise"-type business model. Our field work discovered that the sellers routinely told their employees that "nothing would change" after the sale. This was, of course, patently false—and the sellers knew they were being disingenuous. Indeed, the acquirer had tools to explicitly inform the sellers what would change, when things would change, and how things would change during the integrations. The moral of the story for investment teams is to address employee communications and prepare for the unexpected. The best advice includes being on site when the announcement is made. Again, another tale from the past substantiates the point. The seller called the company employees to the cafeteria. In this case, the employees knew very little about the transaction. The CEO blurted out, sans foundational comments or introduction, "The guys in the suits over there bought the company. Do what they say." He then left the room.

In summary, governance diligence should focus on:

- Board of directors' composition and function.

- Leadership structure verses the workflow. Stated another way, managerial structure should be supportive of the way the company creates value.

- Access to information beneficial to functional management.

- How decisions are made and by whom.

- The objectivity of measurement and rewards.

- Leadership style and organizational cultural markers relative to the general business ecosystem, industry vertical norms, and business objectives.

Endnotes

[1]   Johnson, P. (2011). *Socrates: A man of our times*. New York: Penguin. pp. 98–9.

[2]   Reichheld, F.F. (2006). *The ultimate question: driving good profits and true growth*. Boston, MA: Harvard Business School Press.; Reichheld, F.F. (2004, June). The one number you need to grow. *Harvard Business Review, 82*(6), p. 133; Reichheld, F.F. (2003, December). The one number you need to grow. *Harvard Business Review, 81*(12), pp. 46–54.

[3]   Winston Churchill quotes. (n.d.). *BrainyQuote.com*. Retrieved from http://www.brainyquote.com/quotes/authors/w/winston_churchill_4.html

[4]   Samuel Gompers quotes. (n.d.). *BrainyQuote.com*. Retrieved from http://www.brainyquote.com/quotes/quotes/s/samuelgomp205264.html

[5]   Koch, R. (1998). *The 80/20 principle*. New York, NY: Doubleday.

[6]   Stern, C.W., and Deimler, M.S. (Eds.). (2006). *The Boston Consulting Group on strategy: Classic concepts and new perspectives* (2nd ed.). Hoboken, NJ: John Wiley & Sons.

[7]   Louis Gerstner quotes. (n.d.). *BrainyQuote.com*. Retrieved from http://www.brainyquote.com/quotes/authors/l/louis_gerstner.html

[8]   Stout, M. (2005). *The sociopath next door*. New York, NY: Broadway Books.

Chapter 3

The Private Equity "Operating Partner"

If you can talk with crowds and keep your virtue,
Or walk with Kings—nor lose the common touch,
If neither foes nor loving friends can hurt you,
If all men count with you, but none too much:
If you can fill the unforgiving minute
With sixty seconds' worth of distance run,
Yours is the Earth and everything that's in it,
And—which is more—you'll be a Man, my son![1]

Behind financial engineering, operational improvement was the second private equity innovation.[2] "Operational improvement is private equity's chief source of value."[3] It has to be. The leveraged capital structure creates a "burning platform" sense of urgency because of the narrower margin for error. This is profoundly relevant in the lower end of the middle market, where a little preventive leadership makes for a healthy and productive investment hold period. At a minimum, performance failures may trigger expensive and distracting debt covenant violations, forbearance, cures, and/or renegotiation. Bankruptcy and liquidation are among the worst-case scenarios. At no time during the advent of the private equity model was this made more clear than the recession triggered by the 2008 financial meltdown.[4]

Even the larger firms that once relied entirely on the management team have revisited their strategies. Clayton, Dubilier & Rice (CDR) is one such firm. In recent years, they have added icons to their operational focus to include Jack Welch and Bill Conaty from General Electric (GE).[5] Ironically, lower middle market private equity firms know that the probability is high that certain leadership skills are below expectations within their portfolio companies, yet many have been somewhat lethargic in formally addressing the issue. At a minimum, coaching and development are required for the portfolio execs if the gap is too severe. If portfolio company execs cannot meet the higher operational standards requirements, the positions have to be turned over. This does not even address positions that have to be created because they do not exist at the time of transaction consummation.

Smaller portfolio companies increasingly compete internationally. The higher the direct labor cost of their product, the more likely that global components complement their business model. This reality is but one of the variables that rationalizes some configuration of dedicated private equity-sponsored operational support. In response to the limited partner pressure to address operational execution as a risk mitigating tactic, the lower middle market private equity firms are experimenting with operational excellence strategies. The options include firm "operating partners."

"The only relevant test of the validity of a hypothesis is comparison of prediction with experience."[6] Unfortunately, evidence of private equity operating partner model success stories is scant and anecdotal because firms do not like talking about their track records with this grand experiment. Whereas marque consulting firms and think tanks have published insights on the operating partner role, the content tends to be skewed toward the upper echelons of the middle market. Deductively, one possibility is that if the smaller firms think they have figured it out, they do not wish to divulge trade secrets. Conversely, if firms have not yet figured it out, they do not want to advertise the problem and spook their lending relationships and limited partner investors.

The general idea is that the investment team oversees financial governance while the operating partners steward operational governance. This is synergistic in that each creates value in its own right—but collaboratively, one plus one equals something north of two. The comparative "trick" in private equity is how the measurability of the operational impact is ascribed. Like most other human endeavors, "victory has a million fathers, but defeat is an orphan."[7]

The term "operating partner" lacks a consistent "operational definition." (No pun is intended; this is an engineering definitional convention.) The term is nearly uniquely defined for each firm that has operating partners—or a function tantamount thereto. There are three generic operational models in private equity:

- investment team oversight,

- insourced operators, and

- outsourced operators.

Each will be individually reviewed.

Investment Team Oversight

Typically, three investment professionals comprise an investment team: a senior member who may be on the investment committee, a mid-level member, and a junior member. The roles roughly approximate career-pathing. Junior members embrace heavy workloads, such as spreadsheet modeling and analytics, as a part of on-the-job training. Their performance earns advancement opportunities within the firm.

In some firms, the senior investment professionals are former executives from manufacturing or service companies, and hence possess "operator" credentials. Their pedigree may also logically influence the industry verticals that the firm pursues in search of investment opportunities. Even so, the biggest hazard of the investment team oversight model is Biblical: one cannot serve two masters equally. Therefore, this operating partner model is a pseudo-solution whose flaws are easily understood. First, multitasking generalists are inefficient. Abundant research substantiates that the brain simply cannot multitask. "For the human brain, attention is essentially a zero-sum game: If we pay more attention to one place, object, or event, we necessarily pay less attention to others."[8] The illusion of multitasking is actually a function of how quickly someone may pivot among tasks and achieve laser-focus. Comparatively, specialization enjoys a stronger argument. Ironically, the financial engineers learned these principles in their B-school economics courses.

Second, investment professional skills are more aligned with business development, i.e., the next deal. This takes two forms: a new portfolio company opportunity and/or an acquisition for an existing portfolio company. Indeed, these activities provide the most fulfillment for investment professionals. Not only are operational duties less gratifying, but most also lack the credentials to do it. The temptation is to defer attention on the less fun operational grunt work until it festers into a near-crisis. At this point, the investment professionals are necessarily drawn into the vortex of full-time attention. The only upside is great crisis management experience. The downside is that, more often than not, the crisis could have been averted by proactive measures. Moreover, while the investment team is fully occupied by an operational crisis, business development activity for those investment professionals grinds to a halt. In severe cases, such crises infect the entire firm and hijack its attention.

One of the stronger arguments for investment team oversight, as opposed to supplemental resources, is cost.[9] However, this third reason is a red herring, beginning with the issue of opportunity cost materiality to the firm by misaligning skillsets. By analogy, ophthalmologists do not practice podiatry. Financial engineers do deals. They cannot do deals—at least not effectively— amid a turnaround for an existing portfolio company. Like any other function in any other company, the operating position must provide an adequate return on investment. The math is profoundly in favor of the "right kind" of operators. Analogous to the argument is GE's philosophy on Six Sigma resources. No headcount budget variance is typically allowed for the black belts. They are expected to pay for themselves. In GE's case, their track record vindicates the philosophy.

Insourced Operators

Many firms brandish internal operating partners on their websites. Retired executives are popular. These individuals tend to sit on the boards and bring valuable coaching insights to the portfolio company. There are three primary hazards of this model. First, operational problems sometimes require total line immersion to analyze and resolve the issue. To wit, value-creation efficiencies occur in the trenches. Retired executives may not be sufficiently motivated to engage in this type of heavy-lifting. Conventional thinking is that they have paid their dues and such menial work is beneath their station. Consequently, they either direct existing resources or procure external ones. External resources represent a type of double cost for what the internal operating partner might otherwise handle.

Another hazard entails the firm's cultural dynamic.[10] Private equity firms are primarily "deal shops." Their job is to invest capital in promising opportunities. Except for situations firms, that is, firms that invest in distressed companies, the investment teams tend to "own" the portfolio company relationships. Consequently, there is often counter-productive tension between the investment teams and their operating partners. This is a type of alpha dog phenomenon. The phenomenon is only exacerbated by a likely generation gap. For example, a junior investment team member may be several years younger than the operating partner.

A final hazard regards the relational dynamic between the operating partner and the portfolio company. Despite the alluring credentials of the operating partner, the business card still has the firm's name on it. Consequently, there may be at least some initial reluctance for portfolio company leaders expressing their candid concerns for fear that they are communicating to an investment team spy. It is critical to overcome this perception because the operating partner is often the de facto mensch and mentor to the portfolio company for all things private equity. Indeed, a trusted operating partner will be asked questions that are unlikely posed to the investment team—particularly junior members of the investment team. Simply put, a middle-aged, type-A personality, bootstrapping portfolio company leader does not want to appear ignorant to an investment team member who looks like one of her children.

The arguments in this section may appear thinly theoretical—a fair critique. The retort is practical experience. My practice engaged 30 private equity firms, over 100 portfolio companies, and in excess of 300 deliverables. I am intimately familiar with many more firms than those engaged. First, I offer that I have met only one operating partner in a firm who has mastered the insourced dynamic. Unfortunately for his firm, he is retiring. It remains to be seen how effectively his successors replicate his shtick. Second, roughly half my clients have operating partners. My phone has rung for years to circumvent some of the dynamics described above.

Outsourced Operators

"Outsourced" may not be as clear as it seems. For purposes of the argument, "outsourced" operational support means a subject matter consultant. The question is "Who manages the relationship with the consultant?" Ironically, private equity firms aggressively outsource to diligence vendors, yet are comparatively more reluctant to engage value-creation vendors during the investment hold period. Interestingly, this anomaly may jeopardize the investment thesis.

Even firms with insourced operational support models may outsource based on subject matter. In the insourced model, this may happen for two reasons. First, the expertise required may not align with the operating partner's skillset. Lean manufacturing, multivariate modeling, ERP migration, and regulatory compliance are such examples. Second, the interpersonal dynamic between the firm and the portfolio company suggests that an unaffiliated resource can more easily address the issue because of the "honest broker" phenomenon, that is, the portfolio company leaders may be more comfortable that there is no private equity firm bias. This may occur in many forms but is essentially a trust issue. Let me be crystal clear: trust is a non-negotiable prerequisite to effective cross-functional team problem-solving dynamics. An outside resource brings subject matter expertise to problem-solving. Insiders (portfolio company employees) bring contextual content and perspective to the pool of knowledge. It simply takes too long—which translates into "it costs too much"—for an outsider to "discover" what insiders already know. Such is kryptonite even for the expertise of Peter Drucker and Edwards Deming caliber resources.

Another consideration is the type of advice the investment team is likely to receive from an external source. Whereas the investment and operational professionals are sorting through a myriad of variables for materiality on a decision, research suggests that a trusted outsider is more likely to isolate the primary variable for a good decision.[11] In sizing up the external resource fit by a private equity firm, a good framing question is "What would you do if you were me?" The logical follow-up question is "Why?" An additional, wise vetting question is "Would you share analogous examples for applying this advice?"

Although admittedly anecdotal evidence, my experience is that the private equity firm and portfolio company perspectives on an operational issue are often unaligned. For example, I have been platooned by private equity firms to "fix" a portfolio company problem whose root cause was predetermined (with conviction) by the investment team. However, upon going through diagnostics with the portfolio company, a different root cause was substantiated. The good news is that the problem lent itself to sustainable resolution. The bad news is that this is interpersonally treacherous territory that draws upon diplomatic skills to avoid relational damage—for both the portfolio company and the resource.

An Emerging Hybrid

A hybrid form of the outsourced model that may be gaining some traction in the lower middle market. This regards an operational leader within the private equity firm who is a peer of the senior leaders of the firm. This version of an "operating partner" entails vetting, deploying, and overseeing external resources. The hybrid model contrasts with the investment teams' vetting, deploying, and overseeing external resources.

The vetted resources bear further comment. The lower middle market tends to use boutique vendors for its value-creating functions. This is no slight to the global subject matter experts. Rather, this reflects matching and economic principles. Lower middle market needs are not typically as complex as those of the Fortune 1000s. Moreover, small business budgets are comparatively more Spartan. Consequently, renowned firms like McKenzie & Company, The Boston Consulting Group, and Bain & Company are less prevalent in smaller business venues.

What the Portfolio Company Saw

This section explores the portfolio company perspective: both pre- and post-close. In more robust times, for example, the 1980s, part of the private equity pitch to prospects was that investment teams would not tell portfolio company leadership how to run their business. Of course, this was not an entirely accurate depiction of reality. Non-performance pierces this veil pretty quickly.

There is a more sinister scenario that masks a common problem in the middle market: sellers who eschew operational oversight, and thus deliberately partner with private equity firms who appear to be hands-off. In these situations—even in the face of non-performance, portfolio company executives attempt to fend off perceived interference, despite the fact that they no longer own controlling interest in the company. Instead of being able to work with the existing leadership team, the firm may have to replace at least some of the portfolio execs as a precursor to analysis and rectification. This can consume as much as a year. Even if eventually resolved, the collateral damage to the fund is a lower investment return, wary lenders, and reluctant limited partners.

Conversely, portfolio companies who welcome an operationally focused private equity firm accomplish several objectives, beginning with the deal prospecting activity:

- First, operational excellence may be part of the "branded" investment hold period strategy. This tends to attract foresighted executives who recognize that scaling may entail challenges beyond their experiences. Acquisition integration often fits this description.

- Second, operational resources may be part of diligence activities. Workflow-oriented observations are particularly beneficial. Perhaps the most useful observation is the adequacy and application of technology to workflow.

- Third, firm-aligned operators enjoy early insights from macro diligence that must be addressed post-close. Amid the mix, seasoned operators get a feel for the culture relative to potential challenges when digesting accelerated growth.

- Fourth, a relationship may be established between the private equity firm-sponsored operational resources and the portfolio company leadership team that portends the tenor of mutually beneficial post-close collaboration.[12]

The Right Resources in the Subject Matter Bullpen

The operational excellence argument logically begs the value-creation 80/20 question: "What post-close subject matter resources should the firm have in its arsenal?" I will offer some generic categories and a methodology for specific needs. Returning to the chronic due diligence subjects covered in Chapter 2: Primary Diligence Issues: The Trifecta of Oversight, private equity firms should have pre-vetted resources for information technology—including its application to activity-based costing—and general human asset-related challenges. Other typical expertise needs include process improvement, strategic marketing, sales training, and acquisition integration.

A simple methodology addresses a firm's specific needs. With each successful transaction consummation—a new portfolio company investment, an add-on acquisition, and an investment exit—conduct a formal "lessons-learned" exercise while the issues remain freshly in the minds of the stakeholders. Another ideal tollgate is the firm's typical quarterly portfolio company review. The itemized list will create a Pareto pattern (a version of the 80/20 rule) of the most chronic topics for which the firm should pre-vet resources. The patterns for firms may differ across firms, especially as it pertains to the verticals in which they invest.

One more point is relevant to the subject matter bullpen. Not only do middle market private equity firms tend to favor boutique consulting resources, but they also have an affinity for specific professionals within those firms. Consequently, their allocable bandwidth is a legitimate concern. Investment team professionals may relate to this phenomenon as it is analogous to juggling multiple deal activity. Hence, back-up alternatives are advisable for the preferred primary resource. Beside, a little competition is good for the primary resources, even though they may be reluctant to admit it.

Parting Thoughts: The Operational Perspective

"There is no single operating partner template that will fit every private equity firm."[13] The firm has an obligation to find one that reconciles with its verticals and strategies. Failure to do so jeopardizes portfolio companies, funds, and firms. There is virtue in specialization. Indeed, it is efficient. Investment professionals are quite good at finding and closing attractive investment opportunities. This comes with many ancillary skills such as efficient capital structures with appropriate loan covenants. However, there is a flip side of the Adam Smith logic of specialization. These specialties may come with blind spots. The blind spots may manifest themselves in overlooking otherwise obvious issues that pose impediments to investment thesis execution. These oversights may come in two forms.

The first is overlooking something that the investment professionals are not seeking. The argument is proffered with abundant examples in Christopher Chabris and Daniel Simons' bestseller, *The Invisible Gorilla: How Our Intuitions Deceive Us*. Perhaps the most recognizable example regards their experiment whose footage is easily found on *YouTube*. The gist of the experiment regarded test subjects being asked to count basketball passes between actors whose nondescript attire was black, white, and denim. The real experiment's objective, however, was whether the test subjects noticed someone in a black gorilla suit entering the mix of participants. The experiment and its subsequent recreations have affirmed that half the subjects consistently do not see the gorilla enter or leave the scene. In the experiment, the gorilla actually stops in the middle of the scene and beats his chest.[14] What's the analogous point? When pursuing deals, investment professionals may not see the operational gorillas that will make themselves more conspicuous post-close.

The second form is arguably a corollary to the first and is germane to my consulting practice. I am often asked to coach many junior investment professionals. These are extremely intelligent and highly educated people. What are they missing? In a word, "wisdom." This is not intended to be a criticism, but rather a warning. Several supporting quotes come to mind:

- "Good judgment comes from experience. Experience comes from bad judgment."[15]

- "Experience is not what happens to you. It is what you do with what happens to you."[16]

- "Experience is the name we give to our past mistakes."[17]

- "Experience is what you got by not having it when you need it."[18]

The correlation between age and wisdom might be explained by someone living long enough to experience things in context such that they are more likely to recognize their recurrence the next time it happens—especially if the original lesson learned was painful. Since operators within private equity tend to be a bit older and more experientially seasoned, junior investment professionals should look to them as mentors. Reciprocally and in reverse mentoring fashion, the pups may show the older dogs new tricks. Popular versions of this include desktop technology and social media.

Since operational excellence is tantamount to a non-negotiable in middle market private equity investments, firms would do well to revisit their governance model. There is merit to a specialist examining execution even if the mechanism catalyzes conflict. Effective firm governance embraces diverse perspectives for their dynamic tension attributes. This differs from conflict in that conflict may devolve into interpersonal angst whereby dynamic tension invites collaboration in pursuit of better decisions. Dynamic tension is arguably one of the undergirding mechanisms of Toyota's Total Quality Management system.

Endnotes

[1]   Kipling, R. (2007). If. In *Kipling*. New York: Random House.

[2]   Favaro, K. and Neely, J. The next winning move in private equity. *Booz & Company: Strategy+Business Magazine, 63*, 1–10. Retrieved from www.strategy-business.com

[3]   The 2012 private equity report: Private equity: Engaging for growth. (2012, January). *Boston Consulting Group*. p. 5. Retrieved from https://www.bcgperspectives.com/Images/BCGPrivate_Equity_Jan_2012_tcm80–95414.pdf

[4]   Hemptinne, C. and Hoflack, V. (2009, December). The value of in-house operations teams in private equity. *INSEAD*. Singapore: INSEAD. Retrieved from http://www.insead.edu/facultyresearch/centres/global_private_equity_initiative/students/documents/ISP_Value_of_in_house_operations_teams.pdf

5   Conaty, B. and Charan, R. (2010). *Talent masters: Why smart people put people before numbers*. New York: Crown Business.

6   Milton Friedman quotes. (n.d.). *Thinkexist.com*. Retrieved from http://thinkexist.com/quotation/the_only_relevant_test_of_the_validity_of_a/181848.html

7   John F. Kennedy quotes. (n.d.). *BrainyQuote.com*. Retrieved from http://www.brainyquote.com/quotes/quotes/j/johnfkenn110295.html

8   Chabirs, C. and Simons, D. (2009). *The invisible gorilla: How our institutions deceive us*. New York: Broadway Paperbacks. p. 39.

9   Hemptinne and Hoflack (2009). pp. 15–6.

10 Ibid. pp. 23–5.

11 Heath, C. and Heath, D. (2013). *Decisive: How to make better choices in life and work*. New York: Crown.

12 Hemptinne and Hoflack (2009). pp. 18–9.

13 Quarta, R. (n.d.).The operating partner: An industrial approach to private equity investment. *Clayton, Dubilier & Rice*. Retrieved from www.cdr-inc.com/news/perspectives/operating_partner.pdf. p. 65.

14 Chabris and Simons (2009).

15 Bob Packwood quotes. (n.d.). *Thinkexist.com*. Retrieved from http://thinkexist.com/quotes/like/good_judgment_comes_from_experience-experience/13357/

16 Aldous Huxley quotes. (n.d.). *Thinkexist.com*. Retrieved from http://thinkexist.com/quotation/experience_is_not_what_happens_to_you-it_is_what/145524.html

17 Oscar Wilde quotes. (n.d.). *Thinkexist.com*. Retrieved from http://thinkexist.com/quotes/oscar_wilde/

18 Anonymous. (n.d.). *Thinkexist.com*. Retrieved from http://thinkexist.com/quotation/experience_is_what_you_got_by_not_having_it_when/7189.html

Chapter 4
The DNA of Packs

Now this is the Law of the Jungle—as old and as true as the sky;
And the Wolf that shall keep it may prosper, but the Wolf that shall
break it must die.
As the creeper that girdles the tree-trunk the Law runneth forward
and back—
For the strength of the Pack is the Wolf, and the strength of the Wolf is
the Pack.[1]

"Pack" as used in this chapter heading is an intentionally provocative, primal convention. Alternatively, one could use "team." The point is that closely knit groups have rules of behavior. These rules influence the ability to reliably accomplish an objective. This transcends the limitations of physical organizational design. As Ben Franklin quipped during the American Revolutionary War, "we must all hang together, or assuredly we shall all hang separately."[2] In private equity, "hanging together" has three unique manifestations. First, the private equity firm must have an effective organizational pack. Second, each portfolio company in which the private equity firm invests must have an effective pack. Third, each private equity firm investment team creates a sub-pack dynamic to effectively engage each portfolio company supported so that fiduciary responsibilities may be accomplished during the investment hold period.

The challenge for the investment team is to be a chameleon without losing identity or focus. This point is integral to successfully coaching C-levels (e.g., chief executive officer, chief operating officer, chief financial officer, etc.) within portfolio companies toward improved performance. The private equity firm investment teams are normally comprised of financial engineers—not operators. Moreover, many are junior in age to the C-levels running the portfolio company. The governance dance is delicate. Consequently, the pack metaphor is laced with downside risk of unintended consequences traceable to interpersonal dynamic missteps. Strategic intent may run aground because responsibilities are vague, overlapping, or fragmented. Turf wars may erupt into dysfunction. Opportunities may languish unexploited as managers have to redirect focus to address crises.[3] Talent may also lay fallow and unmotivated.

This may forfeit input from those with the best perspectives for capitalizing on opportunities—as well as problem resolution.[4] Against this backdrop, we will explore key components for creating and nurturing effective packs.

Values and Culture

If your culture doesn't like geeks you are in real trouble.[5]

"Opinion is the medium between knowledge and ignorance."[6] Opinions are shaped by worldviews. Worldview cognizance enables individual understanding to address ignorance in pursuit of shared knowledge for group benefit. A worldview is "a set of presuppositions (assumptions which may be true, partially true, or entirely false) which we hold (consciously or subconsciously, consistently or inconsistently) about the basic makeup of our world."[7] Worldview prisms influence all human interaction. Four worldview variables predominate:

- religion,

- science,

- philosophy, and

- daily life.[8]

There is ample room for conflict in any given category. For example, Islam, Judaism, and Christianity are challenged to coexist. Intelligent design wrestles with Darwinism. Capitalism competes with Marxist economics. "Have-nots" struggle with overcoming poverty without despising the "haves." In dealing with this matrix of ambiguity, "it is the mark of an educated mind to be able to entertain a thought [contradictory to one's worldview] without accepting it."[9]

Worldviews foster values. Values impart "enduring beliefs that a specific mode of conduct or end state of existence is personally or socially preferable to an opposite or converse mode of conduct or end state of existence."[10] Values vary within and across nations.[11] Nine spiritual anchors define values:

- perfection,

- compassion,

- passion,

- inspiration,

- investigation,

- dedication,

- appreciation,

- determination, and

- cooperation.[12]

Moreover, values are influenced by:

- age,

- education,

- occupation, and

- socioeconomic status.[13]

Values are "a system of guiding principles and tenets."[14] "Values tell employees—and the rest of the world—who they are and what they stand for... . [V]alues are the heart and soul of an organization and should be constantly on the minds of the entire workforce."[15] Values are the criteria by which members of an organization hold each other accountable. The same is true of extra-company relationships such as those with vendors and customers. This also applies to relationships between private equity firms and their portfolio companies. Individual and corporate values compatibility are particularly important for professionals operating beyond the line of sight of their leadership structure. These organizational members must comport themselves such that their actions "brand" how the purpose and vision will be realized. (We will revisit purpose and vision later in this chapter.)

Values may be broadly understood in two categories: instrumental and terminal.[16] Instrumental values are enabling. Terminal values are pinnacles, or end states. Values may be espoused, or communicated, versus enacted, or modeled.[17] Logically, instrumental values may be the medium through which the espoused terminal values are reached. In practical terms, middle market portfolio companies and their private equity partners should focus primarily on instrumental values. The rationale has two key points. First, the pace of change is such that enterprise value must be a perpetual obsession, that is to say, organizations are only as good as their last accomplishment. Second, the investment hold period is too brief to think about altruistic, terminal values.

"Values define [a] leader's behavior as well as those who follow."[18] Individuals have values that may differ from peers, subordinates, and bosses. Not only may individual values be diverse, but they may differ from the advocated corporate values. In order to minimize dysfunction and conflict within the organizational culture, a person's values must share sufficient overlap and compatibility with the corporate values. Diametric opposites do well to disassociate. For example, a recovering alcoholic might be a poor fit in a distillery.

Please refer to the Venn diagram in Figure 4.1. The large circle depicts corporate values. The four smaller, darker circles represent four different personal values. Circle 1 represents an individual whose values are a compatible subset of the corporate values, and hence a good fit. Circle 2 is a potential good fit as there is a majority overlap between individual and corporate values. Indeed, this could portend healthy diversification. The question is whether the different values are incompatible. Circle 3 is likely a poor fit, as corporate values are a minority subset of personal values. Circle 4 is a misfit as there are no values in common. Arguably there is a fifth circle not depicted: an identical border between the individual and the organizational values. This might not be desirable. Cultural clones may lead to groupthink derailments. Indeed, there is merit to someone stating the obvious, that is, "the emperor has no clothes."

Middle Market Methods™ coached clients to limit themselves to three values. The rationale is rooted in ample research substantiating two primary points. First, brevity aids retention. Superfluity has an exponentially deleterious impact on retention. Sometimes companies compromise to permit paragraphs explaining the singular words. However, it is the three words—not the verbatim explanatory paragraph words—that enjoy higher retention. Second, if internalized, the values are more likely to influence behavior. In support of this point, companies should include "living the values" in the performance management system.

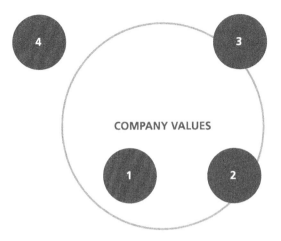

Figure 4.1   The corporate and personal values dynamic

Compatible values between individuals and their organizations engender strong cultures capable of superlative financial results. Culture is "the set of values, norms, guiding beliefs, and understandings that is shared by members of an organization and is taught to the new members."[19] Moreover, culture is

> *a pattern of behavior [that has been] developed by an organization as it learns to cope with its problem of external adaptation and internal integration, [and] that has worked well enough to be considered valid and to be taught to new members as the correct way to perceive, think, and feel.*[20]

Culture entails "values, beliefs, rites, rituals, ceremonies, myths, stories, legends, sagas, language, metaphors, symbols, heroes, and heroines."[21] Culture obliges four primary functions:

- provides "a sense of identity to members [that] increases their commitment to the organization,"

- promotes "a sense-making device for organizational members,"

- reinforces "the values in an organization," and

- serves "as a control mechanism for shaping behavior."[22]

Peter Drucker reminds us that "culture eats strategy for breakfast."[23] All organizations have cultures. However, a company may have never taken the time to describe its culture. Moreover, the company may have forfeited the occasion to contrast what the culture presently is with what it needs to be in order to compete effectively. A useful tool for juxtaposing the present state culture with the desired future state culture is the Organizational Cultural Assessment Instrument. The tool is influenced by the competing values framework and plots teams among four cultural types:

- the hierarchy, based on controlling,

- the clan, based on cooperating,

- the market, based on competing, and

- the adhocracy, based on creating.

Not only does the tool help frame present culture, but it also provides feedback for what the respondents think the culture should be relative to its understanding of the corporate strategy. Indeed, there may be a need to change the culture. All but hierarchical characteristics align with creative teams. To the extent that the indicators skew toward adhocracy, two corresponding attributes are particularly promising: (i) flexibility and discretion; and (ii) external focus and differentiation.[24]

"Meaning and context are inextricably bound up with each other."[25] Consequently, the global economy makes multicultural navigation a preeminent leadership competency. Multicultural proficiency requires understanding in terms of monochronic, polychronic, low-context, and high-context attributes. [26] "Chronic" relates to time. Monochronic cultures tend to be indicative of Western cultures. In monochronic cultures, punctuality is integral to decorum. Moreover, task orientation is an expression of technical competency. Factory assembly lines are monochronic temples of Frederick Taylor's scientific management principles. By contrast, polychronic behavior is Ecclesiastical—"To everything there is a season, and a time to every purpose under heaven … ."[27] Relationships, connectedness, and relativity prevail for polychrons. Interdependency dominates decorum. Expediency is an anathema. Multitasking is preferred despite its inherent inefficiencies. Polychrons are less likely to get entangled in repetitive monotony.

The "contexts" are literal versus nuanced. Low-context cultures are direct—even blunt. The low-context communication style is explicit. Members of these cultures tend to say exactly what they mean. Low context people tend to value independence and individualism. "Most of the [low-context] information must be in the transmitted message in order to make up for what is missing in the context."[28] By contrast, high-context cultures find this offensive. High-context cultures save face and communicate in subtleties and hints. Indeed, the majority of high-context communication is non-verbal. Non-verbal communication includes body language, personal space, eye contact, tactile functions, intonation, inflexion, cadence, and dialect.[29] "High-context transactions feature pre-programmed information that is in the receiver and in the setting, with only minimal information in the transmitted message."[30] In complement of contextual competencies, Geert Hofstede, Gert Jan Hofstede, and Michael Minkov's *Cultures and Organizations: Software of the Mind* (3rd edition) offers six categories for comparing and contrasting dominant country traits:

- power-distance,

- individualism,

- masculinity,

- uncertainty avoidance,

- long-term orientation,

- and indulgence versus restraint.[31]

The categories are most useful for early reads on cultural differences for global executives—especially neophytes. Figure 4.2 uses the categories to juxtapose the United States and China.

The most effective practical navigation between a low-context monochronic and a high-context polychronic I have ever witnessed was a partnership between an English speaking North American and a Spanish speaking Latin American. Both spoke each other's languages fluently. However, to assure that they understood exactly what other one meant, their dialogue embraced role reversal. They addressed each other in the partner's native language, for example, the Latino spoke English and the North American spoke Spanish. They never suffered idiomatic or translational miscues.

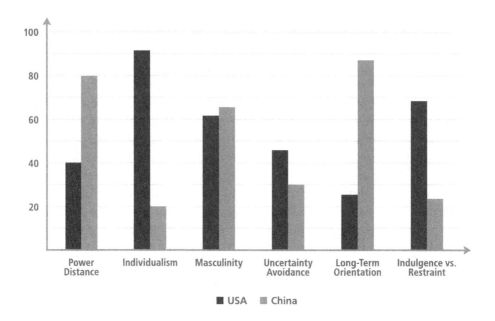

Figure 4.2   Cultural comparison of the US and China

Source: Hofstede, G., Hofstede, G.J., and Minkov, M. (2010). *Cultures and organizations: Software of the mind: Intercultural cooperation and its importance for survival* (3rd ed.). New York: McGraw-Hill.

All values and cultures must be based upon a foundation of trust. Indeed, trust, or some logical corollary thereof, is a common value adopted by organizations. Trust must be earned from deliberate actions over a length of time. Corporate and relationship formation is the best time to start building trust. Indeed, this is analogous to the axiom that there is only one chance to make first impressions. Recall from Chapter 1: Introduction that all teams predictably follow a forming, storming, norming, performing, and adjourning lifecycle.[32] Particularly during the forming and storming phases, trust is a type of mortar that holds the disparate bricks together. Trust works like a bank account for which only tiny deposits are allowed. However, the withdrawals tend to be large—and of necessity infrequent. Therefore, teammates have a vested interest in religiously making deposits in anticipation of the inevitable withdrawals driven by circumstance.[33] Another way to look at trust is dividends versus taxes. Trusting organizational cultures enjoy dividends in the form of a positive group dynamic capable of achieving great feats. Distrustful organizational cultures sustain a tax in the form of lower morale and productivity.[34]

The absence of trust is a fundamental nemesis of team dynamics.[35] The path of earned trust starts with authenticity.[36] The process is enabled by earning credibility through under-promising and over-delivering.[37] Trust includes an element of empathy, that is, the ability to walk in another's shoes. Christianity's Golden rule encapsulates the sentiment: "Therefore all things whatsoever ye would that men should do to you, do ye even so to them … ."[38] Interestingly, every major religion includes a version of the Golden Rule.[39] Trust is one of the four core principles of doing well in a hostile environment.[40] Professionals do not have to agree or share fondness in order to achieve trust. Rather, they must have faith in each other's genuine motivations. This principle includes personal integrity and ethical conduct.

In their book, *Tribal Leadership: Leveraging Natural Groups to Build a Thriving Organization*, Dave Logan, John King, and Halee Fischer-Wright outline five tribal (pack) stages, each with a mantra. Note how trust—by its absence or presence—influences the description of each stage. Stage one tribes (packs) comprise two percent of cultures. Its tag line is "life sucks." Stage two is more personal: "My life sucks." Stage two constitutes a disappointing 25 percent of the workplace environments. Stage three tribes (packs) are mercenary, that is, "I'm great and you're not." This accounts for approximately 49 percent of firm cultures. Stage four discovers outward competitive focus: "We're great [and they're (competitors) not]." Only 22 percent of the workforce fits this description.[41] Leaders should pause here for reflection on the 80/20 principle.[42] Stage four is tantamount to a tipping between from "What's in it for me?" to "What's in it for us?" Obviously, the implied leadership goal for private equity for both the firm and its portfolio companies is stage four tribes (packs). By reversing the population of portfolio company stage fours from one-fifth to four-fifths, the investment fund enjoys competitively differentiable odds. Ideally, tribes (packs) achieve a philosophical "flow,"[43] or corporate chi, whereby all members conclude that their contributions are more effective within a coordinated group effort. Individuals in such tribes (packs) may be intrinsically motivated to pursue "deliberate practice" to become superior performers. Daniel Pink describes contentment with intrinsic motivation toward superior performance as "motivation 3.0."[44] Of course, part of Pink's argument is that the compensation level is sufficient to remove its inadequacy as a demotivator. We will revisit this "hygienic" point with Frederick Herzberg's two-factor theory in Chapter 8: Leadership Choices and Organizational Design.

Logan et al. unexpectedly encountered a fifth tribal (pack) stage that delayed publication of their book. Stage five is not a stable stage. Rather, a stage four tribe (pack) may enter stage five in special circumstances. The philosophy is patently unselfish, that is, "What's in it for mankind?"[45] For example, medical researchers may reach stage five when pursuing solutions to crises. Hence, the focus is on eradicating root cause, making traditional competitors are irrelevant. HIV/AIDS research and treatments fit this description.

Teams have an optimal size, even in flat organizations. The zone ranges from five to 24 members.[46] Six members appear to be the ideal size.[47] Similarly, there is an optimum organizational size. Beyond approximately 250, Logan et al. assert that pack dynamics suffer.[48] More modestly, R.I.M. Dunbar argues that there is a "functional limit [of 150] on interactive groups ... in industrial societies."[49] Consequently, some organizations such as W.L. Gore & Associates, makers of GORE-TEX®, use that size as a signal to create another facility. Similarly, Johnson & Johnson, limits how much it integrates acquisitions in order to preserve the innovative tribal cultures.

When packs focus on external instead of internal enemies, great things are possible. In *Team of Rivals: The Political Genius of Abraham Lincoln*, Doris Kearns Goodwin told the story of President Lincoln's recruitment of formerly bitter adversaries into his cabinet. Lincoln respected their competencies long before they discovered his brilliance. Lincoln stoically endured character assaults, insults, criticism, disrespect, and subterfuge while modeling servant leadership.[50] According to historian Shelby Foote, Lincoln's tenacity recast the United States an "is" rather than an "are."[51] Referring to the United States as a singular noun is so entrenched in American culture that we overlook the obvious syntax problem that may be more common to those outside of our culture. Lincoln united a nation in perilous circumstances and easily ranks among the America's greatest presidents. Indeed, Lincoln enjoys world stature. A monument to Lincoln is prominently perched in Parliament Square in London near Westminster Abbey and the Parliament building.

Generational considerations are also relevant pack variables. Worldviews across these generations differ. This is further compounded by cultural differences across countries. Oddly enough, however, generational material is conspicuously absent from many of the staple management books in business school curricula. "Organizations are essentially networks of personal interconnections ... [that] become a key component of strategic planning."[52] As the Baby Boomers (born 1946–64) enter retirement on one end of the bell curve, Generation Y (born 1981–2000), also known as the Millennials, is arriving on the opposite end of the bell curve. Sandwiched between the tails of the curve is Generation X (born 1965–1980), which now dominates middle management ranks.

"Generation X employees are options thinkers and will therefore listen to other people's points of view rather than "fighting to the death" to have things done their way. Generation Y can use technology to fundamentally re-engineer organizations."[53] Tammy Erikson, author of *What's Next, Gen X?*, explains that Generation X did an analogous thing to Boomers in the 1980s that Generation Y is doing to X's today.[54]

Perhaps one of the most daunting leadership style challenges regards acquisition integration. We will revisit this topic in greater detail in Chapter 8: Leadership Choices and Organizational Design. Indeed, three out of five acquisitions fail to meet financial expectations, and cultural conflict is the primary root cause.[55] Two corporate cultures—not one—have to be understood before attempting integration. One belongs to the acquirer and the other belongs to the acquiree. Of course, nested cultures may reside within each business, further complicating matters. This only gets more aggravated by global integrations.[56] The comparison and contrast of the two organizations reveal potential integration impediments. Cross-referencing these dominant characteristics to leadership models helps frame the culture, and hence the appropriate integration strategy. Leaders have to decide ahead of the purchase which culture and organizational structure will survive—or which parts of each culture form a surviving hybrid.

Cultural due diligence for acquisitions is imperative. Global transactions necessitate navigation in cultural venues for which the acquirer may be unconsciously ignorant. Consider something as seemingly innocuous as the color wheel. The color black symbolizes death in Western and Japanese cultures. However, Chinese consider black a celebratory hue.[57] Words and their translations are also potentially problematic. For example, the British commonly use "lift" to describe an elevator. Body language is another challenge. A hands-on-hips stance is a sign of hostility to Mexicans and Argentines. However, Americans may regard this only as aggressive or "at-the-ready."[58] In response to these potential landmines, three cultural categories offer exploratory guidance:

- basic assumptions,

- values and beliefs, and

- artifacts.[59]

The easy take-away is doing one's homework before entering unfamiliar territory.

The most valuable pack lesson I received involved the transition from GE to a private equity firm in an operational role. GE has an alluring reputation for training. GE employees regularly engage vendors, customers, and subject matter experts in pursuit of differentiable edge. Some of the subject matter experts include the brightest consultants and thought leaders on the globe, for example, McKenzie & Company. One of the unusual, and perhaps unintended consequences, of the rocket scientist banter is a lexicon that only the initiated comprehend. My epiphany entailed literally transitioning from supporting private equity portfolio companies through the Access GE group to supporting some of the same companies as an owner via the private equity firm. One of the first things I was challenged to do was "speak English." Taken aback, I asked for clarification. The portfolio company leaders told me that they did not understand what I was talking about. Of course, I asked why they had waited until now to bring that point to light. The answer was revealing. They told me that they were not about to look stupid to "the world's most admired company" by admitting that they did not understand the jargon. However, now that I had an ownership interest in their success, *I* was the one who should be motivated to speak *their* language. This was one of the single most important lessons learned in developing the operational support role toolbox for the private equity firm. No disrespect is intended to either GE or McKenzie. The point is deeply rooted in change-management principles which both organizations intimately understand.

Purpose Statements

Efforts and courage are not enough without purpose and direction.[60]

Mission statements have enjoyed several luminary protagonists, including the Harvard Business School, Peter Drucker, and Stephen R. Covey. In the rush to adopt them, leaders all too often adulterate their intended impact with verbosity and bloviation. Consequently, mission statements may have lost their luster as a management tool. In lieu of mission statements, purpose statements rediscover the mission statement's original intent. Moreover, purpose statements tend to be more concise. In its most elemental form, a purpose statement explains why we come to work. Of course, there may be more thoughtful explanations for purpose statements.

> [Purpose] statements are enduring statements of [intention] that distinguish one business from other similar firms. A [purpose] statement identifies the scope of a firm's operations in product and

market terms. It addresses the basic question that faces all strategists: "What is our business?" A clear [purpose] statement describes the values and priorities of an organization.[61]

Another way to look at a purpose statement is as follows:

The corporate purpose statement expresses the company's functional reason-for-being … what it does, makes or provides every day. The purpose is never merely "to make money." To make this clear, it helps to add the thought that "by doing this well, we will provide exceptional returns to our employees and shareholders."[62]

Bill George, retired CEO of Medtronic and current Harvard Business School professor, offers further insights on purpose relative to value-creation.

I don't subscribe to the notion that companies exist to create value strictly for their shareholders. I think they are there to create value for their customers, and that gets to the [purpose] of the company. And ultimately, doing that, they create value for society.

If they forget about that, they have no legitimacy, they have no right to exist, no matter how much short-term shareholder value they create. And the shareholder value is misunderstood. It comes as a result of great value for your customers that leads to growth, and that comes from engaged employees that are innovative and provide superior customer service.[63]

An effective purpose statement accomplishes the following four objectives:

- captures the core values,

- specifies the target market,

- encapsulates the value proposition and corresponding points of differentiation, and

- identifies the relevant constituency.[64]

"As private equity firms proliferate and supply chains open up around the world, nothing is more important for complex corporate entities than a clear sense of purpose, a clear sense of why they matter."[65] Those supply chains entail portfolio companies with the same need for clarity of purpose. Simon Sinek wrote a compelling book, *Start with Why: How Great Leaders Inspire Everyone to Take Action*, useful to the purpose and vision argument. Sinek explains "Why?" with a Golden Circle model (see Figure 4.3).[66] Sinek argues that conventional thinking is outside-in, whereby leaders first describe

"What?" they do, then "How?" they do it, in order to rationalize an outcome, or "Why?" The "Why?" for conventionally thinking capitalists is profitability. In contrast, Sinek posits that great leaders, and by implication, great change agents, invert the order of the syllogism. These unconventional leaders begin with an inspirational "Why?" followed by "How?" it will be executed to deliver a "What?," or product. Interestingly, the monetary angle is an afterthought. In the *Richest Man in Town*, Randall Jones explained that money was merely a means of keeping score instead of motivating followers.[67]

Sinek continues that the "Why?" relies upon the brain's limbic system. The limbic system houses the feeling and intuitive functions that lack a verbal outlet. The neocortex controls verbal functions, as well as the analytical and rational capabilities. The argument comes full circle upon realizing that once the leader makes the "Why?" connection with followers, they will help the leader

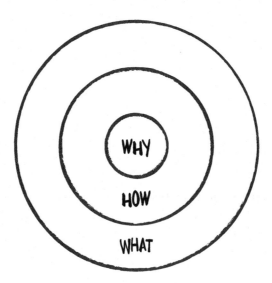

Figure 4.3   Sinek's Golden Circle

Source: From *Start with Why: How Great Leaders Inspire Everyone to Take Action* by Simon Sinek, copyright (c) 2009 by Simon Sinek. Used by permission of Portfolio, an imprint of Penguin Group (USA) LLC.

figure out "how" to transform the "Why?" into tangible activity with fungible results. In the absence of this milestone, we are left with an observation Lewis Carroll made through the Cheshire Cat in *Alice in Wonderland*: "If you don't know where you are going, any road will get you there."[68] Malcolm X offered complementary reasoning for "Why?": "If you don't stand for something you will fall for anything."[69]

"The most viable statements of purpose are easy to grasp and true to a company's distinctiveness."[70] By example, one the best purpose statements I have encountered consists of three words. MedExpress is an urgent care business model headquartered in Morgantown, West Virginia. Its leaders and equity sponsor knew that growth would cover several states. They also understood the purpose, vision, and values contributions to their business model. Their team encapsulated the MedExpress purpose thusly: "Great care. Fast." Those words are painted prominently on the walls of the corporate lobby to greet all visitors. The meaning is etched on the hearts of the employees. Such purpose statement concision often provides an additional measure of utility: the purpose statement may double as the marketing tag line.

Middle Market Methods™ encouraged clients to strive for purpose statements of no more than six words. This is quite a challenge, especially compared to the epistles some companies use for missions statements. However, the challenge compels leaders to focus. The rationale mirrors that for values: retention and behavioral change. Of course, business leaders are obliged to institutionalize the purpose by a myriad of means to elevate the purpose as an effective management tool.

Vision Statements

In order to carry a positive action we must develop here a positive vision.[71]

Purpose and vision are the first and second elements of the foundational triad, and enjoy a symbiotic relationship. Whereas the purpose answers why we come to work, "a vision statement answers the question, 'What do we want to become?'"[72] Effective, crisp vision statements inspire teams toward common objectives by three means:

- guiding principles,

- execution options, and

- motivation.[73]

Essentially, a vision statement defines the expectation for excellently executing corporate purpose for an extended period of time. A vision is an aspirational point in the future at which the individual's complementary purpose reaches something akin to the apex of Abraham Maslow's hierarchy of needs: self-actualization or personal fulfillment. Metaphorically, a vision depicts the summit of the mountain to climb.

A common "vision" question typically emerges in private equity: "Why invest time crafting a vision statement that exceeds the typical hold period of less than five years?" The short answer is "alignment." Near-term actions need to be aligned with longer term aspirations. For example, the National Aeronautics and Space Administration's (NASA) quest to reach the moon in the three-man crew phase of Apollo rocketry was preceded by the Mercury (single astronaut) and Gemini (two astronauts) programs. Potential buyers for a private equity portfolio company need some idea of where the business thinks it is going. Accordingly and in practical terms, a vision statement should describe a vista of at least twice the projected investment hold period. These thoughts should be kept in mind for the foresight principles and scenario analysis that will be discussed in Chapter 5: The Importance of Strategy.

A vision may be just out of reach, yet inspires teams to keep trying because the reward is highly fulfilling. Like Tantalus of Greek mythology, neither the breeze that blew the branch of fruit just beyond his reach, nor the pool that drained beneath his feet as he bent to drink, dissuaded Tantalus from pursuit of his goal. Thus, instead of near-term goals, visions may be perceived as quests in the same manner as the crusades in search of the Holy Grail. Accordingly, a journey is depicted—not a destination.

The utility of visions was not lost on spiritual prophets and leaders. For example, Proverbs 29:18 of the Judeo-Christian tradition communicates the value of a vision in clarion terms: "Without vision, the people perish." Despite ever lofty achievements, the bar must be raised for the next level of competitive differentiation. Should teams ever reach their vision, they must create a new one to avert entropy, that is, disorder that devolves into chaos, and atrophy, that is, institutionalized weakness from comfort with the status quo. This phenomenon presently plagues NASA. Whereas President Kennedy's 1961 goal of a safe moon mission was reached within a decade, NASA struggled with transitioning to the next challenge. The space shuttle program experienced a comparatively protracted timeline and weaker sense of urgency. Presently, absent societal buzz for the next adventure, manned space flight is an easy target for budget cuts for a pathologically overextended federal government.

Dr. Martin Luther King's (MLK) August 28, 1963 "I Have a Dream" speech on the steps of the Lincoln Memorial remains the signature example for understanding the relationship between corporate purpose and vision.[74] MLK's purpose was civil rights. Constitutional parity for people of color had not occurred despite the Thirteenth, Fourteenth, and Fifteenth Amendments to the US Constitution during post-Civil War Reconstruction. Voting rights legislation of 1957 had not ended discrimination either. MLK's speech eloquently communicated a societal vision that his "four little children will one day live in a nation where they will not be judged by the color of their skin, but by the content of their character."[75]

Over my thirty-plus years of entrepreneurial engagement, one example stands out among all others for transforming a purpose and vision into economic success. Dwight England was a spiritual man. While walking his postal route in Michigan in 1964, he experienced a compelling, purposeful pull to the Appalachian Mountains of his native Tennessee to employ a lot of people in an area that needed economic stimulation. Dwight England's vision included building a successful upholstery furniture manufacturing operation. Indeed he did, and punctuated the odyssey with considerable ingenuity and foresight. Dwight England did at least two things that conventional wisdom deemed nearly impossible at the time. First, he ran multiple shifts—and experienced better production quality in the second and third shifts than the first. Second, he engineered the captive trucking unit's operational logistics to guarantee four week delivery for less-than-truckload quantities anywhere in the country, and two weeks for truckloads. Unfortunately, Dwight England succumbed to cancer before seeing his England/Corsair lines reach their zenith. However, he left his signature on the operation with a smooth leadership transition. La-Z-Boy acquired England in 1995. Dwight England's model followed the sentiment encapsulated decades later by Tony Hsieh, co-founder of Zappos: "Chase the vision—not the money. The money will end up following you."[76]

Analogous to purpose statements, Middle Market Methods™ also advised clients to strive for vision statements of no more than six words. In my experiences, leaders struggle more with vision statements than with purpose statements. One of the reasons is that leaders are often so consumed with the immediacy of managing their rapidly growing businesses that it is difficult to focus on something so seemingly nebulous as a vision. However, the generational dynamics explored later in this book should not be overlooked.

For example, the Generation Ys entering the workforce are more influenced by being part of something that aligns with their passions than their baby boomer bosses. Accordingly, leaders ignore the "vision thing" to their talent pipeline peril. It is most gratifying to see executives take their corporate visions seriously. Indeed, it can take months to reconcile the message with the economy of words. Conscientious leaders should take solace in the fact that MLK worked on his "I Have a Dream" vision for years before immortalizing it on the steps of the Lincoln Memorial.

Foundations in Common

When it all boils down, it's about embracing each others' stories and maybe even finding that synergy to collaborate for the common good.[77]

A private equity firm has its own values, purpose, and vision. Moreover, each portfolio company in which the firm invests should have their uniquely suitable values, purpose, and vision. Since the two organizations are highly interactive, the values, purposes, and visions should be understood of one another, as well as enjoy compatibility. For example, conflict is assured if the portfolio company's values, purpose, and vision do not foster value-creation. The encouraging news is that capitalists may do (financially) well doing (societal) good.

In creating values, purpose, and vision cultural foundations, alignment should be monitored. This is both an issue for their initial creation, as well as the evolution of the company as it grows. Accordingly, it is wise to review these concurrent with the strategic planning cycle. Figure 4.4 communicates the point in terms of a three-legged stool. Values, purpose, and vision legs articulate to support corporate culture. If the legs are unaligned (uneven), the culture is problematically imbalanced relative to strategic intent. By contrast, if (evenly) aligned, the culture serves as a guiding "invisible hand" in support of strategic intent.

Figure 4.4 Culture's foundation of purpose, vision, and values

Endnotes

[1] Kipling, R. (n.d.). The law of the jungle. *A complete collection of poems by Rudyard Kipling*. Retrieved from http://www.poetryloverspage.com

[2] The electric Ben Franklin: The quotable Franklin. (n.d.). *USHistory.org*. Retrieved from http://www.ushistory.org/franklin/quotable/quote71.htm

[3] Goold, M. and Campbell, A. (2002). Do you have a well-designed organization? *Harvard Business Review, 80*(3), 117.

[4] Gottfredson, M. and Schaubert, S. (2008). *The breakthrough imperative: How the best managers get outstanding results*. New York, NY: HarperCollins.

[5] Bill Gates quotes. (n.d.). *BrainyQuote.com*. Retrieved from http://www.brainyquote.com/quotes/authors/b/bill_gates_3.html

[6] Plato quotes. (n.d.). *BrainyQuote.com*. Retrieved from http://www.brainyquote.com/quotes/quotes/p/plato382233.html

[7] Sire, James W. (1997). *The universe next door* (3rd ed.). Downers Grove, IL: InterVarsity Press.

[8] Hitt, W. (1996). *A global ethic: The leadership challenge*. Columbus, OH: Battelle. (ISBN: 1574770160). p. 3.

[9]   Aristotle quotes. (n.d.). *Quote DB*. Retrieved from http://www.quotedb.com/quotes/899

[10]   Nelson, D. and Quick, J.C. (2006). *Organizational behavior: Foundations, realities and challenges* (5th ed.). Mason, Ohio: South-Western. p. 127.

[11]   Hofstede, G. (1998, February 1). A case for comparing apples with oranges: International differences in values. *International Journal of Comparative Sociology, 1*, 16–31.

[12]   Karakas, F. (2010, June). Exploring value compasses of leaders in organizations: Introducing nine spiritual anchors. *Journal of Business Ethics, Supplement 1*(93), 73.

[13]   Oyserman, D. (2001). Values: Psychological perspectives in international encyclopedia of social and behavioural sciences. *Elsevier Science*, 16150–3.

[14]   Collins, J.C. and Porras, J.I. (1996, September-October). Building your company's vision. *Harvard Business Review, 74*(5), p. 66.

[15]   Cressey, D.R. and Moore, C.A. (1983). Managerial values and corporate codes of ethics. *California Management Review, 25*(4), 53–77.

[16]   Rokeach, M. (1973). *The nature of human values*. New York, NY: Free Press.

[17]   Nelson and Quick (2006). p. 534.

[18]   Munley, A.E. (2011, March). Cultural differences in leadership. *IUP Journal of Soft Skills, 5*(1), p. 16.

[19]   Daft, R.L. (2007). *Organizational theory and design* (9th ed.). Mason, OH: Thomson South-Western. p. 361.

[20]   Schein, E.H. (1992). *Organizational culture and leadership: A dynamic view* (2nd ed.). San Francisco, CA: Jossey-Bass. p. 9.

[21]   David, F.R. (2005). *Strategic management concepts and cases* (10th ed.). Upper Saddle River, NJ: Pearson Education, Inc./Prentice Hall. p. 118.

[22]   Nelson, D. and Quick, J.C. (2006). *Organizational behavior: Foundations, realities and challenges*. (5th ed.). Mason, Ohio: South-Western. p. 536.

[23]   Heskett, J. (2010, June 2). How do you weigh strategy, execution and culture in an organization's success? *Harvard Business School Working Knowledge*, 1–8. Retrieved from http://www.flextrain.

com.bh/library/How%20Do%20You%20Weigh%20Strategy%20-%20Execution%20and%20
Culture.pdf

24 Cameron, K.S. and Quinn, R.E. (2006). *Diagnosing and changing organizational culture: Based on the competing values framework* (Rev. ed.). San Francisco: Jossey-Bass.

25 Hall, E.T. (1983). *The dance of life: The other dimension of time.* New York, NY: Doubleday; Hall, E.T. (1976). *Beyond culture.* New York, NY: Doubleday; Hall E.T. (1969). *The hidden dimension. Man's use of space in public and private.* London, UK: Bodley Head; Hall's cultural factors. (2012). *Changing Minds.* Retrieved from http://changingminds.org/explanations/culture/hall_culture. htm.

26 Ibid.

27 Ecclesiastes 3:1 (King James Version [KJV]).

28 Hall (1983); Hall (1976); Hall (1969); *Changing Minds* (2012).

29 Dahl, S. (2003). An overview of intercultural research. *Society for Intercultural Training and Research, 2,* 1–13.

30 Hall (1983); Hall (1976); Hall (1969); *Changing Minds* (2012).

31 Hofstede, G., Hofstede, G.J. and Minkov, M. (2010). *Cultures and organizations: Software of the mind: Intercultural cooperation and its importance for survival* (3rd ed.). New York: McGraw-Hill; Hofstede, G. (2001). *Culture's consequences: Comparing values, behaviors, institutions and organizations across nations* (2nd ed.). Thousand Oaks CA: Sage.

32 Tuckman, B.W. (1965). Developing sequence in small groups. *Psychological Bulletin, 63,* 384–9.; Tuckman, B.W. and Jenson, M.A.C. (1977). Stages of small-group development revisited. *Group and Organization Management, 2,* 419–27.

33 Covey, S.M.R. (2006). *The speed of trust: The one thing that changes everything.* New York: Free Press.

34 Ibid.

35 Lencioni, P. (2002). *The five dysfunctions of a team: A leadership fable.* San Francisco, CA: Jossey-Bass.

[36]   Bell, C.R. (2002). *Managers as mentors: Building partnerships for learning.* New York: Berrett-Koehler.

[37]   Deming, E.W. (2000). *Out of the crisis.* Cambridge, MA: First MIT Press; Covey (2004); Drucker (1985).

[38]   Matthew 7:12 (KJV).

[39]   Maxwell, J.C. (2003). *There is no such thing as business ethics: There is only one rule for making decisions.* New York, NY: Warner Books.

[40]   Covey, S.R., Whitman, B. and England, B. (2009). *Predictable results in unpredictable times.* Salt Lake City, UT: FranklinCovey.

[41]   Logan, D., King, J. and Fischer-Wright, H. (2008). Tribal leadership: Leveraging natural groups to build a thriving organization. New York, NY: HarperCollins.

[42]   Koch, R. (1998). *The 80/20 principle: The secret of success by achieving more with less.* New York, NY: Doubleday.

[43]   Csikszentmihaly, M. (2003).*Good business: Leadership, flow and the making of meaning.* New York, NY: Penguin.

[44]   Colvin, G. (2008). *Talent is overrated: What really separates world-class performers from everyone else.* New York, NY: Penguin Group; Pink, D.H. (2011). *Drive: The surprising truth about what motivates us.* New York, NY: Riverhead Books.

[45]   Logan et al. (2008).

[46]   Brickley, J.A., Smith, Jr., C.W. and Zimmerman, J.L. (2007). *Managerial economics and organizational architecture.* (4th ed.) New York: McGraw-Hill Irwin.

[47]   *Is your team too big? Too small? What's the right number?* (2006, June 14). Knowledge@Wharton. 1–4. Retrieved from *http://knowledge.wharton.upenn.edu/articlepdf/1501.pdf?CFID=229450368&CFTOKEN=88199422&jsessionid=a830925615931f6489c14936442346954535*

[48]   Logan et al. (2008).

[49]   Dunbar, R.I.M. (1993). Coevolution of neocortical size, group size and language in humans. *Behavioral and Brain Sciences, 16,* 687.

50 Goodwin, D.K. (2005). *Team of rivals: The political genius of Abraham Lincoln.* New York, NY: Simon and Schuster.

51 Foote, S. (1986). *The Civil War: A narrative.* New York, NY: Random House.

52 Ratcliffe, J. (2002). Scenario planning: Strategic interviews and conversations. *Foresight, 4*(1), 19–30.

53 Hastings, R.R. (2012, September 17).Generations bring unique perspectives to work. *Society for Human Resource Management.* Retrieved from http://www.shrm.org/hrdisciplines/diversity/ articles/pages/generations-bring-unique-perspectives-to-work.aspx

54 Erikson, T. (2010). *What's next, gen X?* Boston: Harvard Business School Press.

55 Sarala, R. (2010). The impact of cultural differences and acculturation factors on post-acquisition conflict. *Scandinavian Journal of Management, 26*(1), 38–56.

56 Harding, D. and Rouse, T. (2007). Human due diligence. *Harvard Business Review, 85*(4), 124–31; Wall, S.J. and Wall, S.R. (2000). *The morning after: Making corporate mergers work after the deal is sealed.* Cambridge, MA: Perseus Publishing.

57 Colors in culture (n.d.). *Information is beautiful.* Retrieved from http://www.informationisbeautiful. net/visualizations/colours-in-cultures/

58 Wu, C. (n.d.). *Cultural gestures.* Retrieved from http://soc302.tripod.com/soc_302rocks/id6.html

59 Schein (1992).

60 John F. Kennedy quotes. (n.d.). *BrainyQuote.com.* Retrieved from http://www.brainyquote.com/ quotes/quotes/j/johnfkenn164001.html

61 David, F.R. (2005). *Strategic management concepts and cases* (10th ed.). Upper Saddle River, NJ: Pearson Education, Inc./Prentice Hall. pp. 9–10.

62 Corporate purpose. (n.d.). *Identityworks.com.* Retrieved from http://www.identityworks.com/ tools/corporate_brand_platforms_purpose.htm

63 Bill George on rethinking capitalism. (2013, December). *McKinsey & Company: Insights and Publications.* Retrieved from http://www.mckinsey.com/Insights/Leading_in_the_21st_century/ Bill_George_on_rethinking_capitalism?cid=other-eml-alt-mip-mck-oth-1312

[64] Zimmerer, T.W. and Scarborough, N.M. (2005). *Essentials of entrepreneurship and small business management* (6th ed.). Upper Saddle River, NJ: Pearson Education. (ISBN: 0536308411). p. 72.

[65] Montgomery, C.A. (2008, January). Putting leadership back into strategy. *Harvard Business Review, 86*(1), 57.

[66] Sinek, S. (2009). *Start with why: How great leaders inspire everyone to take action.* New York: Penguin.

[67] Jones, R. (2009). *The richest man in town: The twelve commandments of wealth.* New York: Hachette.

[68] Carroll, L., Gardner, M. (Ed.) and Tenniel, J. (Il.). (1999). *The annotated Alice* (The definitive ed.). New York: W.W. Norton. pp. 65–6.

[69] Malcolm X quotes. (n.d.). *Goodreads.* Retrieved from http://www.goodreads.com/quotes/362-if-you-don-t-stand-for-something-you-will-fall-for

[70] Montgomery (2008). p.58.

[71] Dalai Lama quotes. (n.d.). *BrainyQuote.com.* Retrieved from http://www.brainyquote.com/quotes/keywords/vision.html#IkjUDqgq6RDO3Pbh.99

[72] David, F.R. (2005). *Strategic management concepts and cases* (10th ed.). Upper Saddle River, NJ: Pearson Education, Inc./Prentice Hall. p. 9.

[73] Zimmerer and Scarborough (2005). p. 71.

[74] King, Jr., M.L. and Washington, J.M. (Ed.). (1991). *A testament of hope: The essential writings and speeches of Martin Luther King, Jr.* New York, NY: HarperCollins. p. 219.

[75] Ibid.

[76] Hsieh, T. (n.d.), *Startupquote.* Retrieved from http://startupquote.com/post/559927259

[77] Dhani Jones quotes. (n.d.). *BrainyQuotes.com.* Retrieved from http://www.brainyquote.com/quotes/authors/d/dhani_jones.html

Chapter 5
The Importance of Strategy

If you do good, people will accuse you of selfish, ulterior motives
  ... do good anyway.
If you are successful, you win false friends and true enemies
  ... be successful anyway.
The good you do today may be forgotten tomorrow
  ... do good anyway.[1]

This may be perceived among the nerdiest chapters of the book. However, the content has merit (there is method to the madness). Strategy is critical to success for any aspiring company—more especially middle market private equity portfolio companies. The credibility of the practical points in this chapter is undergirded with research from branded luminaries. One useful way to digest the content of this chapter may be within the simple "plan, do, check, act" quality principles whose roots trace to Dr. Edwards Deming and Dr. Walter A. Shewhart.[2] Essentially, this compels practitioners to memorialize a roadmap, follow the roadmap, monitor it relative to expected results, and take corrective actions as needed.

Strategy is an ancient concept. The word strategy traces its roots to the Greek "strategos," which regards the warring arts of the army general.[3] Note the word "art" instead of science. The definition implies the exercise of judgment relative to conditions. Stated another way, the art of wisdom is called upon to interpret the science defined by data. There are several possible right answers. Consider that all businesses are experiencing the following changes in their competitive environments:

- the globalization of customers,

- the preference by customers for partnership-type relationships,

- the customers' desire for solutions,

- the omnipresence of electronic commerce, and

- the steady increase in the power of the buyer.[4]

"Strategy" implies a plan. However, the plan may be in the head of a middle market CEO instead of being codified in a document. Moreover, the CEO's supporting cast may not be entirely clear about what is in her head. This phenomenon is further exacerbated by unexpected scenarios of CEO indisposition and other unforeseen phenomena.

"The essence of strategy is choosing what NOT to do."[5] Strategy entails "positioning a business to maximize the value of the capabilities that distinguish it from its competitors."[6] Since there are plentiful viable choices, it is critical to rationalize the best ones relative to a vetting rigor, complemented by leading indicators for appropriate dynamic adjustments. Absent this framework, focus may shift with the winds instead of abiding by persistent and consistent strategic intent.

Long-term business strategy is the pursuit of uniquely differentiable competitive advantage that results in profitable operations.[7] Strategy regards doing something different and differentiable; whereas, tactics regard doing something better than competitors.[8] Accordingly, leaders must continually reconcile the alchemy of these variables:

- "customers purchase comparative value,

- value is a function of price,

- price pressure in the market is relentless,

- firms have more control over their costs than they do over their prices,

- profitability is a function of price and cost, and

- profitability is the prerequisite to employee career possibilities."[9]

Perhaps the single most important strategic guiding principal is strategic intent. President Dwight D. Eisenhower reflected on strategic intent thusly from his experiences as Supreme Allied Commander in the World War II European Theater: "In preparing for battle … plans are useless, but planning is indispensable."[10] Strategic intent compels leaders to:

- prepare for the future,

- anticipate needs,

- use what is available,

- expect surprises,

- think both short and long term,

- dream productively, and

- leverage others' lessons.[11]

Strategic intent—the "What?"—should remain fairly stable. Tactics—the "How?"—may require more fluidity in deference to the issues of:

- speed,

- flexibility,

- integration, and

- innovation.[12]

This chapter will skew its focus toward the fundamentals of strategy as it pertains to private equity portfolio companies, although the principles enjoy universal utility. Strategy is essential to value-creation. The possibilities are influenced by market conditions, or ecosystem—the natural state of things absent the competitive impact of the company. In the wake of ecosystem changes, "the primary [leadership] responsibility … is to determine an organization's goals, strategy, and design, therein adapting the organization to a changing environment."[13] "Understanding the [contrarian views] is not merely nice and morally right; it is a strategic necessity."[14] Three basic strategies are available to leaders:

- cohabitation,

- retrenchment, and

- attack.[15]

"Cohabitation" is indicative of oligopolies whereby a few major competitors dominate the market. This could be used to describe the "big three" automaker era in Detroit: General Motors, Ford, and Chrysler. The defense industry approximates this configuration today. Although cohabitation may seem like a big company scenario, it is quite possible in the lower middle market for niche plays, that is to say, a comparatively modest total addressable market. Cohabitation can be tricky in oligopolistic sectors. For example, temptation occasionally corrupts leadership. Consequently, unflattering headlines may result from nefarious pursuits regarding price fixing and bribery.

"Retrenchment" is the reaction to a firm's conclusion that it cannot effectively compete. An example is major US air carriers who tried to compete with discount carriers like Southwest. Both United's Ted and Delta's Song were discontinued. For many US companies whose products entailed high direct labor content by unskilled workers, market share was lost to Asian interlopers. To avert retrenchment, many US manufacturers outsourced production for domestically created intellectual property to compete more effectively. Apple is an example of this global value chain. Again, retrenchment is not limited to big companies. Even in fragmented lower middle market arenas, the value proposition may be elusive for expanding the core product offering with seemingly complementary products. The new sandbox may be fraught with vicious price competition for a commoditized product. This runs the simultaneous risk of hurting brand equity while diluting execution focus on a less profitable endeavor. Thus, retrenchment becomes a practical option.

"Attack" is most beneficial to consumers. Free market competition provides customers the best products at the most competitive prices. The attack posture is relentlessly Darwinian. A company that rests on its laurels is essentially writing its obituary. This is one of the reasons that innovation is so essential to the strategic mix, as companies have to continually reinvent themselves. The beauty of the attack option in the lower middle market is to define the norms while defragmenting the market and capturing market share.

Consider the example of General Electric (GE). Beginning in the 1980s under Jack Welch, GE modeled both retrenchment and attack. The company determined that it needed to be among the top two providers in any market segment or it would divest the business.[16] This strategy is vindicated by Boston Consulting Group research in terms of economies of scale and pricing leverage. Stable markets result from a dominant player controlling about 50 percent market share, with the remainder controlled by two other dominant players.[17] Interestingly, supply chain efficiency has tilted some US manufacturing away from Asian outsourcing to US repatriation. One of the key competitive drivers for this development is speed.[18] Lean manufacturing principles are an enabler of speed. Favorable outcomes include higher asset turnovers and reduced production costs. Domestic business model efficiencies may now displace the freight costs and ocean-going cargo delays from Asian manufacturers.

The private equity strategic intent rationale for portfolio company value-creation is captured in the "investment thesis." Essentially, the investment thesis is the strategy for realizing a minimum internal rate of return for the investment hold period, typically a three to five year timeframe. The soundness of an investment thesis determines fundamental competitiveness for the portfolio company, and the potential reward to the fund from which the invested capital emanated.

There are two inherent challenges in private equity strategy. The first regards the efficacy of the fund strategy. Firms tend to identify and specialize in short list of industry verticals. Private equity firms make significant investments in specific knowledge (specialization) within industry verticals. Individual investment professionals tend to take the lead in developing marketing channels within industry verticals. Substantial time is devoted to trade shows, conferences, and luminary interaction to hone an investment strategy for a specific industry vertical. This process is a form of Michael Porter's product differentiation.[19] The verticals do not necessarily need to be complementary, but they should avoid outright clash. For example, it may be unlikely that a firm will specialize in both green energy and carbon fuels. The fund strategy affects the types of limited partner prospects that may be courted as fund investors. Indeed, limited partners have their own investment "personalities." In some instances, they are prohibited from certain types of investment because of conflicts rooted in espoused values, investment strategy, or social image. For example, following the Sandy Hook Elementary School shooting in Newton, Connecticut, on December 14, 2012, the California Public Employees' Retirement System (*CalPERS) pressured Cerberus to exit its investment in Freedom Group, Inc., a manufacturer of firearms. CalPERS invests $750 million with Cerberus.*[20]

The second challenge regards the efficacy of the investment thesis for the portfolio company. A popular one, for example, is identifying a promising performer in a highly fragmented industry vertical that serves as a platform. This platform is used to defragment the market via a combination of organic growth and judicious acquisitions. Recall that private equity firms eventually exit their portfolio company investments. Strategic buyers for such exits tend to be preferred over financial buyers (other private equity firms). Noteworthy, however, is that exit investors tend to prefer organic growth over "bought" growth.[21] The reason is simple: demonstrated core competencies in the scalable execution: marketing and selling prowess for which the fulfillment engine keeps up in robust, scalable fashion. We will explore marketing and selling more fully in Chapter 7: Marketing versus Selling.

Strategic buyers are rational acquirers of private equity portfolio companies. Strategic buyer interest in acquiring portfolio companies may be rooted in the target's effectiveness in defragmenting an industry vertical that is complementary to the strategic buyer's aspirations. "Build or buy" is a continual debate in dynamic businesses. Indeed, an acquisition may offer a strategic buyer the path of least resistance toward the best return on investment. As we will explore more fully in Chapter 6: Innovation and Value-creation, smaller companies are effective incubators for innovative value-creation. By contrast, established bureaucratic company cultures may be hostile to disruptively innovative endeavors as a threat to status quo. Consider Microsoft, which may buy a software application's owner instead of building a competing product. Of course, this phenomenon is but one rationale for buying proven value-creation capabilities.

The portfolio company's leadership team must take ownership of its investment thesis and translate it into daily tactical execution. However and ironically, the leadership team may not know it exists. The strategy (investment thesis) for a middle market portfolio company need not be overly complicated for practical reasons. First, the vertical analysis done by the private equity firm preceding pursuit of the portfolio company is leverageable across multiple portfolio company manifestations.

Second, when an investment transaction is entertained, the seller (potential portfolio company) is normally represented by an investment banker or other intermediary. Through proxy, the investment banker, on behalf of the seller, makes a pitch for the value-creating potential of the company. If the two visions—that of the private equity firm and the prospective portfolio company—have sufficient similarity, the courtship continues. The "book" compiled by the investment banker for the prospective portfolio company somewhat bridges the gap between the firm's vertical analysis and the prospective portfolio company's individual strategy. At a minimum, this is "straw man," or hypothetical scenario, for comparative juxtaposition.

Third, the individually tailored investment thesis crafted by the investment banking firm for the prospect, in anticipation of its becoming a portfolio company should the transaction consummate, provides additional insights for what the private equity firm thinks may be accomplished with the investment during the hold period. Post-close, focus pivots to portfolio company ownership for tactical execution of the investment thesis adopted by the private equity firm.

As investment thesis ownership transitions to the portfolio company, leaders have many tools at their disposal when approaching strategy. Among the staples is Michael Porter's Five Forces framework that compels strategist to consider:

- the threat of customers displacing incumbent products with substitutions, e.g., laundry detergent;

- the clout of suppliers with respect to potentially limited resources, e.g., oligopolies or monopolies such as oil refineries;

- the leverage of buyers who may control access to ultimate customers, e.g., big box retailers;

- the threat of new entrants whose disruptive innovation may antiquate incumbent products, e.g., electric car manufacturers; and

- rivalry among existing competitors for access to known markets, e.g., cellular technology versus landlines.[22]

In complement, perhaps two critical thinking questions benefit framing:

- "How can we beat last year's performance?;" and

- "What is [the specific] competition doing, and how can we beat them?"[23]

Corollaries to these framing questions are:

- "What does the company do well versus poorly?,"

- "What unmet customer needs await fulfillment?," and

- "What markets remain untapped?"

Relative to fragmented markets, the objective is keenly focused on accelerated defragmentation before a competitor trumps the move. As in physics, mass times velocity equals inertia.

The portfolio company CEO has three primary strategic responsibilities. First, the CEO should be the chief strategic officer who both seeks options as well as a process for developing those options. Second, the CEO should sponsor a plan that successfully executes in the present with an eye toward future scenarios, including the ability to pivot in response to dynamic ecosystem changes. Third, the CEO should indefatigably pursue new types of competitive edge instead of guarding the status quo.[24] Strategy formulation is comprised of complementary, synergistic elements: strategic thinking and strategic planning. Task-oriented professionals should take note that strategic planning not led by strategic thinking is problematic.[25]

Strategic Thinking and Foresight Principles

> *The future often acts like a drunken monkey stung by a bee—it is confused and disturbing, and its behavior is completely unpredictable.*[26]

Strategic thinking "involves the synthesis of information to identify issues, connections, and the organization more than quantifiable measures."[27] The construct includes seeing ahead, behind, above, below, beyond, and through.[28] Moreover, thoughtful, actionable items from strategic thinking impact individuals within the teams who are responsible for their implementation.[29] Strategic thinking:

- reconciles with purpose, vision, and values;

- regards the "cognitive processes required for the collection, interpretation, generation, and evaluation of information and ideas that shape an organization's sustainable competitive advantage;"[30]

- conjures ideation;

- may be akin to creativity in attempting to pose "What if?" scenarios;

- is focused on creating a vision for the future of the organization and on crafting a clear, concise blueprint for realizing that vision;"[31] and

- bridges "insight about the present and foresight about the future."[32]

In their book, *Blue Ocean Strategy*, W. Chan Kim and Renee Mauborgne metaphorically argue that effective strategic thinking averts "red oceans," or over-fished waters, in favor of "blue oceans," or waters with schools of undiscovered fish.[33] In complement, strategic planning follows thinking to take care of the fishmonger's boat, bait, crew, distribution channels, and customers. Blue versus red ocean tenets are summarized in Figure 5.1 T-account.[34]

Among the benefits of strategic thinking is its ability to break the bonds of convention and reduce the risk of groupthink mistakes. "Teams are subject to groupthink whereby team members focus on a single perspective and reinforce each other even though that perspective is inaccurate."[35] Strategic thinking may be understood in two phases: preparation and process. Preparation for a strategic conclave includes:

- concentration on the big picture,

- focus on the future,

- centering on synergies and efficiencies,

- embracing creativity,

- conducting proper analytics,

- challenging all assumptions, and

- recognizing the fallibility of source material.[36]

(–) CREDITS: *Red Oceans*	(+) DEBITS: *Red Oceans*
Compete in existing markets	Create uncontested markets
Beat the competition	Render the competition irrelevant
Exploit existing demand	Create and capture new demand
Make the value-cost trade-off	Break the value-cost trade-off
Align the business model's activities with its **strategic** choice of differentiation or low cost	Align the business model's activities with the **pursuit** of differentiation and low cost

Figure 5.1   Red and blue ocean T-account comparison

Source: Kim, W.C., and Mauborgne, R. (2005). *Blue Ocean Strategy*. Boston, MA: Harvard Business School Press.

In complement, seven principles benefit the strategic thinking process:

- scrutinizing the entire business model,

- studying the relationship between order and disorder,

- examining unintended consequences of possible catalysts,

- using process mapping to enhance the understanding of workflow (this should be expanded to include both the vendor supply and customer receipt ends of the value chain),

- scouring business sectors for best practice options,

- embracing non-linear analytical thinking, and

- utilizing perspective when encountering turmoil.[37]

Rhetorically, one might criticize the merits of strategic thinking if the futuristic variables have not be adequately pondered. Indeed, "if you can control the future, you do not need to predict it."[38] However, since control is unlikely, a methodology for evaluating possibilities is beneficial. Strategic foresight is such a methodology.

Strategic foresight is a discipline that is complementary to strategic thinking and should precede it. Knowing what strategic foresight is, and what it is not, are equally important. Strategic foresight is different from forecasting or strategic planning by nature of intent and time frame.[39] "Strategic foresight activities are unique among business practices because they deal with the long-term future."[40] "Strategic foresight is based on the principle of planning from the future back to the present, not the typical approach of planning from the present towards the future."[41] Foresight considers long-range possibilities that affect prudent near-term decision-making. Foresight commences with a time frame at least a decade into the future.[42] Effective strategic foresight includes a foundational understanding of constants, trends, issues, and events.[43] With the benefit of the foresight foundation, leaders are better prepared to engage strategic thinking and planning.

At this point, one might legitimately question how to reconcile a foresight perspective of 10 years out with a portfolio company investment hold period of three to five years. There is a simple answer: alignment. Whereas relatively near-term actions are creating results likely to attract a strategic buyer, the actions are more compelling if aligned with longer term vistas. Stated another way, such alignment communicates a value-creating annuity to the buyer. But there is an even bigger "customer" of foresight benefits: the private equity firm. Why? Because foresight principles guide the evaluation of an industry vertical. That is to say, in addition to the traditional homework done to scrutinize a vertical, add foresight principles. The foresight framework aids investment professionals in identifying and evaluating gaps that may otherwise trace back to avoidable root causes for writing off an investment.

Strategic foresight is a mechanism that sheds the deceptive shackles of conventional wisdom. Strategic foresight engages unknowns in scenario analysis. By contrast, strategic planning and forecasting deal with comparatively definitive variables. Foresight is critical to both survival and prosperity. Foresight anticipates the element of disruptive forces that:

- may or may not happen,

- in known or unknown form,

- in order to consider actions that preserve strategic intent.

Ancient mariners used the constellations for seafaring guidance. Foresight functions analogously. While navigation is fluid relative to winds and currents, the constellations were anchoring constants to guide ships' captains toward ultimate destinations. Foresight entails:

- preparing for the future,

- anticipating customer needs,

- using available information when ideal information does not exist,

- expecting the unexpected,

- thinking both long and short-term,

- dreaming productively to connect the ends and means, and

- leveraging others' successes—and mistakes.[44]

Four steps behoove foresight practitioners:

> *The first step in developing contingency plans is to identify possible surprising events... . Second, go beyond isolated events to identify possible surprising developments and alternative futures... . Third, understand the vulnerabilities. Lastly, for substantial threats, develop preventative and eventual strategies.*[45]

Several tools aid the foresight discipline. First, a concept map assists the foresight analyst with a picture of the business model.[46] The technique bears some resemblance to the value stream map within the Lean manufacturing discipline. Another useful tool is Six Sigma's SIPOC. SIPOC is an acronym for suppliers, inputs, processes, outputs, and customers. The objective of all of these tools is perspective so that issues are not overlooked, but rather evaluated in context. (See Figure 5.2.)

Second, those using foresight distinguish constants from trends. Constants are inelastic, that is to say, they do not change over time despite conditions within the ecosystem. For example, humans must constantly breathe oxygen to live. Trends must be distinguished from cycles. Moreover, trends may vacillate, but must not be confused with a cycle.[47] Trends easily last beyond the ten year horizon. Dominant "supertrends" include:

- technological progress,

- economic growth,

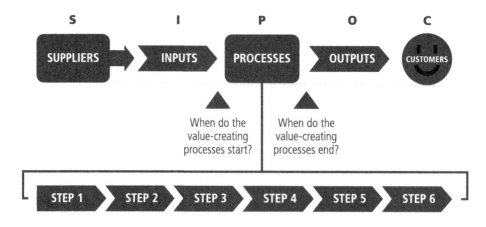

Figure 5.2   SIPOC high-level process map

- improving health,

- increasing mobility,

- environmental decline, and

- increasing "deculturation."[48]

Trends may be hard or soft.[49] Hard trends include:

- existence,

- change,

- patterns, and

- causality.[50]

For example, recessions are cyclical and may "softly" interrupt an underlying hard trend of economic growth. Pop culture may punctuate a hard trend with an adaptation. Additionally, the hard trend of technology enables the soft trends of music enjoyed over an iPod. Supertrends should be the primary focus of the strategist. Returning to our mariner analogy, a rogue wave or typhoon should not be misconstrued as a supertrend. In a Gladwellian sense, a rogue wave is a statistical outlier.[51]

Third, issues must be distinguished from events. An example of an issue is poverty. Implementing a living wage is an event in reaction to poverty. Horizon scanning is useful for keeping a pulse on trends, issues, and events. Industry trade publications, luminaries, thought leaders, think tanks, and academic research should be among the sources tapped. Several media outlets, such as *The Wall Street Journal*, accommodate horizon scanning via programmable notices tailored to topical material. Google also offers utility as its search engine is one of the most versatile and easily used research tools available.

Fourth, the present business strategy's competitiveness may be evaluated using the STEEP technique. STEEP is an acronym whose letters stand for social, technological, environmental, economic, and political.[52] See Table 5.1 for an example of a hypothetical wind turbine company.

Table 5.1   STEEP analysis example for a theoretical wind turbine company

Social	• Renewable energy enjoys favorable publicity as a pollution abatement alternative. However, there is a "not in my backyard" reaction to aesthetics, e.g., deployment on the Cape Cod, Massachusetts, shore.[53]
Technological	• There is no technological issue in running a turbine with wind. The question is power generation efficiency. • Wind turbines only work in an environment with prevailing, sufficient winds. Therefore, certain geographies are predisposed, e.g., Palm Springs, California, whereas others are not.
Environmental	• The ecological impact of wind turbines on air, water, and land is favorable. However, the turbines are attracting negative publicity for killing birds, e.g., bald eagles.[54]
Economic	• As (i) fossil fuel costs rise and (ii) economies of scale and technology drive manufacturing costs lower, product acceptance is likely to improve. • The ability of the US to compete as a global manufacturer of wind turbines must overcome comparatively higher direct labor costs, perhaps through automation.
Political	• Until a cost-effective alternative to fossil fuel and nuclear options emerge, "green" energy is largely propped by government subsidies. Governments tend to be subjective investors prone to poor credit underwriting decisions and scandal, e.g., Solyndra, a solar cell manufacturer and beneficiary of a \$535 million US Department of Energy loan that filed for Chapter 11 bankruptcy protection in 2011.

Functionally similar to the STEEP technique, another useful tool is the SWOT, which stands for strengths, weaknesses, opportunities and threats. Strengths and weaknesses are customer-perspective assessments of an organization's present-state capabilities. Opportunities and threats are company-perspectives of the evolutionary ecosystem over which control may be non-existent and influence may be nominal. See Table 5.2 for an example of applying the SWOT tool to the hypothetical wind turbine company. Both the STEEP and SWOT tools may be used for different angles on evaluating company competitiveness.

Table 5.2   SWOT analysis example for the manufacturing process in a hypothetical wind turbine company

Strengths	• Relationships with research institutions. • Pedigree of research and development unit.
Weaknesses	• Immature global value chain. • High direct labor costs.
Opportunities	• Outsource high direct labor content to developing nation manufacturing sources. • Government subsidies, e.g., enterprise zones, for domestic manufacturing.
Threats	• Possible intellectual property theft if manufacturing is outsourced. • Inability to achieve globally competitive price points absent government inducements benefiting manufacturing and consumption.

The SWOT might be better applied to the key functions of the business model instead of a macro, holistic application of the tool. For example, core competencies in manufacturing may be slipping relative to the competition—a point perhaps lost in applying the tool to the whole business model. Accordingly, a key business model component, or process, SWOT may be more revealing. The generic functions that Middle Market Methods™ asked clients to scrutinize in process SWOT fashion were:

- marketing,

- selling,

- customer service,

- procurement,

- operations,

- logistics (This may be more typical of manufacturing, whereby the product is delivered and, sometimes, installed at the customer.),

- quality,

- compliance (This is more of a regulatory compliance function for industries such as healthcare.),

- human resources,

- finance, and

- information technology.

Between the STEEP and SWOT exercises, a foundation is laid for a "crystal ball," or "What if?" exercise of critical thinking questions.[55]

Sixth, out of these critical thinking questions may emerge thematic signals. Accordingly, a futures wheel, or decision tree, enables the analyst to develop driving forces into first and second order consequences.[56] Decision trees are good visual tools for exploring decisions and their potential implications. While the State Department may not use the tool, per se, the logical construct is certainly how policy options are evaluated for issues such as Iranian nuclear bomb development. The concept may be applied to the events of the 1962 Cuban missile crisis as chronicled in then Attorney General Robert F. Kennedy's *Thirteen Days: A Memoir of the Cuban Missile Crisis.*

See Figure 5.3 for an example of applying to tool to *just one* of the driving forces behind recycled textile fiber adoption.

Seventh, Kurt Lewin's force field analysis is useful for identifying restrainers and enablers of the most compelling driving forces of an issue.[57] Continuing with the example of recycled textile fiber acculturation, See Figure 5.4 for an example of how the force field analysis tool is used.

Eighth, the two most compelling drivers from force field analysis crescendo as foundational elements of scenario analysis. Those two forces are equated with continua axes, each of which is bounded by extreme descriptors. Examples make the point clearer. For one such axis example, consider coal mines in West Virginia. Leaders who thought they were part of the American energy independence equation experienced a dramatic policy reversal between the George W. Bush and Barack Obama administrations. In this case, one of the continua axes might be the regulatory environment. One end depicts laissez faire governance while the opposite is stringent regulation.

Consider a different example: the Keystone XL pipeline project. One of the continua axes might be societal sustainable energy acculturation. One end of such an axis might be zealous environmental activism resisting construction. On the other end of the axis might be interests sympathetic to promoting

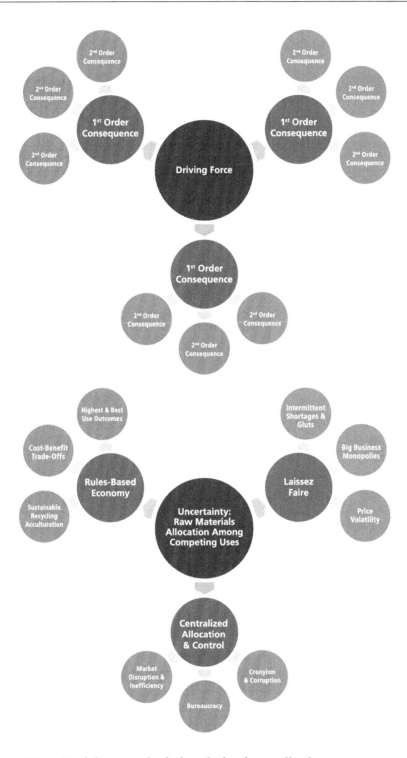

Figure 5.3   Decision tree depicting derivative, ordinal consequences

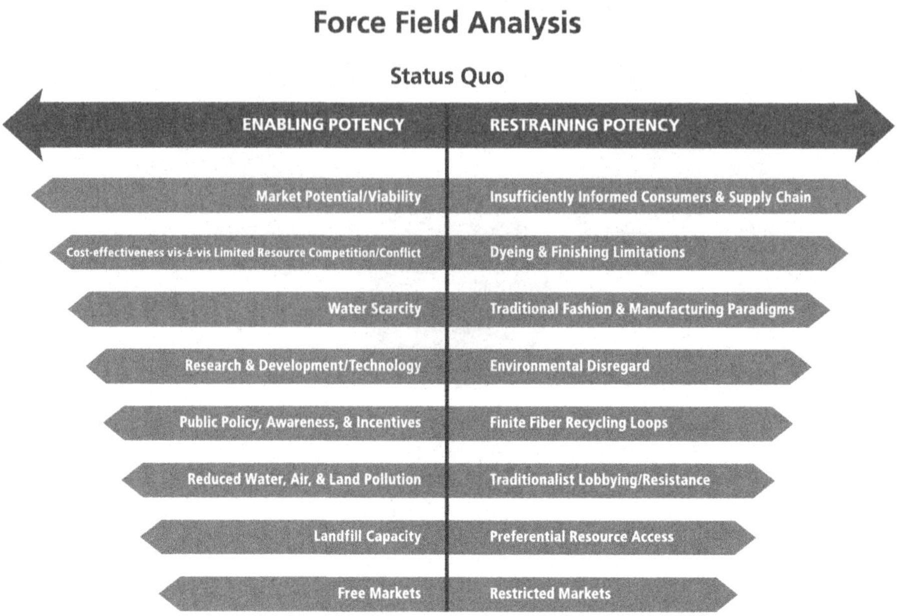

Force Field Analysis

Status Quo

ENABLING POTENCY	RESTRAINING POTENCY
Market Potential/Viability	Insufficiently Informed Consumers & Supply Chain
Cost-effectiveness vis-à-vis Limited Resource Competition/Conflict	Dyeing & Finishing Limitations
Water Scarcity	Traditional Fashion & Manufacturing Paradigms
Research & Development/Technology	Environmental Disregard
Public Policy, Awareness, & Incentives	Finite Fiber Recycling Loops
Reduced Water, Air, & Land Pollution	Traditionalist Lobbying/Resistance
Landfill Capacity	Preferential Resource Access
Free Markets	Restricted Markets

Figure 5.4   Force field analysis
Source: Adapted from Kurt Lewin

the pipeline for its economic benefits and energy independence for national security considerations.

Whatever the framed challenge may be, the point is that the force field analysis tool helps identify the two primary driving forces. Each force is depicted as an axis bounded by extreme positions. Then, the two axes are positioned for 90° intersection at their hypothetical midpoints to form four quadrants, i.e., the axes of uncertainty.[58] Those quadrants are scenarios that will bear names for further vetting. It is important to understand that scenarios are emphasized over variables. (See Figure 5.5 for an example.)

Ninth, once the scenario quadrants are developed, a narrative may ensue for strategic intent relative to the four scenarios. Absent foreknowledge, infallible prediction for a single scenario is elusive. However, that is not the point. Rather, scenario analysis helps leaders avert surprises with predetermined reactions. Users of foresight protocols rationalize three outcomes:

• the expected, or likely, future;

• an alternative future that addresses material variable mutations; and

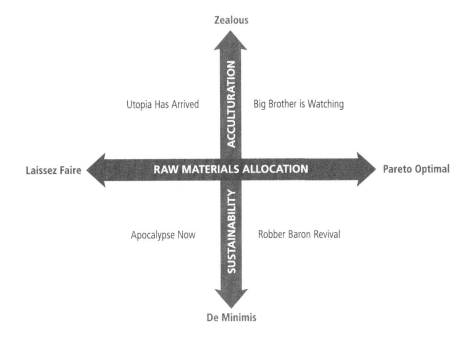

Figure 5.5   Axes of uncertainty example

Source: Lanier, J.A. (2012). LDSL 707 strategic foresight training session deliverable.
Regent University School of Business & Leadership. Virginia Beach, VA: Regent University.

- the unexpected, or surprise future.[59]

Logically, the rigor approximates stock trading algorithms. The strategic "bet" is further hedged by identifying leading indicators for signals foretelling each of the four scenarios.[60] Coming full circle, the analyst returns to horizon scanning as the early warning signal for leading indicators.

Horizon scanning should be used in conjunction with an engineering tool called failure modes and effects analysis, or FMEA.[61] Indeed, FMEA may offer a degree of objectivity in an otherwise subjective function for reconciling expected, alternative, and unexpected scenarios. FMEA sharpens horizon scanning by equating scenario risk with three criteria on a scale of one to 10:

- Consequence, or severity, of an event: A score of one is inconsequential whereas a score of 10 could be associated with death (depending on the context of the exercise). For example, the Chernobyl nuclear reactor incident in Russia would rate a 10.

- Frequency of event occurrence: A score of one equates to the event nearly never happening, whereas a score of 10 represents a very high frequency of occurrence. For example, medieval alchemists logged numerous attempts at turning lead into gold. There endeavors always failed, so this example would rate a 10.

- Ease of failure detection: A score of one equates to the near certain detection whereas a 10 is nearly uncertain and beyond reasonable control. For example, the forensics following the mid-flight explosion in *Apollo 13* traced back to an undetected manufacturing and assembly defect in an otherwise rigorous and highly-controlled process. The *Apollo 13* example may be at nine.

The consequence, frequency of occurrence, and detection scores are multiplied by each other to create a risk priority number from one to 1000. The higher the score, the better the horizon scanning should be aimed at leading indicators. In their book, *Decisive: How to Make Better Choices in Life and Work*, Chip and Dan Heath embrace an analogous technique in something they call a pre-mortem. From a decade hence perspective, a pre-mortem entails asking what disaster might befall an organization whose signals could be detected in the present.[62]

By example, let's return to the Keystone XL Pipeline project to apply FMEA for transporting Canadian crude oil to US refineries using the axes of uncertainty scenarios labeled in Figure 5.5. Whereas in engineering applications FMEA enjoys statistical precision, subjectivity is clearly more evident in scenario analysis. Table 5.3 demonstrates both the conundrum and the need for relevant horizon scanning for leading indicators. Of course, the FMEA must adopt a particular constituency's perspective. Accordingly, the Table 5.3 example will employ the green energy enthusiasts' perspective. (Note: No presumption exists between this example and alignment with any activist's perspective.)

Table 5.3   Failure modes and effects analysis tool

	Scenario 1	Scenario 2
What is the scenario?	Big Brother is Watching	Robber Baron Revival
Coordinates	Pareto optimal raw materials allocation; zealous sustainability acculturation	Pareto optimal raw materials allocation; de minimis sustainability acculturation
What constitutes scenario failure? *Note: "Failure" is the antithesis of the scenario descriptor coordinates.*	The Federal government cannot persuade the electorate on the merits of sustainability and legislation denies Federal regulators purview over pipeline approval.	The Federal government enjoys popular support for throttling carbon fuel processing, but legislation denies Federal regulators purview over pipeline approval.
What is the potential impact for the failure of this scenario to materialize? *Note: This depends on the perspective of the analyst. The assumption for this example is the green energy activist.*	The pipeline proceeds unabated.	The pipeline proceeds until lobbyists successfully influence legislation and regulation.
On a scale of 1–10, what is the consequence or severity of failure?	10	9
On a scale of 1–10, what is the frequency of failure?	5	6
On a scale of 1–10, what is the likely detection of adverse trends?	5	5
Multiply the three numbers above to create the risk priority number.	250	270

	Scenario 3	Scenario 4
What is the scenario?	Apocalypse Now	Utopia Has Arrived
Coordinates	Laissez faire raw materials allocation; de minimis sustainability acculturation	Laissez faire raw materials allocation; zealous sustainability acculturation
What constitutes scenario failure? *Note: "Failure" is the antithesis of the scenario descriptor coordinates.*	The Federal government enjoys popular support for throttling carbon fuel processing, and has the legal and regulatory authority to impose its will on carbon-based energy production—but does nothing.	The Federal government cannot persuade the electorate on the merits of sustainability, but has the legal and regulatory authority to impose its will on carbon-based energy production.
What is the potential impact for the failure of this scenario to materialize? *Note: This depends on the perspective of the analyst. The assumption for this example is the green energy activist.*	The Federal government inexplicably eschews exercising its legal and regulatory authority. The pipeline proceeds.	The Federal government announces that it will not wield its legal and regulatory authority unless and until popular opinion changes. The pipeline proceeds.
On a scale of 1–10, what is the consequence or severity of failure?	8	9
On a scale of 1–10, what is the frequency of failure?	6	6
On a scale of 1–10, what is the likely detection of adverse trends?	7	4
Multiply the three numbers above to create the risk priority number.	336	216

Among the virtues of scenario analysis is the healthy debate within leadership teams to develop contingencies. The team interaction reveals not only what their teammates think, but how their teammates think. These exchanges afford opportunities for factual enlightenment, as well as dispelling positions contradicted by irrefutable factual evidence. Of course, the teams may identify variables for which there are no facts to do either. However, this enigma does not necessarily equate to immateriality. Rather, the team may have stumbled upon something truly important for establishing competitive edge. Keep in mind, it was Royal Dutch Shell that elevated foresight principles to their rightful strategic notoriety by employing them to anticipate and prepare for the Arab oil embargo of the 1970s. Instead of suffering decimation, the company catapulted to a position of strength.[63]

In wrapping up the merits of foresight principles, the question turns to frequency of updates. Two points are offered. First, horizon scanning should be continuous as the data are leading indicators. Many leaders already do forms of horizon scanning although they may not recognize it as such. Relative to foresight scenarios, horizon scanning should be formally referenced quarterly, perhaps in conjunction with board of director meeting cycles and private equity firm portfolio reviews. The actual foresight scenarios should be more deliberately revisited annually for material modifications, as foresight scenarios guide normal strategic planning cycles described in the next section.

Strategic Planning

> *A good plan, violently executed now, is better than a perfect plan next week.*[64]

"Strategic planning is a process used to develop supporting analysis and to communicate and implement the chosen strategy."[65] Strategic planning answers "How?" questions relative to the "What if?" questions of foresight principles. Indeed, strategic planning may be more tactical in nature when applied in conjunction with foresight and strategic thinking principles. Strategic planning translates dreams into value-creating processes. Stated another way, strategic planning transforms thought into actionable roadmaps.

Unfortunately, the majority of typical company employees are detached from their company's strategy.[66] One of the root causes of this phenomenon is their lack of inclusion in the process, exacerbated by poor communication and disconnection from the performance management system. Foresight, strategic thinking, and strategic planning improve by inclusiveness and diversity.[67] Diverse inclusiveness provides numerous benefits, including:

- better decision quality,

- familiarity with strategic intent,

- clarity of execution ownership, and

- risk awareness.[68]

Inclusiveness doubles as a communication medium and quality control mechanism. Indeed, "all of us are smarter than any of us."[69] Moreover, diverse inclusion:

- enhances dispersion of specific knowledge,

- fosters collaboration,

- encourages teamwork,

- enriches personal development, and

- improves the change-management process.[70]

Companies must be competitive in three primary categories:

- products (broadly defined to include services),

- customer relations, and

- operations.

The differentiation extensions of these three primary categories are innovation for products and services, customer intimacy for customer relations, and operational excellence for operations. However, as points of differentiation, the decision becomes either or, not both and.[71] That is to say, if you choose to differentiate through operational excellence, the research indicates that businesses cannot simultaneously differentiate via customer intimacy or innovation. (See Figure 5.6.) Jim Collins described this phenomenon in terms of the "hedgehog principle:"

- knowing what you do in world class form,

- sticking to your passions, and

- knowing the economic levers that tune the effort.[72]

Southwest Airlines, for example, differentiates via operational excellence. Their asset turnover is phenomenal. Their model was designed to compete with ground transportation—not other airlines. Operational excellence is the reason Southwest Airlines does not have first class seats or meals. The objective is low cost per passenger mile. Their stock is one of the all-time best performers in substantiation of their strategy. Similarly, Walmart, FedEx, United Parcel Services, eBay, and Amazon engage operational excellence through their supply chain management.

Several leadership best practices are encapsulated to make strategic initiatives actionable:

- prioritization,

- planning,

Figure 5.6   Treacy and Wiersema's business model differentiation options

Source: Treacy, M. and Wiersema, F. (1995). *The discipline of market leaders*. New York, NY: Perseus.

- delegated responsibility,

- inclusion, and

- communication.[73]

A "4+2" formula strengthens actionable best practices. The "4" regards four prerequisite management practices of:

- strategy,

- execution,

- culture, and

- structure.

In conjunction with the prerequisites, the "2" stands for two of four optional practices:

- talent development,

- innovation,

- leadership, and

- mergers and partnerships.[74]

Prolific writers on the topic of innovation may challenge the notion that it is optional relative to the "4+2" formula, for example, Clayton M. Christensen.

When companies choose among strategic initiatives, leaders must take care to focus on a manageable, vital few for several reasons. Resource allocation is integral to the rationale. Limited access to capital and personnel infer that the same people doing their day jobs are called upon to execute the "new stuff" with a longer payoff. The important naturally competes with the urgent.[75] Consequently, the workload must be managed to avert burnout and turnover from overwhelmed employees. Boiling a pot of water is more practical and manageable than boiling an ocean.

Middle Market Methods™ encouraged its private equity clients to adopt the best practice of a proximal post-close portfolio company strategic session to drive specificity about initiatives and their execution plans. This should also be recognized as the point at which portfolio company ownership of the investment thesis is made clear. The participants should include those who own key functional components of the business model, as well as significant individual contributors. Sessions for Middle Market Methods™ clients were two-day off-sites in a venue isolated from daily distractions. The sessions are preceded by relevant homework assignments relative to the ecosystem in which the company competes.

Most of the time, private equity investment teams participated in the sessions. However, they were encouraged support the session—not drive it. The portfolio company team should own the session and the investment teams should observe the dynamic for coaching clues. The investment teams should prepare for surprises that typically come from including the right people in these sessions. Whereas participants may confirm, complement, and clarify some of the investment thesis and the transaction diligence, they may also refute some of the baseline, as well as reveal things that were totally missed. The investment professionals should be grateful for such enlightenment.

Models are useful for such planning exercises as they provide a rigor to guide the process.[76] Indeed, this may be the first time any of the portfolio leadership team has experienced such a conclave. Middle Market Methods™ referred to these sessions as The Value-creation Roadmap™. Such planning sessions are inherently risk-mitigating in nature.[77] "Dividing meager resources across a host of medium-term operational goals creates mediocrity on a broad scale."[78] Accordingly, Middle Market Methods™ advised the portfolio companies of its private equity firm clients to adopt the Ram Charan and Larry Bossidy's rule of three[79] and identify the highest priority in each of the following categories:

- growth,

- efficiency, and

- culture.

Middle Market Methods™ utilized a 3x3 matrix to facilitate the exercise. (See Figure 5.7.) Growth reconciles acquisitive versus organic pursuits. Efficiency drives focus on keeping up with the growth to achieve economies of scale for improved profitability.

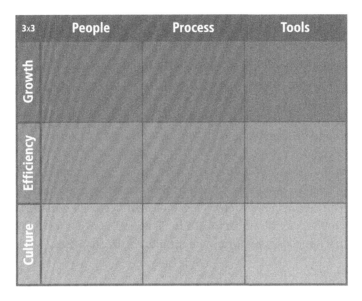

Figure 5.7   A strategic 3x3 framework

Culture was addressed earlier in Chapter 4: The DNA of Packs. Culture encompasses the unique way the members of the organization approach their internal and external deportment. Should the private equity firm investment team participate in the off-site exercise, they derive a contextual glimpse of senior leadership that lends critical insights for value-creation. The CEO sets the cultural tone. Accordingly, the investment team (and the board) should understand who is driving the bus. Relative to culture, four generic CEO responses emerge:

- Rejection: Such CEOs regard cultural initiatives as nonsense undeserving of their time. This attitude is a serious problem. If such leaders do not soon change their attitudes, they simply have to go.

- Imposters: These CEOs talk cultural emphasis, but they do not invest any personal leadership capital in shaping culture to undergird strategy. As in the case of the rejection types described above, they must either change or leave.

- Coachable: These CEOs recognize the merits of the cultural argument, but may not be familiar with best practices for optimizing such utility. They welcome coaching and mentoring to master the skills.

- Visionary: These CEOs are rare and tantamount to Everett Rogers Diffusion of Innovations "innovator" class. They "get it" and only require nominal support for cultural initiatives.

In all three categories—growth, efficiency, and culture, leaders are reminded that the articulation of people, processes, and tools contribute to execution effectiveness and efficiency.

Occasionally, these planning sessions produce a plethora of initiative possibilities. This is a good thing and may represent the ingredients for a multi-year plan. The challenge is identifying the most accretive vital few from the many. Two tools provide efficient utility. The first is a pay-off matrix whose axes are impact and degree of implementation difficulty. (See Figure 5.8.) The

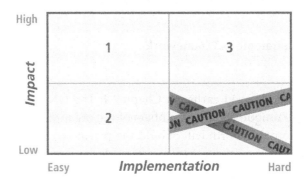

Figure 5.8   Pay-off matrix tool

lines of demarcation on the pay-off matrix between low- and high-impact, as well as easy and hard implementation, must be determined relative to the company's hold period strategy. If discussion around the pay-off matrix cannot triage the list, then Plan B is a criteria-based matrix.[80] (See Figure 5.9.) The process is simple:

- First, identify evaluation criteria.

- Afterwards, each evaluation criterion is weighted on a scale of 1–10, one being the lowest weighting and 10 being the highest weighting. Given the three-to-five-year hold period time horizon, most of the weightings may unsurprisingly approach 10.

- Next, individual options are rated by each evaluation criterion. A low rating corresponds numerically to one, a medium rating corresponds to three, and a high rating corresponds to nine. These are deliberately imbalanced to "manufacture" distinction.

- Then, for each option's evaluation criterion, the weighting factor is multiplied by the rating factor to create an evaluation criterion product, or score.

- Subsequently, the criteria products are summed to determine each option's total score.

- Finally, a "winner" is identified by the option with the highest total score.[81]

Options	Criterion 1		Criterion 2		Criterion 3		Total
	Weighting		Weighting		Weighting		
	Rating: L=1 M=3 H=9	Score	Rating: L=1 M=3 H=9	Score	Rating: L=1 M=3 H=9	Score	
		0		0		0	0
		0		0		0	0
		0		0		0	0
		0		0		0	0
		0		0		0	0
		0		0		0	0

Figure 5.9   Criteria-based matrix tool

Strategic planning is incomplete without implementation and communication. "People don't plan to fail, they fail to plan."[82] Moreover, teams should "plan their work and work their plan."[83] One of the most effective tools is the project plan. Follow-up by virtue of a project plan is rationalized by a simple fact. The strategic planning process argued in this chapter is new to most middle market leaders. Even amid the most conscientious intentions, only about seven in 10 will follow through sans an institutionalized nudge.[84] Project management fills the bill. Microsoft Project is particularly useful to the endeavor. The Gantt chart is a powerful visual tool for conveying time lines and critical path dependencies. These plans tend to be routinely tracked in the reporting metrics and board agendas.[85] The project plan is particularly valuable to portfolio company leadership and investment team discussions about the disruption of an acquisition integration to the critical path of the strategic project plan.

Practical perspective and prudence must not become the casualty of the task-orient passion for performance. Two anecdotes are worth sharing. The first example is general. I initially observed the power of the planning process in a company that enjoyed a double digit EBITDA exit multiple. Indeed, 12 months before the sale, the business was not actually saleable. The CEO confided that strategic planning made *the* difference because it removed the mystery for what was expected of his team by the private equity firm.

The second example corresponds to efficiency initiatives. As a Six Sigma Master Black Belt from GE, I was trained to adhere to 15 steps of a rigor to find root cause to defects and variation. In a large and efficiently managed organization, the odyssey may be protracted in pursuit of needles in haystacks. The justification is rooted in economies of scale associated with substantial enterprises. However, this is nowhere near the case in the middle market. Experienced executives coming out of larger organizations to operate in the middle market must recalibrate their understanding of the 80/20 principle to avoid stepping over $1000 bills to pick up pennies. Since most private equity portfolio companies are breaking out of the norming stage toward performing (see Figure 1.1 in Chapter 1: Introduction), there are promising areas to tackle amid a "target rich" environment. The rule of thumb is deceptively unpretentious: If the action is not measurable and heading in a gratifying direction within 90 days, the odds are high that the priorities are wrong.

Endnotes

[1]   Keith, K.M. (2001). *The paradoxical commandments*. Retrieved from http://www. paradoxicalcommandments.com/

[2]   Moen, R. and Norman, C., (n.d.). Evolution of the PDCA cycle. *Associates in Process Improvement*. Retrieved from http://pkpinc.com/files/NA01MoenNormanFullpaper.pdf

[3]   Sheehan, R. (2005). What is nonprofit strategy? *Prepared for the 34th annual conference of the Association for Research on Nonprofit Organizations and Voluntary Action, Washington, D.C.* College Park: MD: Robert H. Smith School of Business, University of Maryland. Retrieved from http:// www.nationalcne.org/index.cfm?fuseaction=feature.display&feature_id=137

[4]   Galbraith, J. (2002). *Designing organizations: An executive guide to strategy, structure and process.* San Francisco: Jossey-Bass. p. 92.

[5]   Magretta, J. (2011).*Understanding Michael Porter: The essential guide to competition and strategy.* Boston, MA: Harvard Business Review Press. p. 2.

[6]   Porter, M.E. (1980). *Competitive strategy: Techniques for analyzing industries and competitors.* New York, NY: Free Press. p. 47.

[7]   Henderson, B.D. (1980). Strategic and natural competition. In Stern, C.W. and Deimler, M.S. (Eds.). (2006). *The Boston Consulting Group on strategy: Classic concepts and new perspectives* (2nd ed.). Hoboken, NJ: John Wiley & Sons. p. 1.

[8]   De Kluyver, C.A. and Pearce, J.A. (2009). *Strategy: A view from the top (an executive perspective)* (3rd ed.). Upper Saddle River, NJ: Pearson Education. (ISBN: 9780136041405). p. 6.

[9]   Lanier, J.A. (2010, December 12).The leadership waltz: Mentoring vs. discipling between leaders and followers. *Ezine@articles.* Retrieved from http://ezinearticles.com/?The-Leadership-Waltz:-Mentoring-Vs.-Discipling-Between-Leaders-and-Followers&id=5540683

[10]   Dwight D. Eisenhower quotes. (n.d.). *BrainyQuote.com.* Retrieved from http://www.brainyquote.com/quotes/quotes/d/dwightdei164720.html

[11]   Cornish, E. (2004). *Futuring: The exploration of the future.* Bethesda, MD: World Future Society. (ISBN: 0–930242–61–0). pp. 1–8.

[12]   Ashkenas, R., Ulrich, D., Jick, T. and Kerr, S. (2002). *The boundaryless organization: Breaking the chains of organizational structure.* San Francisco, CA: Jossey-Bass. pp. x–xi.

[13]   Daft, R.L. (2007). *Organization theory and design* (9th ed.). Mason, OH: Thomson South-Western. p. 56; Kotter, J.P. (1982, November-December). What effective general managers really do. *Harvard Business Review,* 156–67.; Mintzberg, H. (1973). *The nature of managerial work.* New York, NY: Harper & Row.

[14]   Zweifel, T.D. (2003). *Culture clash: Managing the global high-performance team.* New York: SelectBooks. (ISBN: 1590790510). p. xvii.

[15]   Stalk, Jr., G. (1988). Time-the next source of competitive advantage. In Stern, C.W. and Deimler, M.S. (Eds.). (2006). *The Boston Consulting Group on strategy: Classic concepts and new perspectives* (2nd ed.). Hoboken, NJ: John Wiley & Sons. pp. 63–81.

[16]   Welch (2005); Welch, J. and Byrne, J.A. (2001). *Jack: Straight from the gut*. New York: Warner Business Books.

[17]   Henderson, B.D. (1976). The rule of three or four. In Stern, C.W. and Deimler, M.S. (Eds.). (2006). *The Boston Consulting Group on strategy: Classic concepts and new perspectives* (2nd ed.). Hoboken, NJ: John Wiley & Sons. pp. 31–4.

[18]   Stalk (1988).

[19]   Porter (1980).

[20]   Lattman, P. (2012, December 18). In an unusual move, Cerberus to sell gun company. *DealBook*. Retrieved from http://dealbook.nytimes.com/2012/12/18/cerberus-to-sell-gunmaker-freedom-group/

[21]   Lafley, A.G. and Charan, R. (2008). *The game-changer: How you can drive revenue and profit growth with innovation*. New York: Random House. p. 5.

[22]   Magretta (2011); Porter (1980).

[23]   Welch, J. (2005). *Winning*. New York: HarperCollins. p. 197.

[24]   Montgomery, C.A. (2008, January). Putting leadership back into strategy. *Harvard Business Review*, 86(1), pp. 54–60.

[25]   Sanders, T.I. (1998). *Strategic thinking and the new science: Planning in the midst of chaos, complexity and change*. New York: Simon Schuster. p. 137.

[26]   Chermack, T.J. (2011). *Scenario planning in organizations: How to create, use and assess scenarios*. San Francisco: Berrett-Koehler. p. xv.

[27]   Sanders (1998). p. 162.

[28]   Mintzberg, H., Ahlstrand, B. and Lampel, J. (2005). *Strategy safari: A guided tour through the wilds of strategic management*. New York: The Free Press. pp. 126–8.

[29]   Hughes and Beatty (2005). p. 45.

[30]   Hughes, R.L. and Beatty, K.C. (2005). *Becoming a strategic leader: Your role in your organization's enduring success*. San Francisco, CA: Jossey-Bass. p. 45.

31 De Kluyver, C.A. and Pearce, J.A. (2009). *Strategy: A view from the top (an executive perspective)* (3rd ed.). Upper Saddle River, NJ: Pearson Education. (ISBN: 9780136041405). p. 250.

32 Sanders (1998). p. 52.

33 Kim, W.C. and Mauborgne, R. (2005). *Blue ocean strategy*. Boston, MA: Harvard Business School Press. p. 4.

34 Ibid. p. 18.

35 Shimizu, K. and Hitt, M.A. (2004). Strategic flexibility: Organizational preparedness to reverse ineffective strategic decisions. *Academy of Management Executive, 18*(4), 52.

36 Bacal, R. (2010). What is strategic thinking? *Strategic and Business Planning Free Resource Center.* Retrieved from http://work911.com/planningmaster/faq/thinkingstrategicthinking.htm

37 Sanders (1998). pp. 78–9.

38 Heath, C. and Heath, D. (2013). *Decisive: How to make better choices in life and work.* New York: Crown.

39 Van der Heijden, K. (2005). *Scenarios: The art of strategic conversation* (2nd ed.). Chichester, West Sussex, UK: John Wiley. (ISBN: 978–0–470–02368–6)

40 Hines, A. and Bishop, P. (2006). *Thinking about the future: Guidelines for strategic foresight.* Washington, DC: Social Technologies, LCC. p. 13.

41 Marsh, N., McAllum, M. and Purcell, D., (2002) *Strategic foresight: The power of standing in the future.* Melbourne: Crown Content. (ISBN: 1–74095–004–6). p. 2.

42 Ibid.

43 Gary, J. (2012, May 7). Residency presentation: Strategic foresight. *Regent University Global School of Leadership and Entrepreneurship.* Virginia Beach, VA: Regent University.

44 Cornish (2004).

45 Bishop and Hines (2006). pp. 185–6.

46 Gary (2012).

[47]   Cornish (2004).

[48]   Ibid.

[49]   Burris, D. and Mann, J.D. (2011). *Flash foresight: How to see the invisible and do the impossible*. New York: HarperCollins.

[50]   Cornish (2004).

[51]   Gladwell, M. (2011). *Outliers: The story of success*. New York: Little, Brown and Company.

[52]   Van der Heijden (2005). pp. 183–6; Bishop and Hines (2006). p. 92.

[53]   Zeller, Jr., T. (2013, February 23). Cape wind: Regulation, litigation and the struggle to develop offshore wind power in the US The Huffington Post. Retrieved from http://www.huffingtonpost.com/2013/02/23/cape-wind-regulation-liti_n_2736008.html

[54]   Cappiello, D. (2012, May 14). Why wind farms kill eagles with federal impunity. The Christian Science Monitor. Retrieved from http://www.csmonitor.com/Environment/Latest-News-Wires/2013/0514/Why-wind-farms-kill-*eagles-with-federal-impunity*

[55]   Burchsted, S. and Byrne, J. (2001). *Shaping our future: Facilitator's guide book*. Shelburne, VT: Foundation for Our Future and Center for a Sustainable Future. p. 16–20.

[56]   Ibid. pp. 33–6.

[57]   Gold, M. (Ed.) (1999). *The complete social scientist: A Kurt Lewin reader*. Washington, D.C.: The American Psychological Association.

[58]   Ralston, B. and Wilson, I. (2006). *The scenario-planning handbook: A practitioner's guide to developing and using scenarios to direct strategy in today's uncertain times*. Mason, OH: South-Western Educational. (ISBN: 0324312857). pp. 111–7.

[59]   Bishop, P. (2008, August 15). *Futures studies, University of Houston: Katy ISD*; Gary (2012).

[60]   Schoemaker, P.J.H. (2002). *Profiting from uncertainty: Strategies for succeeding no matter what the future brings*. New York: Free Press. (ISBN: 0743223284). pp. 148–9.

[61]   Pande, P.S., Neuman, R.P. and Cavanagh, R.R. (2002). *The six sigma way team fieldbook: An implementation guide for process improvement teams*. New York: McGraw-Hill. pp. 296–7.

[62] Heath and Heath (2013).

[63] Ralston and Wilson (2006).

[64] Stroup, F. (n.d.). Articles/biographies/military leaders/Patton, George S. *Freeinsociety.com*. Retrieved from http://www.freeinfosociety.com/article.php?id=211

[65] De Kluyver and Pearce (2009). p. 250.

[66] Kaplan, R.S. and Norton, D.P. (2001). *The strategy-focused organization: How balanced scorecard companies thrive in the new business environment*. Cambridge, MA: Harvard Business School Publishing Corporation.

[67] David, F.R. (2005). *Strategic management concepts and cases* (10th ed.). Upper Saddle River, NJ: Pearson Education, Inc./Prentice Hall; Hughes and Beatty (2005); Ratcliffe, J. (2002). Scenario planning: Strategic interviews and conversations. *Foresight*, 4(1), 19–30; Seidl, D. (2007, February). General strategy concepts and the ecology of strategy discourses: A systematic-discursive perspective. *Organization Studies*, 28(2), 197–218; Kotter, J.P. (1996). *Leading change* (1st ed.). Boston, MA: Harvard Business School Press; Brickley et al. (2007).

[68] David (2005). p. 15.

[69] Japanese proverb quotes. (n.d.). *Thinkexist.com*. Retrieved from http://thinkexist.com/quotation/none_of_us_are_as_smart_as_all_of/160488.html

[70] Brickley et al. (2007); Goman, C.K. (2010). Tomorrow's top talent. *Sales & Service Excellence*, 10(10), 4.

[71] Treacy, M. and Wiersema, F. (1995). *The discipline of market leaders*. New York, NY: Perseus.

[72] Collins, J. (2001). *Good to great: Why some companies make the leap and others don't*. New York, NY: HarperCollins.

[73] Drucker, P. (1985). *Innovation and entrepreneurship*. New York: HarperCollins. (ISBN: 9780060851132)

[74] Joyce, W., Nohria, N. and Roberson, B. (2003). *What really works: The 4+2 formula for success*. New York, NY: HarperColllins.

[75] Covey, S.R. (2004). *The 7 habits of highly effective people*. New York, NY: Simon & Schuster.

[76]   De Kluyver and Pearce (2009); Mintzberg et al. (2005).

[77]   De Kluyver and Pearce (2009).

[78]   Hamel, G. and Prahalad, C.K. (1993, March-April). *Harvard Business Review*, 71(2), 79.

[79]   Bossidy, L. and Charan, R. (2002). *Execution: The discipline of getting things done*. New York, NY: Crown Business.

[80]   Pande et al. (2002). pp. 296–7.

[81]   Lanier, J.A. (2012). Transformational organizational design: Appealing to successive generations of workers. *Journal of Strategic Leadership*, 4(1), 29.

[82]   Mackay, H. (1997). *Dig your well before you're thirsty*. New York: Doubleday. p. 287.

[83]   Ibid. p. 171.

[84]   Goldsmith, M. (2007). *What got you here won't get you there*. New York: Hyperion. pp. 164–5.

[85]   De Kluyver and Pearce (2009). p. 250.

Chapter 6
Innovation and Value-creation

"Strong minds discuss ideas. Average minds discuss events. Weak minds discuss people."[1]

Just as the previous chapter on strategy, this, too, may be perceived to be on the nerdier end of the spectrum. Since innovation is essential to value-creation, we do well to understand innovation in a more holistic context. The most compelling reason is that the future belongs to the innovative. Therefore, innovation is non-negotiable.

William Shakespeare's immortal *Romeo and Juliet* penned in iambic pentameter, "What's in a name? That which we call a rose by any other name would smell as sweet."[2] The business prosperity rose is named "innovation." Similar to Shakespeare's plays, innovative value-creation encounters many plot twists—some tragic—in pursuit of customer moments of truth: product purchase, product usage, and repeat purchase.[3] Indeed, as was the case with Shakespeare's Montagues and Capulets, occasional irreversible pain is the price paid for counterproductive attitudes toward the prevailing competitive environment. Innovators prefer the alluring fragrance of the rose despite its threat of thorns.

"People want to be part of growth, not endless cost cutting."[4] Growth is exciting and promises a tomorrow. Innovation is a necessary part of inventing tomorrow. Civilization depends on innovation; "innovation rescued humanity from privation."[5] However, the data are discouraging to the fainthearted:

- "As many as 60 percent of new product development initiatives are cancelled before they come to market, and of the 40 percent that do come to market, 40 percent of them fail to make a profit."[6]

- New product initiatives relate to existing products about 75 percent of the time.[7] This infers that only about 25 percent of innovation regards new products.

- About 60 percent of that 25 percent directly challenges existing competition.

- Deductively, only about 10 percent of innovation entails new products for new markets.[8]

Nurturing creativity and innovation is a vital leadership competency.[9] "Companies cannot build a culture of innovation without cultivating people who do."[10] There are three innovation myths:

- innovation is limited to products,

- the players are exclusionary and preordained, and

- only the loaded (wealthy) may ante up.[11]

The stakeholders of private equity investments create both extrinsic and intrinsic value by applying to the innovative process Tom Morris' "seven Cs of success in business" described in *The Art of Achievement*:

- *conceiving* a plethora of both incremental and disruptive innovation applied to both products and processes,

- exuding *confidence* in developing markets toward commercial viability,

- *concentrating* on first mover advantage and customer satisfaction,

- *consistently* pursuing excellence in low cost production,

- *committing* to superior quality and continual reinvention,

- exercising *character* in doing the right things in the right way as supply chains are cultivated to scale the market, and

- creating the *capacity* to have fun amid the intrepidity of the value-creation odyssey.[12]

Steven R. Covey's *7 Habits of Highly Effective People* may also be applied to the innovative crucible:[13]

- proactively engage innovation for its value-creating potential,

- begin with the end in mind, i.e., the problem the firm is trying to solve for present and potential customers,

- sieve hubris to prioritize the "important" over the "urgent,"

- think in terms of mutual wins between the company and its customers—not exclusively in terms of profitability,

- ask the right customer-focused questions to understand potential innovative benefits before attempting to sell them,

- encourage dynamic interaction of seemingly disparate parts to discover solutions and synergies, and

- embrace a learning culture to benefit from mistakes.[14]

Interestingly, however, innovation tends to be greeted poorly within organizations—much like antibodies to a virus.[15] Leaders resolved to make innovation successful within their organizations must foster five change-management corporate traits:

- courageousness (to challenge status quo),

- connectedness (to things that matter to customers),

- collaboration (with inter- and extra-organizational resources),

- curiosity (about the possible), and

- openness (to discrediting conventional wisdom and the epiphany of quantum leaps in value-creation discovery).[16]

Best practices support the objective. For example, "agnostic marketing" entails observing potential customers in their ecosystems. This may lend perspective on what a customer would "hire" a product to do.[17] Agnostic marketing may be accomplished via:

- questioning,

- networking,

- observing, and

- experimenting.[18]

Innovative choices are complex. More than one right choice is possible. So is making no right choice. In his book, *Thinking Fast and Slow*, Daniel Kahneman describes System 1, or heuristic decision making, versus System 2, or contemplative decision-making. Kahneman imparts an example of a boss hearing 20 ideas that his collective cadre of middle managers killed. The boss would have done them all because he looked at risk in a macro perspective.[19] The boss's model mirrored venture capital: Out of 10 companies, two fail outright, six are walking wounded, and two justify the entire investment pool.[20] Like baseball, times at bat matter because no one knows which two innovative initiatives will be successful.

Entrepreneurship, Startups, and Inventions

A pessimist sees difficulty in every opportunity; an optimist sees opportunity in every difficulty.[21]

Entrepreneurs are more comfortable with calculated risk than most people. Indeed, they may not view risk the same as others. Startups are not prerequisites to entrepreneurship, as entrepreneurial leadership is also a major element of continued business success. A startup is just what it sounds like: a brand new company with no previous commercial activity.

An invention is something new, and sometimes patentable. Invention sometimes catalyzes a startup to promote its commercialization. However, both entrepreneurism and startups may occur absent invention. Established businesses, too, may be active inventors. Indeed, whereas invention may have been the reason for the startup, continuous invention may be what perpetuates the company. Entrepreneurism benefits both.

This discussion is not circular logic, but rather symbiosis in action. Comparison and contrast between entrepreneurship, startups, and inventions may benefit by using the Kano Model.[22] (See Figure 6.1.) The foundation of the Kano Model is two axes: customer reaction and product functionality.

Four quadrants are formed. Beginning in the northeast corner and proceeding clockwise, they are:

- customer satisfaction and product functionality,

- customer dissatisfaction and product functionality,

- customer dissatisfaction and product dysfunctionality, and

- customer satisfaction and product dysfunctionality.

Three curves are depicted in the model. Must-bes are non-negotiables that determine product salability. The best it can ever be is functional, or sufficient. Must-bes only differentiate by their absence, much like Herzberg's hygienic factors of personal motivation that will be discussed later in the

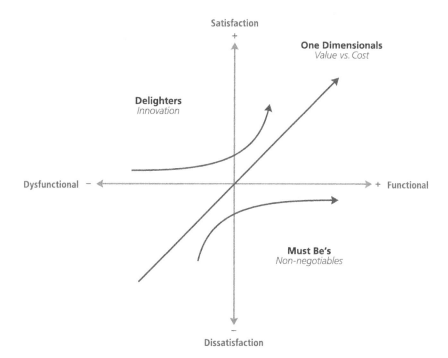

Figure 6.1   The Kano model

Source: Adapted from Pande, P.S., Neuman, R.P., and Cavanagh, R.R. (2002). *The Six Sigma Way Team Fieldbook: An Implementation Guide for Process Improvement Teams*. New York: McGraw-Hill. pp. 296–7.; Pande, P.S., Neuman, R.P., and Cavanagh, R.R. (2002). *The Six Sigma Way Team Fieldbook: An Implementation Guide for Process Improvement Teams*. New York: McGraw-Hill. pp. 296–7.

Chapter 8: Leadership Choices and Organizational Design. Must-be absence is not a favorable differentiation! One-dimensionals equate to economies of scale. Customers enjoy perceived value when they can get more quantity per unit price—of course, assuming no diminution of quality. Delighters are new. The initial market reaction is suspect. Concurrent with Simon Sinek's argument about Everett Roger's Diffusion of Innovations curve (see Figure 6.2), the innovators and early adopters have to grasp the vision of product utility to reach a traction tipping point; markets are made when early majority customers buy the product.[23] Over time, the innovations (inventions) of the northwest quadrant (satisfied dysfunction) normalize and drift toward the commoditization of the southeast corner (dissatisfied functionality).

Consider the power windows invention in cars. Power windows were invented by the erstwhile Packard Motor Car Company, a luxury price point manufacturer. At one point, just like all other businesses, Packard was a start-up (in 1899). Upon the advent of power windows (the northwest quadrant), the product was greeted with the skepticism, as rolling down the window to escape a car driven into a lake was not an option. (The argument regarded

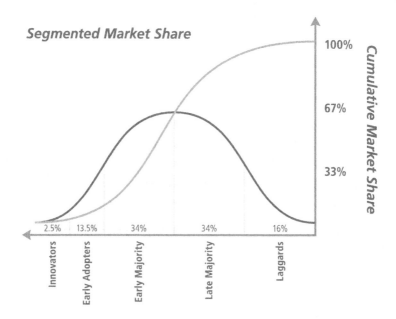

Figure 6.2   Roger's Diffusion of Innovations categories and accumulation

Source: Reprinted with the permission of Simon & Schuster Publishing Group from the Free Press edition of *Diffusion of Innovations*, 5th Edition by Everett M. Rogers. Copyright © 1962, 1971, 1983 by The Free Press. All rights reserved.

electrical failure.) However, friends of innovators and early adaptors observed the convenience of safely lowering the rear windows without pulling over to enjoy a refreshing spring afternoon. Of course, the entrepreneurial skills in the equation were evident in how the benefits of the power window feature were promoted. This was the tipping point that triggered the one-dimensional phase. Demand undergirded the economies of scale that resulted in the inclusion of power windows in options packages at reasonable prices—to include other luxury competitors that had to offer the feature to avoid losing customers. Overtime, power windows migrated from luxury options to standards, along with customer dissatisfaction with the absence of a perfectly reliable accessory (the southeastern quadrant of the Kano model). Today, it is more difficult to find a new car without power windows than with them. The power windows saga evolved at a glacial pace compared to present high tech consumer products whose half-life is treacherously abbreviated.

Let's now dive a little deeper on some terms, beginning with invention.

> *An invention is a new idea that is often turned into a tangible outcome, such as a product or a system. An innovation is the conversion of a new idea into revenues and products. An idea that looks great in the lab and fails in the market is not an innovation; it is, at best, a curiosity… . Invention is needed for innovation to take place. But invention is not innovation.*[24]

An invention need not be authored by a start-up. Although invention entails something new, the market may not value the creation. The concept of "new" might not even be sufficiently clear. "An inventor creates a technical capability that can be used to create products or features that solve a customer problem or market need."[25] New skills may be part of the success formula.[26] Invention rests on four steps:

- the perception of an unsatisfactory pattern,

- the setting of the stage,

- the primary act of insight, and

- critical revision and development.[27]

Invention is only worthwhile if it solves a customer problem. Sometimes, however, the customer does not recognize that they have a problem. Moreover, the customer paradigm might be that the problem is without solution.

Consider intermittent windshield wipers. The patented product was invented by an entrepreneur, Robert Kearns. Ford Motor Company violated Kearns' protected intellectual property. The story inspired the 2008 movie, *Flash of Genius*, a David and Goliath story of Kearns successfully defending his patents, albeit at great personal toll over a protracted period.[28] Intellectual property rights protection is considered by The US Patent and Trademark Office if the invention has novel and non-obvious uses.[29] However, "in [point of] fact, there is no correlation between the number of corporate patents earned and financial success."[30]

Startups do not necessarily require product invention. "A startup's job is to:

- rigorously measure where it is right now, forming the hard truths that assessment reveals, and then

- devise experiments to learn how to move the real numbers closer to the ideal reflected in the business plan."[31]

"Finding the right balance between passion, patience, and a practical respect for market feedback is probably a more realistic formula for startup success."[32]

Consider two types of startups. Suppose a neighborhood kid observed elderly neighbors walking their dogs and decided that offering a service solved two problems. First, it relieved the pet owners from something they deemed necessary, but would rather not do. In this case, their economic opportunity cost is the price of walking the dog instead of doing something else with that 30 minutes—like savoring a cup of coffee while watching the morning news on cable TV. Second, it solved the budding entrepreneur's problem by providing an income opportunity to fund a major desire—perhaps a new iPad. This may be an example of a start-up for a unique business model.

Consider another start-up example: franchising. The franchisor may have proved an alluring business model. However, the franchisee for a new location is engaged in another type of start-up: repetition for an otherwise proven business model in an untested venue. Of course, there are agreements to be negotiated, seed capital to source, and working capital financing issues. The entrepreneur in this case scratched a capitalistic itch through the risk mitigating medium of franchising. One of my former colleagues and did this with Baskin-Robbins ice-cream franchises as a sideline to his primary career in a financial institution. Some franchises are near certain winners, such as McDonald's.

If entrepreneurism punctuates both invention and startups, what exactly is an entrepreneur? One definition is a person (or group of persons) who "creates a new business in the face of risk and uncertainty for the purpose of achieving profit and growth by identifying significant opportunities and assembling the necessary resources to capitalize on them."[33] Entrepreneurs possess a differentiable set of attributes. Specifically, the profile includes:

- a desire for responsibility,

- a preference for moderate risk-taking,

- confidence in the ability to succeed,

- a thirst for immediate feedback,

- a high level of energy and stamina,

- an orientation toward the future,

- skills in organizing, and

- the emphasis of achievement over monetary gain.[34]

Sometimes entrepreneurism, or investing, is compared to gambling. Economists see a distinct difference. The entrepreneur believes her talents mitigate risk en route to a profitable likelihood. By contrast, gambling entails unalterable statistical chance.

Entrepreneurs, startups, inventions, or some combination thereof, may fail. These failures often draw criticisms from people unqualified to make such judgments.

> It is always easy to critique failure after the fact, but it is not always fair. An unfair critique focuses on the failure and criticizes management for the outcome. It focuses on the specific choices made. A fair critique focuses on the way that choices were made. It offers an approach that

could reasonably have been used to arrive at defensible recommendations before the outcomes were known.[35]

Such "fair critiques" are signs of effectively-led companies. Three topics should be covered in fair post mortems:

- capabilities (of the business model and its employees),

- customers (their appetite for the entrepreneurial value proposition), and

- competition (the ability to attract customers to the exclusion of available alternatives).[36]

Since people learn more from mistakes than successes, the pool of knowledge benefits by such case studies to avert repeat mistakes for the next attempt in the value-creation odyssey. Indeed, many iconic leaders who are celebrated for their successes both learned from and overcame failures that received much less attention.

Creativity versus Innovation

There is no innovation and creativity without failure.[37]

George Bernard Shaw pronounced, "We need men who can dream of things that never were and ask 'Why not?'"[38] This speaks to the heart of the symbiosis between creativity and innovation. Creativity is self-contained, that is, an end unto itself.[39] Creativity is fuel for innovation, but distinct from it.[40] "Creativity is the playing with and [the] 'reordering' of objects or concepts in such a way that no foregone result is achieved."[41] "Behind every successful innovation is an unexpected insight,"[42] or creativity. Mihaly Csikszentmihaly framed five steps for the creative process:

- preparation by way of study and immersion,

- incubation, during which the juices flow subconsciously and non-linearly,

- insight, or the conscious connection of components for potential solutions,

- evaluation, when insights are scrutinized for practical application, and

- elaboration, the laborious necessity of packaging implementation.[43]

Creativity may be considered in two categories: conceptual and experimental.[44] There is no magic age at which creativity is most ripened for its creator.[45]

Both creativity and innovation rely on different types of intelligence. "General intelligence ... is a genetic endowment—[25–40 percent], but creativity is not. Nurture trumps nature as far as creativity goes."[46] Creativity is housed in the brain's right hemisphere, but must become actionable.[47] Another way to look at this is applied intelligence in the laboratory of the competitive ecosystem through three avenues of experimentation:

- experiences,

- dissection to understand how things work, and

- prototypes.[48]

"Creativity ... consists largely of rearranging what we know in order to find out what we do not know."[49] Creativity may result from the articulation and conflation of three types of logic:

- deductive, i.e., "logic and analysis, typically based on past evidence;"

- inductive, i.e., "based on directly observable facts;" and

- abductive, i.e., "imagining what could be possible."[50]

"Creativity is 80 percent context and 20 percent technique."[51] Companies that proactively solicit supplier, customer, and academic feedback tend to perform better within their industries than do those who seek input across industries.[52] However, the line is drawn at receptivity from insightful sources—not directives.[53]

Collectivism is the enemy of creativity. Collectivism may also explain why some cultures dishonor patented and copyrighted intellectual property.

Individualism is the ally of creativity.[54] This at least partially explains the innovative edge of Western cultures. Five discovery skills behoove creativity:

- associating the "not obvious,"

- questioning conventional wisdom,

- observing an ecosystem for its exploitable secrets,

- networking to leverage existing discoveries, and

- experimenting to identify the optimal design.[55]

Creativity pursues the "elegant design," comprised of:

- the utterly unexpected,

- the amazingly competent,

- the aesthetically exquisite, and

- the conspicuously conscientious.[56]

In contrast to creativity, innovation is "something different that has impact."[57] Stated another way, creativity is credited as innovative upon being successfully commercialized. Innovation may respond to the hard or soft trends reviewed in the strategic thinking and planning processes.[58] "Knowing how to identify hard trends gives us the ability to see the future. Knowing how to identify soft trends gives us the ability to shape the future."[59] "Innovation is the intentional development of a specific product, service, idea, environment, or process for the generation of value."[60] Researchers and authors have compiled a plethora of descriptors to frame the innovative arena. Innovators may be distinguished among five genres:

- Rockets: "young companies that have been boosted aloft by wacky new business models."

- Laureates: "companies [that] innovate year after year, albeit in narrow, technologically oriented domains."

- Artistes: "smaller … companies that are in the creativity business—innovation is their primary product."

- Cyborgs: "endlessly inventive and strategically flexible [such] that they seem to have come from another solar system."

- Born-again innovators: established firms that, by necessity, have sobered to the necessity of "reordering their priorities and reassessing lifelong habits" in order to reverse a negative trajectory toward ultimate demise.[61]

Alternatively, innovators may fall within four generic categories:

- "startup entrepreneurs … ,

- corporate entrepreneurs (those who launch an innovative venture from within the corporation),

- product innovators (those who invent a new product or service), and

- process innovators (those who author a paradigm-shifting alternative for creating value)."[62]

Additionally, innovation may be regarded as one of two types: process and product.[63] The two may converge to produce synergies. For example, GoToMeeting.com is an innovative product offered via an innovative process: a Citrix-hosted cloud application. Finally, innovation may be viewed as sustaining versus disruptive.[64]

Daniel Burris and John David Mann offer seven innovation ideological points:

- start with certainty, i.e., use hard trends to see what's coming;

- anticipate, i.e., base your strategies on what you know about the future;

- transform, i.e., use technology-driven change to your advantage;

- take your biggest problem and skip it because it is probably not the real problem, i.e., bootstrapping is a creative financing alternative to conventional capital sources;

- go opposite, i.e., look where no one else is looking to see what no one else is seeing and do what no one else is doing;

- redefine and reinvent, i.e., identify and leverage your uniqueness in new and powerful ways; and

- own the destiny of your future to insulate self-determinism over reactionary captivity.[65]

Keen innovators comprehend what the customer might accomplish with the new widget.[66] Three techniques offer guidance to innovators:

- immersion, i.e., observing ecosystem functionality;

- convergence and divergence of ecosystem evolution; and

- adaption, i.e., ecosystem adjustment.[67]

Accordingly, high failure rates for ideas-first and needs-first innovation may be averted. That is to say, outcomes-based innovation has better odds.[68] Using the rapid prototyping approach reveals quick failures that allow course corrections to preserve developmental budgets.[69]

Invention may be necessary to innovation, but the litmus test for meaningful innovation is traction in the market.[70] Two types of customer signals matter to engineering a market response: (i) conscious needs; and (ii) latent needs.[71] Successful innovators decipher four elusive, yet key principles:

- unchallenged orthodoxies,

- underappreciated trends,

- unleveraged competencies and assets, and

- unarticulated needs.[72]

Timing is germane to the creative spark that results in innovation. Leonardo da Vinci was a creative genius. "One of the paradoxes of creativity is that in order to think originally, we must first familiarize ourselves with the ideas of others."[73] Da Vinci's work included sketches of flying machines. Da Vinci's vision preceded applied physics by a few centuries. The Wright brothers mastered fixed wing flight and Sikorsky developed rotary wing flight.

Peter Drucker outlined seven generic and potentially overlapping sources of innovation:

- unexpected successes and failures that reveal opportunities,

- the incongruity between actual and potential reality,

- needs of the business model machinations,

- changes in the competitive environment,

- demographics,

- culture, and

- information.

The first four are within organizational context; the last three are extra-organizational, respectively.[74] Two points loom large in an organization's value chain of innovation capabilities.

First, a company's innovation capability is only as good as the weakest link in this chain.... . Second, the strongest link in the chain is also a weakness: by viewing a strong link as a company's core capability, managers set out to further strengthen this part of the innovation value chain, which can make things worse.[75]

Innovation may be the prescription to solve:

- "wicked problems," i.e., complexity that defies simple solutions;[76] and

- "x-problems," i.e., uniquely mysterious, profoundly consequential, and exponentially rewarding to the problem solvers.[77]

X-problems further contrast with wicked problems as follows:

> *the presence of competition, and competitors that are getting better and more diverse; the need to satisfy more demanding customers and provide superior customer experiences; the need to integrate products of diverse types and origins into comprehensive, coherent systems for customers; and clarity about the problem emerges slowly, as with wicked problems, but iterative approaches to solving them are necessary, in contrast to the one-shot deal of wicked problems.[78]*

Many tools are available to help the creative and innovative process. One such tool is the fishbone diagram developed by Kaoru Ishikawa (see Figure 6.3).[79] In complement, Six Sigma's "five whys" may be applied to offer some structural guidance to problem-solving. In reality, the tool may be applied to diverse scenarios. The real point is structured problem-solving to identify legitimate root causes or impediments whose solutions may yield profitable opportunities.

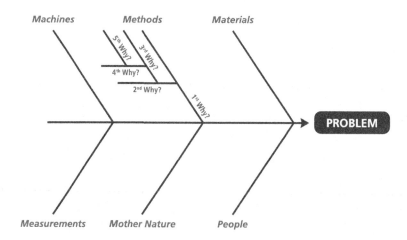

Figure 6.3   The fishbone diagram for pursuing the "five why's"

Source: Adapted from Ishikawa, K. (1986). *Guide to quality control* (2nd ed.). Tokyo, Japan: Asian Productivity Organization; Tague, N.S. (2005).*The Quality Toolbox* (2nd ed.). Milwaukee, WI: American Society for Quality. pp. 247–9.; Fishbone (Ishikawa) diagram. (n.d.). American Society for Quality. Retrieved from http://asq.org/learn-about-quality/cause-analysis-tools/overview/fishbone.html

Product versus Process Innovation

Innovation and best practices can be sown throughout an organization—but only when they fall on fertile ground.[80]

Charles Handy's Sigmoid Curve (see Figure 6.4) conveys the business lifecycle of a thriving company. Whereas cycles ebb and flow, the trend line through the sine-wave cycles has a slope of positive trajectory—provided the company generally makes good strategic (innovative) decisions.[81] Successfully innovative companies have pipelines of activity intended to unleash the next widget to catalyze a new growth curve before the previous one peters out. This description applies to any industry. Microsoft and Apple are but two marque technology examples.

Innovation lends itself to two generic descriptors: product (including services) and process.[82] For example, Henry Ford's assembly line brandished process innovation. The advent of the hypermarket is another form of process innovation. The hypermarket delivers high volumes of merchandise in supply chain artistry. Joy's Law "assumes innovation will occur elsewhere."[83] This is not necessarily a bad thing for process innovation. Great processes

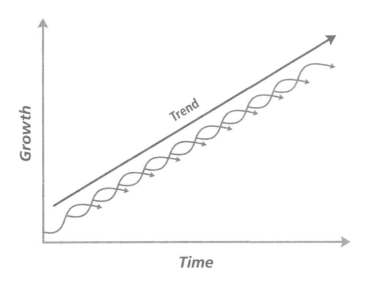

Figure 6.4   Positive trending of Handy's sigmoid curves

Source: Handy, C. (1995). *The Age of Paradox*. Boston, MA: The Harvard Business School Press.

may be transferred to other industries. For example, Toyota's Total Quality Management system was the genesis for Lean manufacturing whose principles permeate a global plethora of manufacturing and service industries.

Middle Market Methods™ observed that middle market companies are target-rich environments for both process improvement and innovation. Indeed, process improvement and innovation dominated the firm's engagement deliverables. Returning to Tuckman's evolution of organized teams depicted in Chapter 1: Introduction (see Figure 1.1), process improvement and innovation are an integral part of both norming and performing. Consultants with broad industry exposure often encounter process ideas in one industry that may be cross-pollinated to another industry, that is, the consultants are the bees. One should not split hairs delineating process improvement from process innovation. Whereas a cross-pollinated process may be the norm in one industry, another industry may regard it as transformationally efficient. Indeed, uniqueness and originality may occur. However, the sole criterion should be differentiable value-creation.

Proctor & Gambles' odor eating Febreze is indicative of product innovation. Google's search engine dominance is another form of product innovation. How the product provides customers satisfaction may be more important than the product itself.[84] The product lifecycle may include iterations of incremental innovation. Incremental "product innovation takes established [products] in established markets to the next level. The focus can be on performance increase …, cost reduction …, usability improvement …, or any other … enhancement."[85]

A great example of middle market product innovation is MTS Medication Technologies. MTS invented its niche. MTS's founders recognized the opportunity to offer blister packaging to skilled nursing facilities to assist in long-term medication administration. The product also facilitated compliance, something keen to Medicare administrators, the biggest payer of skilled nursing care. MTS modified a silk screen printer for its inaugural machine to press covers over the blister packs. Today, MTS utilizes high speed robotics to create blister packs with proficiency and efficiency. The company's innovative product line is a classic razor-razorblade model in that it manufacturers the packaging machines, and supplies the disposable blister packs.

"Technology risk is primary [in product innovations] while the market risk is secondary. That is, in the early stages of product development, technology risk is very high, but it flattens in later stages when the market risk begins to soar."[86]

With the marketplace forming its expectations for a product in terms of features, form, and capabilities, the bases on which product innovation can take place become much fewer, and the focus of research and development narrows to incremental innovations on existing features.[87]

"Many organizations still have difficulty with sustained product innovation, or managing a number of product innovations over time."[88]

Complementary to Handy's work, James M. Utterback produced a Dynamics of Innovation Curve[89] (see Figure 6.5) to explain the evolution of product innovation yielding to process innovation to extend the life of a maturing product through cost reduction without adulterating its quality.[90] Interestingly, prior to product and process market performance achieving the "norming" stage for complex, multifaceted products, the aggregated product marketing approach inures to the creator's benefit. After component norms are established for multifaceted products, however, component marketing proves more profitable.[91] The caveat is that if the competitive entrant only adds incremental functionality to an existing product or component, the incumbent usually prevails.[92]

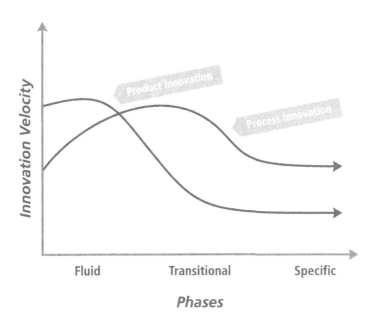

Figure 6.5   Utterback's Dynamics of Innovation curves

Source: Utterback, J. (1994). *Mastering the Dynamics of Innovation*. Boston: Harvard University School Press. p. 91.

Process innovation often complements product innovation to overcome inaugural production inefficiencies. Indeed, "too much variation leads to waste and inefficiency; too little variation can lead to stagnation, atrophy, and dissolution."[93] Process innovation utilizes techniques, such as Lean manufacturing or invention, to enhance supply chain efficiency—in part or en toto.[94] Process innovation potentially liberates resources that may be redirected to product innovation.[95] A good example is AxelaCare, a B2C healthcare home infusion provider. The company's intake process (insurance verification) innovation efficiencies helped self-fund product development for its CareExchange® product that provides prescribing physicians outcome assessment technology to help physicians evaluate the efficacy of medication therapies.

Process innovation is an enabler of emergent innovation. "Emergent innovation does not impose new and foreign innovation techniques on company employees, but instead seeks out, recognizes and helps promote useful innovation methodologies already at work in the organization."[96]

Process innovation suffers four ambiguities:

- innovation is by nature a process even if its result is a product;

- product innovation invariably includes improved processes, i.e., process innovation;

- the process, e.g., consulting, may be the actual product—or an indistinguishable aspect of the product; and

- process innovation may improve the competitiveness of the familiar products concurrent with the "specific phase" of Utterback's Dynamics of Innovation curve (see Figure 6.5).[97]

Sustaining versus Disruptive Innovation

Innovation distinguishes between a leader and a follower.[98]

"Understanding a question is half an answer."[99] The question is "What is the product hired to do?"[100] Whether product or process, innovation may be further described as sustaining or disruptive.[101] "There is no harm in repeating a good thing."[102] Incremental, or sustaining, innovation "simply improves what is"[103] as a medium of repeating a good thing. Incremental innovation accomplishes economies of scale resulting in lower prices on commoditized items. Another form of incremental innovation is the addition of features on core products, for example, new and improved Tide detergent, or liquid Tide concentrate.

Incremental innovation dominates a typical organization's developmental focus— approximately 90 percent.[104] Moreover, half of a typical company's sales come from products within five years of their introduction.[105] Sustaining innovation organizations

> *systematically invest in a wide variety of low-cost experiments to continuously probe new markets and technologies; they pace the rhythm of change to balance chaos and inertia by applying steady pressure on product development cycles and market launches; and they maintain speed and flexibility by calibrating the size of their business units to avoid the chaos that is characteristic of too many small units and the inertia associated with most large bureaucracies. This kind of continuous innovation can be found not only in high-tech firms, but also in so-called staid academic institutions.[106]*

Product refreshing and continuous process improvements are compatible with sustaining innovation.[107] A shortcoming of sustaining innovation is that there is "acceptable effectiveness but excessive focus on small, safe projects. Many consumer packaged goods companies fit into this category, with their bias for relatively safe and less expensive line extensions to existing brands."[108]

Reliable standards for incremental innovation may be impediments to disruptive innovation. One such example is the stage gate product development process. There are two primary explanations. First, stage gate presumes product conceptualization and supporting technology. Second, management is typically predisposed to support incremental innovation.[109] Comparatively, disruptive innovation includes a "fuzzy front end" absent developmental standards.[110] Minimally viable products (MVPs),[111] or the "good enough" threshold,[112] is a rational disruptive development response to elicit market acceptance reactions, but with two caveats:

- "any effort that is not absolutely necessary for learning what customers want should be eliminated," and

- "customers don't care how much time something takes to build; they care only that it serves their needs."[113]

Customers tend to tolerate imperfections for inaugural launches of disruptive products because there is no comparative benchmark norm, provided, however, product utility meets an overt or latent need.

> *Disruptive [innovations] bring to market a very different value proposition ... . Generally, disruptive [innovations] underperform established products in the mainstream markets. But they have other features that ... new, fringe (and generally new) customers value. Products based on disruptive technologies are typically cheaper, simpler, smaller, and, frequently, more convenient to use.*[114]

Disruptive innovation should "hurt" competitors—not customers. Disruptive innovation pursues overshot and undershot customers, as well as non-consumption customers. Overshot customers' product selections provide more than they need. Undershot customers are not offered any options—or the options may be so inferior that there is no motivation to buy. Non-consumption customers who did not know they desired the product because it did not exist.[115]

Technology is a predominant component of disruptive innovation. Consider motion pictures. Thomas Edison's projector introduced silent film entertainment. "Talkies" obsoleted silent films. Color displaced black and white. VCRs threatened movie theaters. Blockbuster modeled bookstore-type distribution of films. Tape gave way to CDs. Netflix and Redbox dethroned Blockbuster. Now movies may be piped into homes via broadband technology through cable vendors like Comcast or web portals like Netflix.

Disruptive innovation captivates the imagination. Disruptions seem to "appear as if from nowhere, creating massive new sources of wealth ... [from] ... technological discontinuities."[116] The overriding objective of disruptive innovation is growth over profits. Even so, the impatience for, and eventual necessity of, profits hone focus on commercialized applications.[117] Clayton M. Christensen is an indefatigable writer on the topic of innovation. Christensen teamed Michael E. Raynor to write *The Innovator's Solution: Creating and Sustaining Successful Growth*, in which five principles of disruptive innovation are enumerated.

- Resource dependencies influence options, i.e., customers effectively control the patterns of resource allocation in well-run companies.

- Small markets don't solve the growth needs of large companies. (This point was made in Chapter 1: Introduction using Merck as an example.)

- The ultimate uses or applications of disruptive technology are unknowable in advance. Failure is an intrinsic step toward success.

- Organizations have capabilities that exist independent of the capabilities of people who work within them. Organizational capabilities reside within their processes and values—and the very processes and values that constitute their core capabilities within the current business model also define their disabilities when confronted with disruption.

- [Innovation] supply may not equal market demand. The attributes that make disruptive technologies unattractive in established markets often are the very ones that constitute the greatest value in emerging markets.[118]

At best, disruptors may hypothesize markets. They are inventing the rules, not abiding by known rules. Traction for disruptors rests upon first mover advantage. As mentioned earlier and relative to Everett Rogers' Diffusion of Innovations curve, disruptors must persuade the innovator and early adopter audiences[119] to reach escape velocity for market development.[120] Especially in the era of social media, the phenomenon draws upon Metcalf's Law: "the value of a network as a whole is proportional to the square of the number of its participants."[121]

The Annuity of Serial Innovation

Innovation is the calling card of the future.[122]

"Managers at all organizational levels are challenged by the vortex of inertia creeping up on innovation."[123] A potential cure is serial innovation. Unlike the one-hit wonders that make a big, single splash before cashing out to an acquirer to avert foundering, serial innovators are an annuity. Serial innovation is arguably tantamount to capitalist Nirvana. Serial innovators are a CEO's delight, provided the CEO knows how to lead them.

> *Serial innovators are individuals who have conceived ideas that solve*
> *important problems for people and organizations, have developed those*
> *ideas into breakthrough new products and services, inventing new*
> *technologies to do so as needed, and then have guided those products*
> *and services through the corporations' commercialization process and*
> *into the market.*[124]

These special professionals enjoy working on "interesting problems"[125]—repeatedly. Serial innovators do not necessarily aspire to notoriety. Rather, they are content to work in environments where their efforts are appreciated, plus they are left alone to do their own thing. Serial innovators will take unusual risks if they think they are correct in their convictions. Losing their jobs does not bother them as much as may be the case for other types of innovators. Serial innovators are motivated by the articulation of preparation, perspective, and personality; moreover, they are influenced (hindered or helped) by organizational politics and legacy business model processes.[126]

The serial innovators' alchemy of invention and validation is governed by:

- finding the right problem to solve,

- developing a deep understanding from the customers' perspective,

- creating a market-palatable solution, and

- executing from concept to delivery.[127]

Indeed, this process highlights at least two distinguishing characteristics of serial innovators:

- a non-linear and seemingly schizophrenic approach that contrasts sharply with incremental innovation, and

- involvement from inception to market stability.[128]

The latter is a form of double-loop learning.[129] Ultimately, serial innovators thrive on three ecosystem criteria:

- solvable problems,

- high impact solutions, and

- producers and customers benefiting jointly.[130]

While somewhat altruistic, serial innovators are definitely capitalists as they know the outcome must be rationalized by profitability.

The Role of the Teams in Innovative Organizations

Talent wins games, but teamwork and intelligence wins championships.[131]

"None of us is as smart as all of us;"[132] however, there are practical limits to the size implied by "all of us." When the number exceeds an upper boundary of two dozen, dysfunction tends to creep into the dynamic. The sweet spot appears to be about a half-dozen members.[133] Assuming teams embrace modest size to preserve agility, the issue of team composition looms large, that is to say, skills commensurate with the challenge. Diversity of perspective is a worthy inclusion criterion.[134] This includes age diversification. Younger people tend to be more creative.[135] This at least partially explains the magic of Silicon Valley.

Trust is the essential building block of effective innovation teams. The ability for teammates to trust may rest upon the teammates "scores" in the categories of competence, reliability, transparency, and empathy.[136] T-shaped attributes of teammates are virtuous: breadth of perspective and depth of specific topics.[137] Project management remains critical to innovation. However, the degree of difficulty is higher for herding the creative cats toward synergistic alignment.[138]

Four healthy habits prepare effective innovative teammates:

- experiential variety,

- studying pioneering individuals, e.g. Thomas Edison and Steve Jobs,

- reading eclectic material, and

- tapping into luminaries and thought leaders.[139]

Three resume enhancements are also noteworthy:

- expatriate experience,

- multi-functional or multi-disciplinary credentials, and

- differentiable new skills.[140]

Professionals with expatriate experience have a 35 percent more likely innovative edge.[141] The American "melting pot" innovative teams need to be cognizant of Edward T. Hall's polychronic versus monochronic, and low-context versus high-context, styles.[142] (These will be explored more thoroughly in Chapter 8: Leadership Choices and Organizational Design.)

A familiar model will be revisited here relative to innovation. Team development—including innovative ones—entails forming, storming, norming, performing, and adjourning.[143] Forming may include both conscription and voluntary selection. Storming regards group dynamics. Norming includes:

- conflict resolution,

- problem-solving,

- communication concision and clarity,

- decision-making,

- goal-setting,

- planning,

- task execution, and

- performance management.[144]

Performing accomplishes results through consistent execution with robust processes. Innovative teams need time to think, something that from an outsider's perspective may look deceptively unproductive. This may include a reprieve from the performing routine business model processes.

Since team cultural evolution influences innovative productivity, establishing a baseline for perspective is a wise option. Four critical innovation mindsets are beneficial to a project team:

- being externally focused;

- recognizing that one's first idea is usually wrong;

- realizing one's "inner Edison" and start sweating toward solutions; and

- breaking the sucking sound of the core business, i.e., the black hole of complacency.[145]

In their book, *Organizing Genius: The Secrets of Creative Collaboration*, Warren Bennis and Patricia Warren Biederman itemize 15 lessons of superlative teams, or "great groups:"

- Greatness starts with superb people who tend to be deep generalists—not specialists—and problem solvers.

- Great groups and great leaders create each other.

- Every great group has a strong leader, but not necessary a supervisor. The leader may be more of a coordinator for highly motivated people. Moreover, the leader tends to shelter productive people from the inane aspects of the core business's bureaucracy. This is how J. Robert Oppenheimer, a gifted scientist in his own right, managed the Los Alamos National Laboratory as part of the Manhattan Project that produced the first nuclear bomb during World War II. One of the more interesting aspects of the leader-follower dynamic is the 80/20 reality that leaders are actually leading a minority of the time and followers produce a majority of results,[146] i.e., true leadership proactively defers to those with superior knowledge or insightful contextual perspective.

- The leaders of great groups love talent and know how and where to recruit it.

- Great groups are full of talented people who can work together.

- Great groups think they are on a mission from God. When they understand their role in context, they need less supervision and are more productive.

- Every great group is an island, but an island with a bridge to the mainland, i.e., the organization.

- Great groups see themselves as winning underdogs.

- Great groups always have an enemy. This hones focus and aligns with Dave Logan et al.'s stage four and five tribes discussed in Chapter 4: The DNA of Packs.[147]

- People in great groups brandish blinders to tune out distractions.

- Great groups are optimistic—not realistic. Eustress, or motivating stress, is their fuel.

- In great groups, the right person has the right job.

- The leaders of great groups give their teammates what they need to meet the challenge and shield them from hindrances.

- Great groups ship, i.e., deliver results.

- Great work is its own intrinsic reward.[148] This aligns with Herzberg's motivating factors discussed more fully in Chapter 8: Leadership Choices and Organizational Design.

Great teams model two more noteworthy characteristics. First, they tend to break up after completing the project. In some instances, for example, religion, the teams never disband because the innovative mission is never completed. Second, teams need an occasional outlet to relieve the stress of pressure.[149] Paintball "maneuvers" and whitewater rafting are such examples.

Innovation in Private Equity

Innovation comes from the producer—not from the customer.[150]

The innovative success that attracted private equity investment in a portfolio company may become collateral damage as a function of risk aversion traceable to a leveraged balance sheet.[151] As an antidote to this scenario, good marketing efforts may identify unmet customer needs that lead to new product development opportunities. Private equity firms tend to be more comfortable when these opportunities are sustaining and process innovations. Occasionally, a disruptive opportunity is identified, replete with the vagueness of potential addressable market because customers may not know they need "it," that is, the disruptive product. Private equity firms would typically be challenged by these scenarios if pursuing the disruption posed material downside risk to performance, and thus threatened loan covenant violations. Venture capital firms more typically invest in disruptive technology start-ups. Private equity investors become more interested after new products gain traction, perhaps as an exit vehicle for sponsoring venture firms.

The enigma is that innovation has to occur. The global economy eventually makes cost an issue for all products. Consequently, the ability to innovate efficiently is increasingly important to private equity. A potential solution for private equity firms is a risk mitigating methodology for innovation. In his book, *Lean Startup: How Today's Entrepreneurs Use Continuous Innovation to Create Radically Successful Businesses,* Eric Ries offers a palatable model defined by five principles:

- Entrepreneurs are everywhere.

- Entrepreneurship is management and "requires a new type of management specifically geared to its context of extreme uncertainty."

- Validated learning is essential. "Startups exist not just to make stuff, make money, or even serve customers. They exist to learn how to build a sustainable business."

- The basic model is build-measure-learn. "The fundamental activity of a startup is to turn ideas into products, measure how customers respond, and then learn whether to pivot (punt) or persevere."

- Innovation accounting behooves managerial necessities. Such metrics should be tailored to reflect the dynamics of the process. Good technique will "measure progress, how to set up milestones, and how to prioritize work."[152]

Ries continues with three phases for lean startups:

- Vision, comprised of starting, defining, learning, and experimenting.

- Steering, consisting of leaping, testing, measuring, and pivoting or persevering. Another way to look at this is a build-measure-learn feedback loop. Herein lays one of the core principles of the lean startup: the minimally viable product introduced earlier in this chapter. Since there is no product standard at this juncture, the crude product both establishes a market beachhead and elicits customer feedback for iterative improvement.

- Accelerating, including batching, growth, adaptation, and innovation.[153]

Resources, processes, and values (philosophy[154]) define the innovative posture of the organization.[155] Note that philosophy is different from culture as discussed in Chapter 4: The DNA of Packs. However, they are compatible. Leaders for both the private equity firm and the portfolio company set the tone for the organization before either should realistically expect the team to expose themselves to the risk and ridicule of challenging status quo.[156]

The proper attitude toward innovation is perhaps best encapsulated by Andy Grove: "Only the paranoid survive."[157] Physics again offers metaphorical insights. Sir Isaac Newton's first law of motion explains that objects in motion tend to remain so, the same as objects at rest, unless resisting forces alter the objects state.[158] Customer-focused innovation is either limited or promoted by organizational architecture, supporting systems, and prevailing conditions.[159] Innovation is the most potent alternative to the threat of entropy, atrophy, apathy, and complacency. By necessity, the investment thesis must accommodate innovation to position the portfolio company for a successful investment exit.

Endnotes

[1]   Socrates quotes. (n.d.). *Goodreads.* Retrieved from http://www.goodreads.com/quotes/472923-strong-minds-discuss-ideas-average-minds-discuss-events-weak-minds

[2]   Shakespeare, W. (2005). *Romeo and Juliet.* Clayton, DE: Prestwick House. Act 2, scene 2, line 40, p. 45.

[3]   Lafley, A.G. and Charan, R. (2008). *The game-changer: How you can drive revenue and profit growth with innovation.* New York: Random House. pp. 5, 21.

[4]   Ibid. p. 24.

5   Hamel, G. (2012). *What matters now: How to win in a world of relentless change, ferocious competition, and unstoppable innovation.* San Francisco: Jossey-Bass. p. 42.

6   Richardson, A. (2010). *Innovation x: Why a company's toughest problems are its greatest advantage.* San Francisco: Jossey-Bass. p. 60.

7   Barczak, G., Griffin, A. and Kahn, K.B. (2009, January). Perspective: Trends and drivers of success in NPD practices: Results of the 2003 PDMA Best Practices Study. *Journal of Product Innovation Management, 25,* 3–23.

8   Griffin, A., Price, R. and Vojak, B. (2012). *Serial innovators: How individuals create and deliver breakthrough innovations in mature firms.* Stanford, CA: Stanford Business Books. p. 17.

9   Dyer, J., Gregersen, H. and Christensen, C.M. (2011). *The innovator's DNA: Mastering the five skills of disruptive innovators.* Boston, MA: Harvard Business School Publishing. (ISBN: 9781422134818)

10   Lafley and Charan (2008). p. 24.

11   Ibid. pp. 24–6.

12   Morris, T. (2002). *The art of achievement: Mastering the 7 c's of success in business and life.* Kansas City, MO: Andrews McMeel Publishing.

13   Covey, S.R. (2004). *The 7 habits of highly effective people.* New York, NY: Simon & Schuster.

14   Senge, P.M. (2006). *The fifth discipline: The art and practice of the learning organization.* New York, NY: Doubleday.

15   Christensen, C.M. and Raynor, M.E. (2003). *The innovator's solution: Creating and sustaining successful growth.* Boston, MA: Harvard Business School Publishing.

16   Lafley and Charan (2008). p. 243.

17   Christensen and Raynor (2003). p. 78; Dyer et al. (2011); Richardson, A. (2010). *Innovation x: Why a company's toughest problems are its greatest advantage.* San Francisco: Jossey-Bass; Christensen, C.M. (1997). *The innovator's dilemma: When new technologies cause great firms to fail.* Boston, MA: Harvard Business School Press. pp. xv, 157.; Anthony, S.D. (2012). *The little black book of innovation.* Boston: Harvard Business Press.

18   Anthony (2012). pp. 33–4.

[19] Kahneman, D. (2011). *Thinking fast and slow*. New York, NY: Farrar, Straus and Giroux.

[20] Christensen and Raynor (2003). p. 8.

[21] Winston Churchill quotes. (n.d.). *BrainyQuote.com* Retrieved from http://www.brainyquote.com/quotes/authors/w/winston_churchill.html

[22] Pande, P.S., Neuman, R.P. and Cavanagh, R.R. (2002). *The six sigma way team fieldbook: An implementation guide for process improvement teams*. New York: McGraw-Hill. pp. 89–91.

[23] Sinek, S. (2009). *Start with why: How great leaders inspire everyone to take action*. New York: Penguin.; Rogers, E.M. (2003). *Diffusion of innovations* (5th ed.). New York: Free Press. pp. 279–85.

[24] Lafley and Charan (2008). p. 21.

[25] Griffin et al. (2012). p. 24.

[26] Usher, P.A. (1955) Technical change and capital formation. In Universities-National Bureau (ed.). *Capital formation and economic growth*. Princeton, NJ: Princeton University Press. (ISBN: 087014197X). p. 528.

[27] Ibid. pp. 527–8.

[28] Birnbaum, R., Barber, G., Bliss, T., Lieber, M. (Producers) and Abraham, M. (Director). (2008). Flash of genius [Motion picture]. USA: Spyglass Entertainment and Strike Entertainment.

[29] Patents. (n.d.). *The United States Patent and Trademark Office*. Retrieved from http://www.uspto.gov/patents

[30] Lafley and Charan (2008). p. 21.

[31] Ries, E. (2011). *Lean startup: How today's entrepreneurs use continuous innovation to create radically successful businesses*. New York: Crown Business. p. 114.

[32] McGinn, D. (2012, September). Too many pivots, too little passion: What's wrong with today's entrepreneurism. *Harvard Business Review, 90*(9), 35.

[33] Zimmerer, T.W. and Scarborough, N.M. (2005). *Essentials of entrepreneurship and small business management*. (4th ed.) Upper Saddle River, New Jersey: Pearson/Prentice Hall. p. 3.

[34] McClelland, D. (1961). *The achieving society*. Princeton, NJ: Van Nostrand. p. 16.

[35]   Adner, R. (2012). *The wide lens: A new strategy for innovation*. New York: Portfolio Hardcover. (ISBN: 1591844606). p. 35

[36]   Ibid. p. 32.

[37]   Brene Brown quotes. (n.d.). *BrainyQuote.com*. Retrieved from http://www.brainyquote.com/quotes/authors/b/brene_brown.html

[38]   George Bernard Shaw quotes. (n.d.). *Thinkexist.com*. Retrieved from http://thinkexist.com/quotation/we-need-men-who-can-dream-of-things-that-never/1273373.html

[39]   Anthony (2012). p. 17.

[40]   Anthony (2012).

[41]   Oster, G.W. (2011). *The light prize: Perspectives on Christian innovation*. USA: Positive Signs Media. p. 18.

[42]   Silverstein, M.J. (1995). From the insight out. In Stern, C. W. and Deimler, M.S. (Eds.). (2006). *The Boston Consulting Group on strategy: Classic concepts and new perspectives* (2nd ed.). Hoboken, NJ: John Wiley & Sons. pp. 174–5.

[43]   Csikszentmihaly, M. (1996). *Creativity: flow and the psychology of discovery and invention*. New York: HarperCollins. pp. 79–80

[44]   Gladwell. M. (2009). *What the dog saw and other adventures*. New York: Little, Brown, & Company. p. 304.

[45]   Ibid. pp. 295–313.

[46]   Lafley and Charan (2008). p. 22.

[47]   Dyer et al. (2011).

[48]   Ibid. pp. 137–8.

[49]   Michalko, M. (2006). *Thinkertoys: A handbook of creative-thinking techniques* (2nd ed.). Berkeley, CA: Ten Speed Press. (ISBN: 1580087736). p. 100.

[50]   Lafley and Charan (2008). p. 106.

[51] Cook, P. (1998). The creativity advantage—is your organization the leader of the pack? *Industrial and Commercial Training, 30*(5), 180.

[52] Inauen, M. and Schenker-Wicki, A. (2011). The impact of outside-in open innovation on innovation performance. *European Journal of Innovation Management, 14*(4), 509.

[53] Lafley and Charan (2008). p. 60.

[54] Dyer et al. (2011). pp. 168–70.

[55] Ibid. 168–70.

[56] Hamel (2012). pp. 56–7.

[57] Anthony (2012). p. 16.

[58] Burrus, D. and Mann, J.D. (2011). Flash foresight: How to see the invisible and do the impossible. New York: HarperCollins.

[59] Ibid. p. 19.

[60] Oster (2011). p. 3.

[61] Hamel (2012). pp. 47–51.

[62] Dyer et al. (2011). p. 4

[63] Drucker, P. (1985). *Innovation and entrepreneurship.* New York: HarperCollins. (ISBN: 9780060851132)

[64] Griffin et al. (2012); Lafley and Charan (2008); Christensen and Raynor (2003).

[65] Burrus and Mann (2011). pp. xx–xxi.

[66] Christensen and Raynor (2003). p. 78.

[67] Richardson (2010). p. 24.

[68] Ulwick, A.W. (2005). *What customers want: Using outcome-driven innovation to create breakthrough products and services.* New York: McGraw-Hill; Ulwick, A.W. (2009). An introduction to outcome-driven innovation. *Strategyn, Incorporated,* 1–10. Retrieved from http://ebookbrowse.com/

an-introduction-to-outcome-driven-innovation-strategyn-uk-2009-pdf-d12258785;   Ulwick, A.W. (2009, March 15). What is outcome-driven innovation? *Strategyn, Incorporated*, 1–17. Retrieved from http://innovbfa.viabloga.com/files/Strategyn___what_is_outcome_driven_ innovation___2010.pdf

[69] Jonash, R.S. (2005). Driving sustainable growth and innovation: Pathways to high performance leadership. *Handbook of Business Strategy, 6*(1), 201–2.

[70] Lafley and Charan (2008). p. 21.

[71] Ibid.

[72] Hamel (2012). pp. 64–72.

[73] Ibid. p. 85.

[74] Drucker (1985).

[75] Hansen, M.T. and Birkinshaw, J. (2006, October 31). *University of Hamburg Digital Library*, 2. Retrieved from http://cosmic.rrz.uni-hamburg.de/webcat/hwwa/edok07/f10844g/SIM50.pdf

[76] Rittel, H.W.J. and Webber, M.W. (1973). Dilemmas in a general theory of planning. *Policy Sciences, 4*, 155–69.

[77] Richardson (2010). p. 24.

[78] Ibid.

[79] Ishikawa, K. (1986). *Guide to quality control* (2nd ed.). Tokyo, Japan: Asian Productivity Organization.

[80] Marcus Buckingham quotes. (n.d.). *BrainyQuote.com*. Retrieved from http://www.brainyquote. com/quotes/authors/m/marcus_buckingham.html

[81] Handy, C. (1995). *The age of paradox*. Boston, MA: The Harvard Business School Press. pp. 50–56.; Vannevar. (2009, January 5). Riding the sigmoid curve. *What Would Vannevar Blog*? Retrieved from http://vannevar.blogspot.com/2009/01/riding-sigmoid-curve.html

[82] Drucker (1985).

[83]   Blaxill, M. and Rivette, K. (2004). Acquiring your future. In Stern, C.W. and Deimler, M.S. (Eds.). (2006). *The Boston Consulting Group on strategy: Classic concepts and new perspectives* (2nd ed.). Hoboken, NJ: John Wiley & Sons. p. 189.

[84]   Richardson (2010).

[85]   Moore, G.A. (2004, July–August). Darwin and the demon: Innovating within established enterprises. *Harvard Business Review, 82*(7–8), 86–92.

[86]   Mascarenhas, O. (2009, May 12). Strategic innovation management. *University of Detroit-Mercy.* p. 19. Retrieved from www.udmercy.edu

[87]   Utterback, J. (1994). *Mastering the dynamics of innovation*. Boston: Harvard University School Press. (ISBN: 0875847404). p. 81.

[88]   Dougherty, D. and Hardy, C. (1996). Sustained product innovation in large, mature organizations: Overcoming innovation-to-organization problems. *Academy of Management Journal, 39*(5), 1120.

[89]   Utterback (1994). p. 91.

[90]   Ibid. 90–97.

[91]   Richardson (2010).

[92]   Christensen and Raynor (2003).

[93]   Miller, H. (1998). Variation, innovation and dynamic quality. *The TQM Magazine, 10*(6), 447–51.

[94]   Moore (2004). pp. 86–92.; Johne, A. (1999). Successful market innovation. *Journal of Innovation Management, 2*(1), 6–11.

[95]   Lafley and Charan (2008).

[96]   Oster, G. (2009). Emergent innovation: A new strategic paradigm. *Journal of Strategic Leadership, 2*(1), 40.

[97]   Utterback (1996). pp. 90–7.

[98]   Steve Jobs quotes. (n.d.). *BrainyQuote.com*. Retrieved from http://www.brainyquote.com/quotes/quotes/s/stevejobs173474.html

[99] Socrates quotes. (n.d.). *Goodreads*. Retrieved from http://www.goodreads.com/quotes/196632-understanding-a-question-is-half-an-answer

[100] Christensen and Raynor (2003).

[101] Christensen (1997).

[102] Plato quotes. (n.d.). *BrainyQuote.com* Retrieved from http://www.brainyquote.com/quotes/quotes/p/plato398878.html

[103] Mascarenhas (2009). p. 20.

[104] Day, G.S. (2007, December). Is it real? Can we win? Is it worth doing? Managing risk and reward in an innovation portfolio. *Harvard Business Review, 85*(12), 110.

[105] Portfolio management. (n.d.). *Product Development Institute, Inc*. Retrieved from http://www.prod-dev.com/portfolio_management.php

[106] Huy, Q.N., Mintzberg, H. (2003, Summer). The rhythm of change. *MIT Sloan Management Review*, 44(4), 83–4.

[107] Chandrasekar, D. and Mehmood, C.S. (2010, June). *Value of innovation in a company* (Master's thesis, University of Gävle, Gävle, Sweden). Retrieved from http://urn.kb.se/resolve?urn=urn:nbn:se:hig:diva-8040

[108] Kandybin, A. (2009, Fall). Which innovation efforts will pay? *MIT Sloan Management Review, 51*(1), 58.

[109] Grffin et al. (2012). p. 18.

[110] Ibid. pp. 18–9.

[111] Ries (2011).

[112] Christensen and Raynor (2003).

[113] Ries, E. (2011, October). Build measure learn. *Inc.*, 33(8), 56–63.

[114] Christensen (1997). p. xv.

[115] Christensen, C.M., Roth, E.A. and Anthony, S.D. (2004). *Seeing what's next: Using theories of innovation to predict industry change*. Boston: Harvard Business School Press.

[116] Moore (2004). pp. 86–92.

[117] Christensen and Raynor (2003).

[118] Ibid. p. 99.

[119] Rogers, E.M. (2003). pp. 279–85.

[120] Sinek (2009).

[121] Ries (2011). p. 39.

[122] Ann Eshoo quotes. (n.d.). *BrainyQuotes.com*. http://www.brainyquote.com/quotes/quotes/a/annaeshoo505472.html

[123] Tushman, M. and O'Reilly, C. (2002). *Winning through innovation: A practical guide to leading organizational change and renewal*. Boston: Harvard University School Press. (ISBN: 1578518210). p. 2.

[124] Griffin et al. (2012). p. 2.

[125] Ibid. p. 39.

[126] Ibid. pp. 29–34.

[127] Ibid. pp. 32–4.

[128] Ibid. p. 39–40.

[129] Senge (2006); Argyris, C. (1977, September-October). Double loop learning in organizations. *Harvard Business Review, 55*(5), 115–25.

[130] Griffin et al. (2012). p. 41.

[131] Michael Jordan quotes. (n.d.). *BrainyQuote.com*. Retrieved from http://www.brainyquote.com/quotes/keywords/teamwork.html

132 Japanese proverb quotes. (n.d.). *Thinkexist.com*. Retrieved from http://thinkexist.com/quotation/none_of_us_are_as_smart_as_all_of/160488.html

133 Brickley, J.A., Smith, Jr., C.W. and Zimmerman, J.L. (2007). *Managerial economics and organizational architecture*. (4th ed.) New York: McGraw-Hill Irwin. p. 343.; Is your team too big? Too small? What's the right number? (2006, June 14). *Knowledge@Wharton*. 1–4. Retrieved from http://knowledge.wharton.upenn.edu/articlepdf/1501.pdf?CFID=229450368&CFTOKEN=8819 9422&jsessionid=a830925615931f6489c14936442346954535

134 Kelly, T. and Littman, J. (2000). *The art of innovation: Success through innovation the IDEO way*. New York: Currency.

135 Burkus, D. (2013). *The myths of creativity: The truth about how innovative companies and people generate great ideas*. San Francisco, CA: Jossey-Bass. pp. 67–86.

136 Williams, S.L. (2001). *The relationship between shared work values and interpersonal trust among individuals in selected work settings* (Doctoral dissertation, University of Illinois at Urbana-Champaign). Retrieved from http://www.worldcat.org/title/relationship-between-shared-work-values-and-interpersonal-trust-among-individuals-in-selected-work-settings/oclc/48839692

137 Kelly and Littman (2000).

138 Lafley and Charan (2008).

139 Anthony (2012). pp. 132–3.

140 Dyer et al. (2011).

141 Ibid.

142 Hall, E.T. (1983). *The dance of life: The other dimension of time*. New York, NY; Doubleday; Hall, E.T. (1976). *Beyond culture*. New York: Doubleday; Hall E.T. (1969). *The hidden dimension. Man's use of space in public and private*. London, UK: Bodley Head; Hall's cultural factors. (2012). *Changing Minds*. Retrieved from http://changingminds.org/explanations/culture/hall_culture.htm.; Dahl (2003).

143 Tuckman, B.W. and Jenson, M.A.C. (1977). Stages of small-group development revisited. *Group & Organization Management*, 2, 419–27.

[144] Gilley, J.W., Morris, M.L., Waite, A.M., Coates, T. Veliquette, T. (2010, February). Integrated theoretical model for building effective teams. *Advances in Human Development Resources*, 12(1), 7–28.

[145] Cameron, K.S. and Quinn, R.E. (2006). *Diagnosing and changing organizational culture: Based on the competing values framework* (Rev. ed.). San Francisco: Jossey-Bass. p. 70.

[146] Kelley, R.E. (1992). *The power of followership: How to create leaders people want to follow and followers who lead themselves.* New York: Doubleday Currency.

[147] Logan, D., King, J. and Fischer-Wright, H. (2008). *Tribal leadership: Leveraging natural groups to build a thriving organization.* New York, NY: HarperCollins.

[148] Bennis, W. and Biederman, P.W. (1997). *Organizing genius: The secrets of creative collaboration.* New York: Perseus. (ISBN: 0201339897). pp. 197–218.

[149] Ibid. (1997).

[150] W. Edwards Deming quotes. (n.d.). *BrainyQuote.com.* Retrieved from http://www.brainyquote.com/quotes/keywords/innovation_9.html

[151] Tushman and O'Reilly (2002). p. 14.

[152] Ries (2011). pp. 8–9.

[153] Ibid. pp. 10–11.

[154] Dyer et al. (2011).

[155] Christensen (1997).

[156] Evans, J.H. and Greenleaf, W. (Ed.). (2007). *The bright sales book on closing* (1st ed.). West Yorkshire, UK: Vista House.

[157] Grove, A.S. (1996). *Only the paranoid survive.* New York, NY: Doubleday.

[158] Newton, I. and Hawking, S. (Ed.). (2002). *Principia.* Philadelphia, PA: Running Press. p. 11.

[159] Lafley and Charan (2008).

Chapter 7
Marketing versus Selling

Get someone else to blow your horn and the sound will carry twice as far.[1]

Revenue growth for a private equity portfolio company is a function of organic and acquisitive growth. We will focus on organic, although some of the points in this section are applicable to making the most of acquired growth. Organic growth is the third wave of private equity innovation.[2] To be clear, organic growth is autonomously accomplished by a company through developed marketing channels with its own sales professionals. As alluded in Chapter 5: The Importance of Strategy, "organic growth ... is less risky than acquired growth and more highly valued by investors."[3] There are five Ps of strategy to be considered in attacking organic growth:

- a plan, or deliberate set of actions;

- a ploy, or purpose of the plan;

- a pattern, or pronounced style of execution, that is, the way things are done within the organization;

- a position, or differentiation among other players in the ecosystem; and

- a perspective, or worldview for rationalizing strategy.[4]

These five strategic Ps may be considered in conjunction with Michael Porter's basic model of general product differentiation, general cost leadership, or narrowly defined focus in either category.[5] (See Figure 7.1.) Irrespective of the strategic focus, the yardstick of success is profitable sales.

"Marketing" and "sales" are often interchangeable synonyms within the middle market. Moreover, when the two are communicated as separate functions, the relationship between marketing and sales is typically backwards.

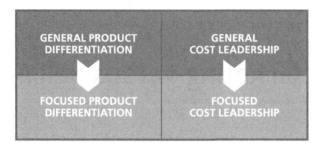

Figure 7.1   A depiction of Porter's basic strategies

Source: Reprinted with the permission of Simon & Schuster Publishing Group from the Free Press edition of *Competitive Strategy: Techniques for Analyzing Industries and Competitors* by Michael E. Porter. Copyright © 1980, 1988 by The Free Press. All rights reserved.

For example, a business card might brandish "vice-president of sales and marketing." When the term "marketing" is used, it is commonly subservient to sales. In these instances, "marketing" is tantamount to marketing communications—not strategic marketing. Marketing communications includes activities such as social media blasts in advance of an industry trade show to remind prospects and customers where to find the company's booth. The value of marketing communications is not discounted here. Rather, the point is not to confuse it with strategic marketing. Indeed, marketing communications is an integral part of strategic marketing.

The correct relationship between marketing and sales is similar to that between strategic thinking and strategic planning. The former is strategic (marketing and thinking) and the latter is tactical (sales and planning). Ideally, the marketing and sales functions should recognize themselves as partners in a three-legged race.

Marketing

> *The population is by nature fickle; it is easy to persuade them of something, but difficult to confirm them in that persuasion. Therefore, one must urgently arrange matters so that when they no longer believe, they can be made to believe . . . .*[6]

Marketing strategy is developed and executed in existing and potential markets. According to Richard L. Daft, there are four stages of global market development. The first is domestic, which is germane to the home country. The second is international, often commenced by simple exporting before considering joint ventures, acquisitions, or greenfield operations. The third is multinational, whereby duplicative efforts pepper the globe. The fourth is global, in which a boundaryless, integrated company defers to the core competencies of the business model units based on economics—irrespective of geography.[7] Competing in an increasingly boundaryless environment demands that strategy must encompass the issues of speed, flexibility, integration, and innovation.[8]

> *All else being equal, countries whose economic systems facilitate and motivate [disruptive innovation] have better long term growth prospects, and [leaders] should expect companies that follow the principles of disruption when they expand oversees to have high growth potential. Finding simple ways to reach non-consumers in developing markets provides tremendous room for growth.[9]*

Marketing strategy (not to be confused with general strategy) is often juxtaposed against a different set of five P's than mentioned above:

- product,

- placement,

- promotion,

- pricing, and

- packaging.[10]

The five marketing P's must reconcile—or fit—with customer target markets, as well as navigating the externalities imposed by governments in the form of laws and regulations. Concurrent with the depiction of the Kano model (see Figure 6.1 in Chapter 6: Innovation and Value-creation), all products tend to commoditize over time. This condemns product comparison to price. Since perceived value eclipses general satisfaction for predictive customer loyalty,[11] it is imperative that marketers dial in to the customers value proposition DNA. Otherwise, customer retention may yield to price-catalyzed attrition. Businesses generally suffer 10 percent annual attrition.[12] Adding insult to injury, acquiring replacement customers, that is, customer acquisition cost, regularly exceeds five times the cost of retaining a customer.[13]

The antidote to price competition is customization. Better yet, shrewd marketers inoculate their products in advance of price competition by repositioning the price P as value. Value is validated by the customer conviction of superior utility relative to the quantity purchased. This abides by Warren Buffett's axiom that "price is what [customers] pay; value is what [customers] get."[14]

Value-based marketing requires a keen understanding of the product's value proposition from the customers' perspective. The value proposition is "the whole cluster of benefits the company promises to deliver."[15] Fine tuning the value proposition is akin to the innovative discussion in Chapter 6: Innovation and Value-creation, that is to say, understanding what the product is "hired" to do. However, in this case, a known product has to be tailored to address a customer need in a differentiable solution that nullifies price pressure. By example, consider the commodity of sheep manure, a less pungent natural plant fertilizer alternative to the traditional cow option. Repositioning the "product" with the Baa Baa Doo brand gained traction with organic gardeners. Another clever adaptation regards cars. Do you remember when cars became pre-owned instead of used? Upscale brands like Mercedes Benz even "certify" pre-owned cars in attestation to their mechanical reliability.

Middle market private equity firms salivate over fragmented markets. As covered in Chapter 5: The Importance of Strategy, private equity firms seek an anchor, or platform, for prosecuting a defragmentation strategy via organic and acquisitive means. The fragmentation phenomenon is, indeed, one of the reasons that marketing is underdeveloped in the middle market. Hot products may sell themselves. Misguided order takers, masquerading as rainmakers, may develop a false sense of complacency until the product becomes passé. This is particularly relevant to fashion or faddish merchandising. Consider by way of example the season to season antiquation of couture fashions found in posh settings like Rodeo Drive, Los Angeles, California.

Strategic marketing for a business resembles military reconnaissance in that ground forces need to know what lays over the hill beyond the line of sight. Professional marketers attempt to answer several questions, including purchasing decision drivers. The marketing discipline applies several types of "listening" to identify latent and overt customer needs. This feedback has to be translated to the product development function for new opportunities and the sales force for existing products.

The inability to empathize with customer perspective can be disastrous. By way of analogy, consider the parable of the blind men and the elephant handed down from Indian tradition.[16] Six blind men encountered an elephant, each palpating a different part of the pachyderm—and consequently deriving a micro, myopic perspective:

- a leg was mistaken for a pillar,

- the trunk a tree branch,

- a tusk was a pipe,

- the tail a rope,

- the thorax a wall, and

- the ear a large fan.

The point is that the holistic perspective individually eluded each man. By comparing notes and despite the benefit of one of the key evaluation senses (sight), the men might have surmised something more articulated and complete, thus yielding a more enlightening truth about this ecosystem phenomenon. So it is with customers.

Customer purchasing decisions are rooted in four general criteria: value, quality, speed, and customer service. Market share is created and/or captured when the five marketing P's align with the customer's decision criteria. Consider the symbiosis between the two as push and pull. To wit, when the pull is understood (customer purchasing decisions), marketers push product toward customers with an appealing five P's algorithm.

Useful customer metrics for analysis may be scarce within middle market companies. Moreover, some of the measures evade universal definition. Customer service, for example, may be defined quite differently for individual customers. When surveys are conducted, they are usually poorly structured and biased. A personal experience proves the point. A car dealer surveyed each sale with the promise of a free tank of gas for customers who provided perfect survey scores. When it costs $100 to fill-up, the temptation to fudge can be overwhelming. Consequently, the feedback is worthless. The dealer in question in this example is out of business even though the survey data "proved" that the dealership was exceptional.

Traditional marketing metrics are becoming obsolete. Upon the advent of micromarketing enabled by social media, the metrics may be unique to the customer. Consider software as a service (SaaS) vendors who supply customized solutions in complex scenarios. In these instances, the relationship may include initial revenue associated with installation, followed by recurring revenue for support. Service level agreements are common. Metrics should appropriately evolve from these agreements.

Longer-term, there is only one survey question that has any statistical validity. Generically, the wording is "Would you recommend the product to family and friends?" The reason it is that the respondent is required to invest personal capital in the response. Most people will not run the risk of endorsing a product for which the likelihood of dissatisfaction jeopardizes a personal relationship, or personal credibility among valued social networks. The concept is called "Net Promoter® score."[17] Two complementary questions are apropos. First, "If so, why so?" imparts differentiable feedback. Second, "If not, why not?" is a signal to fix a problem—or else!

The Net Promoter® score feedback facilitates the discovery of points of differentiation and parity used in marketing efforts.[18] Parities are equalizers, for example, wheels on cars. Parities relate to the must-bes discussed above relative to the Kano model (see Figure 6.1 in Chapter 6: Innovation and Value-creation). Differentiators distinguish and separate from the competition, for example, automatically piloted cars. These are the delighters of the Kano model. Leaders must remain vigilant within their ecosystems because today's delighters may be tomorrow's must-bes. "The more alike two products are, the more important their differences become."[19] Once a competitor duplicates a differentiator, or antiquates it with a superior offering, credibility is at risk for erroneously continuing the promotion of the first-mover as differentiable.

As mentioned above, because all products tend to commoditize over time, good marketing intelligence should keep tabs on competitor parity and differentiation. The secret shopper technique is one such mechanism. For example, Sam Walton, founder of Walmart, personally and regularly checked out competing retailers. Moreover, best practices were promptly disseminated across the entire organization in weekly quick market intelligence, or QMI, debriefs. When all of the product attributes devolve to must-bes, the product is a commodity susceptible to cutthroat price competition. When marketing discovers that a competitor is brandishing parity as a differentiator, the sales force may be alerted for appropriate tactical adjustments. This does not mean that the sales force engages in taboo badmouthing. Rather, the customer dialogue may be modified to accomplish the objective more discretely, for example, "As you know, (Ms. Customer), all of the major competitors now offer this feature … ."

The diligence regimen often engages consultants who endeavor to nail the customer value proposition for the business model's products. Even so, the private equity investment team should be reminded that such research confirms what worked in the past as opposed to what may work in the future. Extrapolations in marketing are just as problematic as they are in statistics.[20] Buggy whip manufacturers were antiquated by the advent of the automobile. Similarly, e-commerce is knocking a dent in mall traffic. If direct customer contact is not done as a diligence item out of concern for spooking the customers, it should follow as a post-close exercise. Eschewing such "homework" is risky behavior. The exercise is highly complementary to the quality of earnings scrutiny of accounting diligence. Notwithstanding the timing of such homework, prospect and portfolio company market positions should not be overanalyzed either because the sector may be in the early stages of the norming phase (see Figure 1.1 in Chapter 1: Introduction). It is more important to frame the customer's opinion of you, prioritize marketing channels, and dominate market share through sales. Indeed, one of the most critical objectives of strategic marketing is identifying efficient marketing channels.

Market channels are avenues through which prospective customers are reached. In the "good ole days," buying air time on one of the three major television networks was a slam dunk to sell Ivory soap. The *Mad Men* TV drama reminds us of this era. However, over time, media outlets proliferated and audience share diluted. Presently, social media is one of the channel darlings, but it is not a panacea for all industries by any stretch of the imagination. Indeed, marketing channels may have 80/20s for industries. However, players within those industries may emphasize channels uniquely. Ultimately, when marketing leadership identifies the optimal approach, it develops the training and tools for the sales force. Essentially, marketing should be the discipline that positions the sales force to succeed.

Sales

> To the victors belong the spoils.[21]

Samuel Goldwin gave us: "The harder I work, the luckier I get."[22] "We are what we repeatedly do. Excellence then, is not an act, but a habit."[23] Why not institutionalize good sales habits? What if the hard work was first scrutinized to make sure it was smart work, or likely to produce the right results through quality—not quantity—of actions. In his book, *The Power of Habit: Why We Do What We Do in Life and in Business*, Charles Duhigg imparts that a significant portion of human actions are rooted in habit according to a model of cue, behavior, and reward.[24] Institutionalizing this model into a routine can result in cravings. Since bad habits are not easily broken, the sales leader's challenge is to institutionalize good habits that result in a craving for rewarded excellence whose byproduct is market share. Consider these points in substantiation of habits:

- Eighty percent of all buy decisions are made after the fifth call. (This presumes that the call abided by best practices according to the sales methodology.)

- About half of sales people only call a customer once. About one quarter make a second attempt. (This figure tells us nothing about whether the "suspect" was properly qualified or disqualified as a prospect.)

- One tenth of the sales force is indefatigably intrepid. This effort produces four fifths of a typical company's revenue.[25]

Reliable sales training statistics in the middle market are elusive. One of the reasons is the operational definition of the term "sales training." Ambiguity prevails between product training versus sales methodology, even though the two have a necessarily symbiotic relationship. In 2013, AXIOM Sales Force Development, LLC, and Training Development, Inc., published finding from a sales survey of 120 companies, 56 percent of which had over 500 employees. Eighty percent of the respondents were sales and human resource professionals. Sixty five percent of respondents consider their sales training programs effective, although the demarcation criteria are unclear. Among the types of training provided, product training was the most important type of training, with coaching a close second, at 56.7 percent and 52.9 percent, respectively. The explanation of coaching is tantamount to "technique" training.[26] Comparatively, the *Encyclopedia of Business* (2nd Edition) communicates that "most sales training emphasizes product, company, and industry knowledge. Only about 25 percent of the average company training program, in fact, addresses personal selling techniques."[27] Sadly, Middle Market Methods™ observed that only about one in ten sales professionals are trained in an institutionalized methodology—not to be confused with product training. These sales people tend to receive such training from the larger organizations from which they were recruited. Even then, such training may have been an event instead of a continuous improvement orientation. By analogous comparison, certain professions, for example, certified public accountants, must receive minimum continuing education credits within certain time frames as a condition of licensure. However, this type of continuous training is tantamount to product training. Clearly, differentiation awaits middle market companies who address the institutional deficiency of sales training, coupled with continuous process improvement.

Daniel Pink's book, *To Sell is Human: The Surprising Truth about Motivating Others*, offers some interesting framing data points:

- One out of every nine jobs in the economy is sales. Neither cyclical downturns nor the information age has affected this ratio.

- Among non-sales positions in a typical company, 40 percent of their time is attributable to sales support activities, e.g., customer service.

- One fifth of societal sales descriptors are negative. Interestingly, this abides by the 80/20 rule. One reason is the historical asymmetry of information skewed in favor of sellers. The advent of bisymmetry over the web changed the customer relationship dynamic from caveat emptor (let the buyer beware) to caveat venditor (let the seller beware).

- A counterintuitive issue regards the personality profile. Gregarious type-As have traditionally been preferred to build friendly customer relations. However, there is no statistical validation of this practice. Indeed, ambiverts have an edge. Ambiverts have the IQ (cognitive intelligence), EQ (emotional intelligence in reading other people) and PQ ("the control you have over your own mind and how well your mind acts in your best interest" [28]) to adjust their style to the audience. When the signals suggest passivity is good judgment, the introvert appears. When, aggressiveness is warranted, the extrovert appears. Ambiverts are also comfortable in deferring to their technical support when they discover that this is the best way to consummate a transaction. Alternatively, an insecure sales person may be vulnerable to the customer discounting as hubris the salient technical points that came from a non-technical person.

- The best sales professionals in the future will embrace attunement with their customers, buoyancy despite intermittent setbacks, and clarity for how their product addresses customer needs better than alternatives. Pink provides an interesting metric in substantiation of buoyance toward this objective: a 3:1 positive to negative ratio on commentary depicting attitudinal posture.[29] Stated another way, the great sales professionals of the future will see their glass at least have full 75 percent of the time.

Bain & Company complements Pink's insights thusly:

> *Mobilizing back-office resources to augment field reps' efforts is a powerful force multiplier. "Customer-facing time," not administration, is where the selling organization earns its paycheck. The best sales organizations therefore measure customer-facing time and use internal support to create more. In fact, shifting to a well-trained team to qualify leads, pitch in with outbound selling and help close deals can add as much as 30 percent back to a rep's day.[30]*

"Selling suffers from an image crisis—largely of its own making."[31] Aversion to this odiferous aura has compelled some organizations to adopt all manner of euphemisms to avoid the "S" word. B2C healthcare business models seem particularly vulnerable to this malady. Surrogates include "marketer" and "liaison." Root causes may include bad personal experiences with the proverbial high-pressure, used car salesman approach. Truly, customers do not like being sold. Lost in the fog is that customers do like to buy—when the product addresses their issues.

Some companies describe themselves in terms of a sales culture. This has virtue, provided certain principles are embraced. Without customers, there is no business. A "sales culture" may mean that customer satisfaction is a primary focus. Even this is a matter of perspective. Some so-called sales cultures push what they have. Taken to extremes, this approximates the primary protagonist in the play turned movie, *Glengarry Glen Ross*, whose mantra was ABC: always be closing.[32] This is an unscrupulous model of peddling what a vendor has irrespective of customer benefit.

Customers prefer doing business with people they like.[33] Professional sales people find genuine means of becoming a trustworthy friend. This phenomenon also ties into a comment made by Zig Ziglar: "People don't buy for logical reasons. They buy for emotional reasons."[34] When customer options are plentiful—and perhaps ambiguous, the relationship tips the scales.

Sales should be focused on solving customer problems. This may be understood in the context of moments of truth, or what happens each time the customer encounters the product.[35] Good salesmanship goes a step beyond the Golden Rule to the Platinum Rule: "Do unto others as they'd like done unto them."[36] This should be an integral part of an organization's brand equity. Indeed sales professional behaviors and concurrent customer service quality brand an organization more definitively than any catchy marketing tag line. One of my favorite client stories regards Chuck Bell, founder and CEO of AIS Pharmacy in Ridgeland, Mississippi. Chuck's first date with his future bride included a detour to service a patient. He was also late for their wedding pictures in order to take care of patients. Lucky for him, his bride also has a passion for the Platinum Rule. They have been happily married over 20 years.

The Hippocratic Oath offers some analogous points: (i) first do no harm and (ii) solve a problem. This is something Middle Market Methods™ applied as its version of the "Rule of Three" in solving customer problems. If the customer issue is not in the competency strike zone, the sales professional's network should be strong enough to identify a solution for the customer within three phone calls. Even though the sale was missed, a relationship was built that may result in a future opportunity. This activity builds brand equity through trust, an underestimated and potent form of credibility.

Most communication is non-verbal. Trained sales professionals look for cues. These cues are more easily detected when the mouth is in neutral and the eyes and ears are engaged. Socrates agreed: "Nature has given us two ears, two eyes, and but one tongue—to the end that we should hear and see more than we speak."[37] Socratic Method mimics the pull methodology of Lean manufacturing whereby customer needs are identified and a solution is crafted in response.[38] When a need is discovered and validated, the sales professional positions key benefits of a proposed solution. Additional benefits are revealed as needed. A sales professional need not spew the entire inventory of solution benefits—only the ones that suffice from the customer's perspective. Seasoned pros quip that a good sales person never misses a good opportunity to shut up, or buy back the order just written. Customer curiosity about the means by which a benefit is derived entails the positioning of prime features. Again, a litany is not necessary—only sufficiency. Herein lays the solution to a chronic conundrum in selling: the confusion between features and benefits. Features explain how a benefit is produced.

Solving a problem extends beyond the Socratic method of asking prospects questions until they identify a problem to be solved. Indeed, the Socratic approach relies upon prospect awareness of an unmet need. However, prospects may have needs beyond their cognizance. This provides a sales professional an opportunity to become an anticipatory problem solver. The entre may be phrased by the sales professional as "Have you ever considered a scenario whereby … ." Of course, the prospect might dismiss the notion. The opposite extreme is also plausible: immediate recognition that the scenario presently applies. More likely, though, is that the prospect will ruminate over the scenario—consciously or subconsciously. This may or may not evolve as a near term order. However, the encounter may catalyze a different type of interpersonal relationship as the prospect may regard the sales professional as thinking ahead for the benefit of the prospect. This is differentiable. The potential benefits to the sales professional are not isolated to the specific prospect. Indeed, the sales professional may be identified as a problem solver within the prospect's personal network. That makes possible a "first order" from a party other than the prospect to whom the scenario was originally posited. This should be recognized in terms of the Net Promoter® score. However, instead of being reactive to inquiry, the prospect has pivoted to proactive advocacy.

Delighting customers seems to be a crusade for some companies. Actually, this is a waste of time and money.[39] Customers will settle for satisfaction. One of the primary reasons is that customers do not believe the "delighting" hubris anyway. Besides, it is hard to measure the difference between satisfaction and delight. Customers expect mistakes. Resolving customer complaints accomplishes retention in the half to three quarters probability range; however, prompt resolution bumps retention to 95 percent. This is the essence of customer service—an axiom ignored to the detriment of the vendor. Unfortunately for vendors, only about four percent of customers complain—to the vendor.[40] However, unhappy customers are comparatively unimpeded in telling their networks about a bad experience. The advent of social media outlets increases the "reach" both exponentially and globally. Problem ownership and resolution are practical means of building trust. "Nothing is ever gained by winning an argument and losing a customer."[41]

Whether closing a deal or responding to a customer complaint, effective negotiation is a staple of good customer relations. *Getting to Yes* is a must have for any sales professional's bookcase. The book itemizes three fairness criteria for negotiation:

- a wise agreement,

- an efficient agreement, and

- an agreement that preserves civility between the parties.[42]

The book also offers three simple steps for win-win outcomes to conflict resolution commonly encountered in sales negotiations:

- state the other party's position in terms by which they agree that you listened to them and understood their position,

- itemize the points on which you agree, and

- state your position and desired outcome.

Points on which the vendor-customer dynamic differ may be rooted in transaction, or execution, risk. Once identified, the sales professional may isolate and error-proof the root causes to mitigate the probability of occurrence. This may remove a key obstacle to writing the order.[43]

World class sales professionals share something in common with other world class professionals: a desire for improvement feedback, including customer feedback. This is a first cousin to customer service: preemptive solicitation that dispels mythical misconceptions rooted in assumption. One on the most colorful and effective characters in American politics, New York City Mayor Ed Koch, had a signature approach for soliciting such feedback. As he canvassed the five boroughs, he asked "How'm I doin'?" New Yorkers were not shy about telling Mayor Koch either. It must have worked for the major as he served three consecutive terms.

Unlike general customer service feedback, there is an Ecclesiastical timing for referral positioning feedback by sales professionals. Among the more opportune moments is when the customer expresses satisfaction with a transaction outcome. Savvy sales professionals thank them for the feedback, and pivot to "Would you introduce me to people in your professional network who would appreciate similar satisfaction?" Indeed, it would be pretty awkward for the customer to say "no" at this point.

There is absolutely no substitute for effectively managing a sales force. A common middle market mistake is promoting a rainmaker to manager. However, managerial skills are different from sales skills. Great sales managers need not be great sales people. In her book, *Quiet: The Power of Introverts in a World That Can't Stop Talking,* Susan Cane points out that extroverted sales managers are more effective with introverted sales subordinates; whereas, introverted sales managers are more effective with aggressive, self-directed subordinates.[44] The take-away appears to be that the manager or sale force may have a dominant personality, but not both. One might further speculate that introversion in both groups may lead to unsatisfactory outcomes.

The sales manager's objective is training, development, and topgrading (sic). Bradford D. Smart defines topgrading as "filling every position … with an A player at the appropriate level of compensation."[45] Topgrading works much like spring training in Major League Baseball. Talent is continually evaluated to field the best team each season within the constraints of the budget. David Anderson describes the sales management process as training, nurturing performers, and terminating non-performers.[46] Effective execution for this responsibility requires time in the field for contextual perspective. Sales positions typically come with relatively stout travel and entertainment expenses. Managers should be held accountable for quickly addressing performance problems that are only exacerbated by high support costs. Especially in the middle market, indulging sales non-performance is unacceptable because the relative impact is so pronounced.

One of the biggest hazards of sales management is the compensation mechanism. There is no silver bullet, yet the organization has a sacrosanct interest in getting it right relative to its business model. Generally speaking, short cycled sales should be more leveraged toward commissions, and long cycle sales should be leveraged toward salary. Leaders should beware tying commissions to transactions when sales people have discretion over pricing. When sales professionals are empowered to negotiate price, their incentives should be tied to a profitability metric, such as the contribution margin. For any incentive, the backdrop should be the critical thinking question: "What happens in extreme cases?" This is a form of Six Sigma's potential problem analysis. Incentivized behaviors are the ones the manager will get from her people. It is better to stress test the incentive package before sustaining an embarrassing (and possibility illegal) surprise.

Another noteworthy hazard is intellectual property. Wise leaders obtain non-compete agreements to guard against intellectual property theft. Even wiser leaders go the extra steps of legally protecting trademarks and service marks, copyrighting material, and applying for patent protection. Whereas non-compete agreements may lack solid enforceability depending on state to state case law, the point is making a former employee think twice about hijacking intellectual property.

The process of sales management is made easier by a customer relationship management (CRM) tool. Unfortunately, the track record for successful CRM implementation is abysmal. My first experience with a customer relationship management was in the 1980s with a lumbering software called Paradox. Over the years, I have implemented several systems—and overhauled just as many implementation disasters—covering the following partial list of software in both off-the-shelf and customized varieties: ACT!, Goldmine, Lotus Notes, Saleforce.com, SalesLogix, and Siebel. Two problems loom chronic. The first is a function of change-management. Requisite minimum PC skills to navigate the software should not be assumed—particularly for older professionals who grew up sans technology tools. Moreover, changing old habits without a compelling case of personal benefit is problematic. Second, the application often "overshoots" the need. The required information is relatively simple and distills to the type of prospect contact, for example, gatekeeper versus a decision-maker, and the timing of defined steps in the rigor. The managerial analytical objectives should be:

- conversion rates, i.e., how many "operationally defined" calls preceded the sale;

- cycle times, i.e., how long it takes to make each sale;

- lost deal analysis for the benefit of improved conversions; and

- won deal analysis for the benefit of cross-pollination.

Lost and won deal analyses are more important than they may appear. Whereas an occasional loss within a sales professional's territory may be dismissed to chance, recurrence across several territories may signal a developing trend. Fifth century BC Greek philosopher Antisthenes warned us to "pay attention to [our] enemies, for they are the first to discover [our] mistakes."[47] More complex analytics may be done without disrupting the sales force using relational database technology. For example, the Microsoft Office suite includes Access, a powerful desktop analytics tool well suited to this activity. There is a final worthy point about CRMs: intellectual property. The company needs to archive customer contact information to protect itself from inevitable attrition, punctuated by data theft and/or destruction.

CRMs should be a reliable source of information for the best practice of account reviews. Of course, these data may be complemented by data from both the operating and financial system modules. Account reviews are especially wise for major accounts. Account reviews analyze past activity in the relationship as a basis for discussing the future. Such reviews glean insights about things such as growth opportunities, vendor consolidation plans, product development insights, quality concerns, and/or service issues. Account reviews also lend credibility to budgeting and forecasting.

Ultimately, the competitive tenor and personal accountability for the sales force are set by company leadership. Indeed, the tone must permeate the entire organization. The livelihood of a company is reliant on profitable relationships with loyal, satisfied customers. An effective middle market sales force is encapsulated in the parable of the lion and the gazelle.

> *Every morning in Africa, a Gazelle wakes up. It knows it must run faster than the fastest lion or it will be killed. Every morning a Lion wakes up. It knows it must outrun the slowest Gazelle or it will starve to death. It doesn't matter whether you are a Lion or a Gazelle ... when the sun comes up, you'd better be running.*[48]

Endnotes

[1]   Will Rogers quotes. (n.d.). *Thinkexist.com*. Retrieved from http://thinkexist.com/quotation/get_someone_else_to_blow_your_horn_and_the_sound/186490.html

[2]   Favaro, K. and Neely, J. The next winning move in private equity. *Booz & Company: Strategy+Business Magazine, 63*, 1–10. Retrieved from www.strategy-business.com

[3]   Lafley, A.G. and Charan, R. (2008). *The game-changer: How you can drive revenue and profit growth with innovation*. New York: Random House. p. 5.

[4]   Mintzberg, H. (1987). General strategic theory: The strategy concept I: Five Ps for strategy. *California Management Review*, 11–24.

[5]   Porter, M.E. (1980). *Competitive strategy: Techniques for analyzing industries and competitors*. New York, NY: Free Press.

[6]   Machiavelli, N. (1994). *The prince*. New York: Barnes & Noble. p. 52.

[7]   Daft, R.L. (2007). *Organizational theory and design* (9th ed.). Mason, OH: Thomson South-Western.

[8]   Ashkenas, R., Ulrich, D., Jick, T. and Kerr, S. (2002). *The boundaryless organization: Breaking the chains of organizational structure.* San Francisco, CA: Jossey-Bass. pp. x–xi.

[9]   Christensen, C.M., Roth, E.A. and Anthony, S.D. (2004). *Seeing what's next: Using theories of innovation to predict industry change.* Boston: Harvard Business School Press. p. 207–08.

[10] Kotler, P. and Keller, P.L. (2006). *Marketing management* (12th ed.). Upper Saddle River, New Jersey: Pearson Education, Inc. pp. 19–20, 393–4; Pande, S. (2010, February 21). Packaging, the 5th p of marketing. Business Today, 19(4), 18; Stahlberg, M. and Maila, V. (2012). *Shopper marketing: How to increase purchasing decisions at the point of sale* (2nd ed.). Philadelphia: Kogan Page Limited.

[11] Reidenbach, R.E. (2010, July 13). Growing market share through customer retention. *Quality Digest.* Retrieved from http://www.qualitydigest.com/inside/quality-insider-column/growing-market-share-through-customer-retention.html

[12] Kotler and Keller (2006). p. 156.

[13] Ibid.

[14] Warren Buffett quotes. (n.d.). *Goodreads.* Retrieved from http://www.goodreads.com/author/quotes/756.Warren_Buffett

[15] Kotler and Keller (2006). p. 148.

[16] Elephant and the blind men. (n.d.). *Jainworld.com.* Retrieved from http://www.jainworld.com/education/stories25.asp

[17] Reichheld, F.F. (2006). *The ultimate question: driving good profits and true growth.* Boston, MA: Harvard Business School Press; Reichheld, F.F. (2004, June). The one number you need to grow. *Harvard Business Review, 82*(6), p. 133; Reichheld, F.F. (2003, December). The one number you need to grow. *Harvard Business Review, 81*(12), pp. 46–54.

[18] Kotler and Keller (2006).

[19] Regis McKenna quote. (n.d.). 175 great quotes on business, entrepreneurship, marketing, and sales. *Slideshare.net.* Retrieved from http://www.slideshare.net/stephendaviscxo/175-great-quotes-on-business-entrepreneurship-marketing-and-sales

[20]   Ries, A. and Trout, J. (1990). *Bottom-up marketing*. New York: Plume.

[21]   *TheFreeDictionary*. (n.d.). Retrieved from http://idioms.thefreedictionary.com/To+the+victors+b elong+the+spoils

[22]   Samuel Goldwyn quotes. (n.d.). *BrainyQuote.com* Retrieved from http://www.brainyquote.com/ quotes/authors/s/samuel_goldwyn_3.html

[23]   Aristotle quotes. (n.d.). *Thinkexist.com*. Retrieved from http://thinkexist.com/quotation/we_are_ what_we_repeatedly_do-excellence_then-is/12820.html

[24]   Duhigg, C. (2012). *The power of habit: Why we do what we do in life and business*. New York: Random House.

[25]   Reddy, P. (n.d.). 10 powerful secrets of a successful salesman. *Preserve Articles*. Retrieved from http://www.preservearticles.com/201101173467/10-powerful-secrets-of-a-successful-salesman. html

[26]   The guide to sustaining the impact of sales training: Using effective coaching methods to improve sales performance. (2013, May). *AXIOM Sales Force Development, LLC, & Training Development, Inc.* Retrieved from http://www.trainingindustry.com/media/16427396/sustaining_the_impact_ of_sales_training_report_final.pdf

[27]   Sales management. (n.d.). *Encyclopedia of business* (2nd ed.). Retrieved from http://www. referenceforbusiness.com/small/Qu-Sm/Sales-Management.html

[28]   Chamine, S. (2012). *Positive intelligence: Why only 20% of team and individuals achieve their true potential and how you can achieve yours*. Austin, TX: Greenleaf, R.K. and Spears, L.C. (Ed.). (1998). *The power of servant leadership*. San Francisco, CA: Berrett-Koehler Publishers. p. 6.

[29]   Pink, D.H. (2012). *To sell is human: The surprising truth about moving others*. New York: Penguin.

[30]   How leaders get the most out of their sales force. (2011, March 11). *Insights*. Boston, MA: Bain & Company. Retrieved from http://www.bain.com/publications/articles/how-leaders-get-the-most-out-of-salesforce.aspx

[31]   Lanier, J.A. (2013, 1st quarter.). Caveat venditor. *Middle Market Methods™*. Retrieved from www.middlemarketmethods.com

[32]   Mamet, D. (1994). *Glengarry Glen Ross: A play* (Reissue ed.). New York: Grove Press.

33 Gitomer, J. (2005). *Little red book of selling*. Austin, TX: Bard. p. 81.

34 Zig Ziglar quotes. (n.d.). *BrainyQuote.com* Retrieved from http://www.brainyquote.com/quotes/authors/z/zig_ziglar.html

35 Carlzon, J. (1987). *Moments of truth: New strategies for today's customer-driven economy*. New York: Ballinger.

36 Alessandra, T. and O'Connor, M.J. (1998). *The platinum rule: The four basic business personalities and how they can lead you to success*. New York: Grand Central Publishing. p. 4.

37 Socrates quotes. (n.d.). *Thinkexist.com*. Retrieved from http://thinkexist.com/quotation/nature_has_given_us_two_ears-two_eyes-and_but_one/297595.html

38 Lanier (2013).

39 Dixon, M., Freeman, K. and Toman, N. (2010, July-August). Stop trying to delight your customers. *Harvard Business Review, 88*(7/8) 116–22.

40 Kotler and Keller (2006). pp. 155–6.

41 Norton, C.F. (n.d.). Thoughts on the business of life. *Forbes.com*. Retrieved from http://thoughts.forbes.com/thoughts/winning-c-f-norton-nothing-is-ever

42 Fisher, R. and Ury. W. (1991). *Getting to yes* (2nd ed.). New York: Penguin. p. 4.

43 Gitomer (2005). p. 153.

44 Cane, C. (2012). *Quiet: The power of introverts in a world that can't stop talking*. New York: Crown.

45 Smart, B.A. (1999). *Topgrading: How leading companies win by hiring, coaching, and keeping the best people*. Paramus, NJ: Prentice Hall. p. 11.

46 Anderson, D. (2001).*Three key lessons in leadership: Re-train your leaders, feed your eagles, trim your turkeys* [mp3 recording]. USA: Creative Broadcast Concepts.

47 Antisthenese quotes. (n.d.). *Finestquotes.com*. Retrieved from http://www.finestquotes.com/author_quotes-author-Antisthenes-page-0.htm

48 *Quotations book*. (n.d.). Retrieved from http://quotationsbook.com/quote/42333/#sthash.cjKDQoMz.dpbs

Chapter 8

Leadership Choices and Organizational Design

A good leader inspires people to have confidence in the leader; a great leader inspires people to have confidence in themselves.[1]

Leadership Choices

… But I have promises to keep,
And miles to go before I sleep …[2]

"There is not one universal, unified definition of leadership. Leadership has diverse connotations in different cultures, and most of them are misleading myths."[3] Moreover, there is no evidence supporting a single best leadership style.[4] Among the false assumptions about leadership is that it is reserved for managers. "Leadership is not management… . Management is efficiency in climbing the ladder of success; leadership determines whether the ladder is leaning against the right wall."[5] The process of management includes three core functions:

- planning,

- staffing and organizing, and

- directing and controlling.[6]

Leadership is not confined to rank. Titles are a tool of managers who need position power. Effective leaders use influence. In a word, leadership is "persuasion."[7] By definition, a leader needs followers. Wise people have known for centuries that honey attracts higher caliber of fly than vinegar. Metaphorically, this differentiates persuasion from directives.

Voltaire instructed us to "love truth, but pardon error."[8] Indeed, "a life spent making mistakes is not only more honorable, but more useful than a life spent doing nothing."[9] The real leadership challenge is how much and what kind of error is tolerated along the path of follower development without violating values and ethical standards. The "best" leadership style depends on the desired leader dynamic relative to the ecosystem. Good leadership decisions tend to be rooted in relevant experience, and relevant experience may emanate from past mistakes. For example, Thomas Edison failed many times trying to master the incandescent light. Edison described his failures in terms of ruling out options that did not work.[10] Theodore Roosevelt framed is thoughts on perseverance thusly:

> It is not the critic who counts, not the man who points out how the strong man stumbles or where the doer of deeds could have done better. The credit belongs to the man who is actually in the arena, whose face is marred by dust and sweat and blood, who strives valiantly, who errs and comes up short again and again, because there is no effort without error or shortcoming, but who knows the great enthusiasms, the great devotions, who spends himself for a worthy cause; who, at the best, knows, in the end, the triumph of high achievement, and who, at the worst, if he fails, at least he fails while daring greatly, so that his place shall never be with those cold and timid souls who knew neither victory nor defeat.[11]

Global leaders are not born with genetic predispositions for greatness. Rather, "global leaders are born, then made."[12] "Leadership cannot be taught, but it can be learned."[13] There are four leadership myths:

- everyone can lead,

- leaders always deliver results,

- leaders always wind up in charge, and

- leaders make great coaches.[14]

The decision to pursue leadership excellence is a continuous, multifaceted endeavor.

> [Leadership is] the process of diagnosing where the work group is now, and where it needs to be in the future, and formulating a strategy for getting there. Leadership also involves implementing change through developing a base of influence with followers, motivating them to

commit to and work hard in pursuit of change goals, and working with
them to overcome obstacles to change.[15]

A person's ability to engage another individual is characterized in three categories: security, anxiousness, and avoidance. Not only is it beneficial for the leader to have self-awareness, but it is also beneficial for coaches and followers to be dialed into the leaders psyche. One reason psychologists ask leaders about their childhoods is that it has a bearing on their interpersonal propensities, although early childhood development is not the only variable. Despite someone's possible discontentment with their personal proclivities, the odds of changing are only about 25 percent.[16] This is eerily similar to the 80/20 principle and has some bearing on the axiom that great leaders are in the minority.

"Leadership strategy describes the organizational and human capabilities needed to enact the [organizational] strategy effectively."[17] A rigor improves the results:

- "prioritizing the decisions that must be made;

- examining the factors involved in each;

- designing roles, processes, systems, and behavior to improve decisions; and

- institutionalizing the new approach through training, refined data analysis, and outcome assessment."[18]

Double-loop learning is beneficial to this process.[19] Organizational design should be engineered to learn from mistakes without risking the business. Moreover, those mistakes should become part of the organization's pool of knowledge.

> *People in [an] organization often interpret a lack of immediate success*
> *as failure and this interpretation is a key threat to building momentum*
> *and expanding the stretch of influence. The strategic leader must*
> *preempt those interpretations by setting appropriate expectations*
> *inside and outside the organization.*[20]

"Few organizations have so clear a picture of their global business strategy that it can be translated into specific developmental needs"[21] for members of the organization responsible for executing the strategy. The Global Results Pyramid™ (see Figure 8.1) provides some clarity by conveying the foundation-to-apex alignment of relationship, vision, strategy, and action.[22] The pyramid begins with people for the simple reason that they do the work. These people must buy into a vision. This does not happen unless they have cause to trust its personal impact. These same people have to execute a strategy that they understand. Actions have consequences. Responsible people have to enjoy a degree of confidence that these actions make sense.

Leadership is increasingly a team sport.[23] The term leader refers to an individual person enacting a particular role as "leader" or from a particular role exerting leadership behavior. In this context, the term "leadership" refers to a function, which may be, but is not necessarily, fulfilled by a single person. Leadership can be shared and exerted by a group, for example, or, may be part of an organization's culture. The same distinction can be made with respect to the terms "follower" and "followership."[24]

There simply is not leadership without followers. Followers can make or break leaders.[25] Accordingly, leaders should encourage feedback from followers. Reciprocally, followers should:

Figure 8.1   Zweifel's Global Results Pyramid™

Source: Zweifel, T.D. (2003). *Culture Clash: Managing the Global High-performance Team.* New York: SelectBooks.

- embrace the responsibility,

- serve purposefully,

- challenge that which violates their values and/or appears in error,

- invest themselves in transforming the company, and

- do the right thing.[26]

Additionally, followers should "work with others when appropriate, ... get the job done, ... stand up for what is right, ... care, ... and know when enough is enough."[27] The most effective followers model "enthusiasm, intelligence, and self-reliance."[28]

People own accountabilities for corporate initiatives. High performance organizations rely on symbiosis between good leaders and followers. Effective leaders know when to defer to followers' subject matter expertise. Indeed, leaders follow 90 percent of the time.[29] The leader-follower dynamic trumps all other performance variables, including type of industry, size of business, or age of business.[30]

Effective teams know when and how to defer to each other relative to situations and skills. This is core to successful private equity investment. Private equity firms seek good investment opportunities in proven business models. Investment teams effectively wield persuasion with portfolio company management. Similarly, the scalability of the portfolio company rests upon leadership persuasion. Sometimes this entails the founder-leader persuading herself to delegate in flatter organizational structures.

Trust seems simple enough in principle, but how do leaders earn trust? In his book, *Managers as Mentors: Building Partnerships for Learning*, Chip Bell imparts that trust starts with authenticity.[31] Stephen M.R. Covey adds in *The Speed of Trust: The One Thing that Changes Everything* that trust is a function of credibility.[32] By making commitments and delivering against expectations, credibility is methodically and incrementally earned over a period of time. Edwards Deming, Stephen R. Covey (the father of Stephen M.R. Covey), and Peter Drucker refer to the process of earning credibility as under-promising and over-delivering.[33] This works within and across leader and follower roles. Covey warns that whereas trust creation is a slow process, trust decimation may occur with one careless act. Patrick Lencioni cites the absence of trust as the fundamental nemesis of team dynamics in his book, *The Five Dysfunctions of Teams*.[34] (See Figure 8.2.) Lencioni posits trust as foundational in a structure that progresses through unfiltered conflict around ideas, commitment to decisions and plans of action, holding teammates accountable for execution, and focusing on achievement of collective results. In *Predictable Results in Unpredictable Times*, Stephen R. Covey and Bob Whitman cite trust as one of the four core principles of doing well in a hostile environment.[35] Again, from *Managers as Mentors*, Bell expounds on servant leadership tenets by reminding practitioners that the best leaders not only develop their teams, but they also share the publicity and rewards of successes with their teams.[36]

Leaders must contend with the "judgment domains" of people, strategy, and crisis.[37] Since people execute the business strategy and defuse crises, the people domain trumps the other two.[38] Irrespective of leadership style, the first obligation is to communicate ecosystem reality. Subsequently, followers should be positioned and empowered for success. Finally, the leader should say "thanks" when the goals are accomplished.[39] An even better way to say "thanks" is by celebrating to mark the milestone.

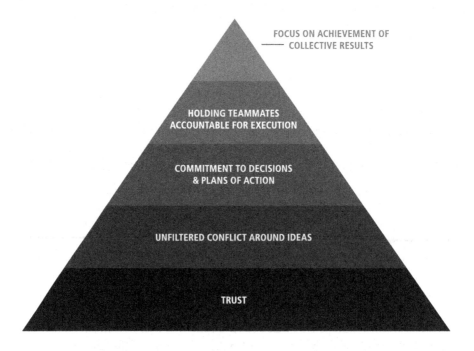

Figure 8.2   Lencioni's five dysfunctions of teams

Source: Lencioni, P. (2002). *The Five Dysfunctions of a Team: A Leadership Fable*. San Francisco, CA: Jossey-Bass. Reproduced with permission of John Wiley & Sons, Inc.

Second guessing is among the leader's biggest enemies. Doubt can be debilitating. Neither perfect information nor perfect decisions exist. Experienced leaders may do no better than their gut instinct when they have access to practically available information. Exhaustive analysis beyond that point does not improve the quality of the decision—certainly not when the additional time and cost are considered.[40] The primary caveat to this is single versus multiple options. Decisions substantially improve when multiple options are available.[41] Even so, when leaders go with their gut, they should temper the call with candid feedback from intimates before pulling the trigger and while implementing the decision. The research shows that leaders decide to change course much less frequently than their teams think they should.[42]

Abraham Lincoln said, "Nearly all men can stand adversity, but if you want to test a man's character, give him power."[43] "Circumstances do not determine a man [or woman], they reveal him [or her]."[44] How, then, must a leader wield authority wisely? In international relations, President Teddy Roosevelt thought it meant "Speak softly and carry a big stick … ."[45] Collectively, these sentiments are symptomatic of "power school" dogma—in other words, macro and micro power preservation.[46] Like the "great man" theory to which it aligned, "power school" dogma is antiquated.

Timeless precepts foster better outcomes. Leaders and followers do well to define and embrace them, but this is easier said than done. Integrity and character aid the cause. Integrity is "the quality of honesty and trustworthiness."[47] "Character is always about consistently aligning words … and [daily] modeled actions."[48] The relationship between integrity and character may be explained thusly: Integrity is doing the right thing; character is doing the right thing when no one is looking. In Hamlet, Shakespeare penned an apt line for Polonius about character that he probably borrowed from Socrates: "This above all: to thine own self be true."[49] (Socrates' version was "To know thyself is the beginning of wisdom."[50])

Ethics and values also play a role in the solution. "Ethics is concerned with the kinds of values and morals an individual or society finds desirable or appropriate."[51] Values were elaborated upon in Chapter 4: The DNA of Packs. "Business ethics can be defined as principles of conduct within organizations that guide decision-making and behavior."[52] There are five principles of ethical leadership:

- modeling respect for others,

- serving others,

- demonstrating work environment justice,

- institutionalizing honesty, and

- building community.[53]

Many leadership theories permeate academic debate. Leadership theory is "a set of interrelated concepts, definitions, assumptions, and generalizations that systematically describes and explains regularities in behaviors."[54]

The variables are dynamic—not static. Were they static, theories would become axioms or laws. Naturally, it follows that a particular leadership theory suffices until a change in at least one variable renders it moot. Leadership includes:

- competencies,

- literacies,

- dynamics, and

- problem-solving.

All four of these may be further explained. The four leadership competencies are:

- inquisitiveness,

- character,

- perspective ("embracing uncertainty and balancing tensions"[55]), and

- savvy (street smarts).[56]

The four leadership literacies are:

- personal ("understanding and valuing yourself"[57]),

- social (effective interpersonal dynamics),

- business (stewarding the organization toward executing strategy), and

- cultural (forging an organizational culture conducive to strategy).[58]

Finally, the two leadership dynamics are:

- global dispersion and

- duality (reconciling global thinking and local operations).[59]

Leaders also lean problem-solving types. There are two:

- technical (applied knowledge) and

- adaptive (invented knowledge).[60]

Espoused leadership styles should consider the organization relative to the ecosystem in which it operates. An effective leadership style for an organization may be:

- driven by the necessities or prerequisites of the operating environment,

- motivated by the individual's behavioral traits,

- influenced by the alignment between one's values and the role's combination of intrinsic and extrinsic levers, and

- motivated by the individual's mandatory and optional preparation for the role.[61]

Personality proclivities are complex. Otherwise, psychologists would have little to do. The leader's personality style may influence her leadership style.[62] A simple means of describing leadership propensities is:

- "me," or charismatic;

- "we," or transformational;

- "thee," or servant; and

- "it," or transactional.

If leaders do not explain what they are trying to do, followers will label it as they understand it.[63]

No single leadership style is effective in all scenarios.[64] A tidal wave of overwhelming inputs creates a data "garbage can" through which leaders must sift for relevance.[65] Leaders tend to have primary styles, but default to fallback styles under duress.[66] Self-awareness is a defense against such slippage, especially when the fallback style inflicts collateral damage. A winning leadership style today enjoys no guarantee of relevance tomorrow. Indeed, leadership dynamics shift as cultures evolve across generations. Transactional leaders barter with followers to promote the interests of both parties.[67] These leaders may function in active, passive, or exceptional modes.[68] Transactional leadership is compatible with agency, whereby a principle engages an agent to perform certain acts for remuneration.[69]

A leader's personal style has bearing on his adaptability to a suitable leadership style. Moreover, the personal styles of the leader's team affect the viability of leadership style choices. Leadership style motivators form a continuum whose boundaries are people orientation and task orientation.[70] Robert R. Blake and Anne Adams McCanse modified a Managerial Grid® originally constructed by Blake and Jane S. Mouton that explores the people-task interaction.[71] A matrix resulting from their endeavors reveals seven profiles (see Figure 8.3):

1.   impoverished management that is derelict in both people and task terms (coordinates 1,1);

2.   authority-compliance management that emphasizes task to the exclusion of interpersonal concern (coordinates 9,1);

3.   middle-of-the-road management which moderately emphasizes both people and task issues (coordinates 5,5);

4.   country club management that emphasizes people to the exclusion of task (coordinates 1,9);

5.   team management that exerts strong emphasis on both people and task concerns (coordinates 9,9);

6.   paternalism/materialism management whose benevolent dictatorship vacillates between country club and authority-compliance styles; and

7.   opportunistic management that is Machiavellian, i.e., the end justifies the means.

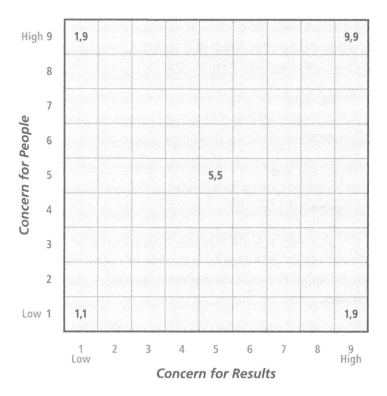

Figure 8.3   Blake and McCanse's Managerial Grid®

Source: Blake, R.R., and McCanse, A.A. (1991). *Leadership Dilemmas-Grid® Solutions: A Visionary New Look at a Classic Tool for Defining and Attaining Leadership and Management Excellence.* Houston, TX: Gulf Publishing Company.

Peter G. Northouse's *Leadership Theory and Practice* discusses four leadership profiles that have particular utility in acquisition integration settings:

- situational,

- contingency,

- transformational, and

- team.[72]

In their book, *Leadership and the One Minute Manager: Increasing Effectiveness through Situational Leadership*, Kenneth Blanchard, Patricia Zigarmi, and Drea Zigarmi impart that situational leadership progresses through four styles:

- delegating,

- supporting,

- coaching, and

- directing.[73]

A situation may be sufficiently complex to draw upon all four profiles. In middle market private equity, this may be true of the investment transaction for the private equity firm. For the portfolio company, a common example is acquisition integration.

Contingency leadership style reacts algorithmically to environmental cues, resulting in the leader's level of empowerment versus directives toward subordinates.[74] An example of the "if, then" logic occurs when order backlog falls below an established threshold, resulting in possible lay-offs. Contingency theory may be appropriate in a recessionary environment as the necessity of a turnaround often skews decisions toward task-orientation at the expense of people orientation. Thus, command and control may be rationalized due to urgency. However, autocratic leadership may be counterproductive in a full-employment economy. Even so, contingency theory does have its redeeming qualities.

The most impressive contingency theory application I encountered in my consulting practice regarded Dale Cole, founder of CTW, now a unit of Tegra

Medical, a contract medical device manufacturer. Cole is a true innovative entrepreneur in every sense of the word. CTW experienced a catastrophic fire. The first thing Cole did was assure his employees that their compensation would not be interrupted. Cole prioritized the preservation of the highly skilled team he built. When told by a general contractor the time and cost to rebuild the plant, Cole rejected the option and resolved to function as his own general contractor. Cole drew upon team dynamics to address a crisis. His employees pitched in as construction workers. The plant came back on line in record time to the delight and surprise of his customers. Cole's leadership cemented him as a cultural folk hero. Cole nurtured corporate culture in novel ways. The new plant includes a picnic patio. At its corner is perched a stainless steel custom smoker of commercial proportions. During his tenure, Cole personally cooked for his employees each month.

Transformational leaders seek to achieve high performance by developing their followers' potential.[75] Transformational leadership shares some attribution to servant leadership. This brand of leadership is "attentive to the concerns of their followers and empathizes with them,"[76] and endeavors to do "the right thing at the right time for the right reason."[77] Transformational leaders coach their followers to a higher plane of achievement. Transformational leadership requires the leader to rally followers around a superlative future state, for example, the post-acquisition integration vision. Transformational leaders help their followers see past the task-people conflict toward a new reality, for example, the tipping point of disruptive innovation adoption.[78]

Team leadership describes a group sharing a common goal, but without necessarily having a designated senior person.[79] Such teams may sometimes be described as self-directed. Shared leadership is yet another common descriptor.[80] The team leadership model relies on articulating functional roles:

- a navigator whose contribution is charting the logical deliverable course,

- an engineer who provides efficient structural guidance,

- a social integrator who wields emotional intelligence insights for effective interpersonal dynamics, and

- a liaison who networks adroitly for stakeholder persuasion and resources.

Functional roles provide different levels of contribution throughout a deliverable. Role overlap and sharing may be beneficial in the team model, whereas role changing tends not to be beneficial.[81]

Non-leadership styles bear mention. Laissez-faire leadership constitutes "absence of leadership,"[82] and "abdicates the authority and responsibility of the [leadership] position."[83] This "anything goes" style of leadership is the opposite of transformational leadership, and may devolve into chaos.[84]

Hierarchical and "great man" leadership theories were among the norms for "the Greatest Generation." Baby Boomers are not so inclined and responded more favorably to situational, contingency, and agency theories. Generations X and Y are more attuned to transformational, team, and open leadership styles. Six approaches are recommended for Boomers in connecting with Generations X and Y—especially Y:

- transparency,

- career customization,

- overt recognition,

- mentoring,

- integrated technology, and

- participation.[85]

GE's Jack Welch described leadership as "It's not about you. It's about them."[86] During his tenure as CEO, Welch also promoted candor—brutal honesty. If he thought discussions were avoiding conflict, he played devil's advocate. He challenged his team to be their best. His style may have only worked at GE during his era, but that is at least partially the point. He was an intrepid change agent whose style fit the need of the company in its ecosystem during his tenure. Whether it would work today is irrelevant. He is retired.

"When the student is ready, the teacher will appear."[87] Several avenues are available to leaders for positioning followers to succeed. Training and experience loom large. Perhaps nothing prepares a leader for global perspective better than foreign assignments necessitating total immersion in the host culture.[88] Mentoring is another proven learning medium. Homer's *Odyssey* coined "mentor" as a trusted advisor. Mentoring is an informal, infrequent, and non-conformist learning process by which mentors share insights and perspectives to mentees who are free from reprisal for eschewing the gift.[89] "Mentoring is a brain to pick, an ear to listen, and a push in the right direction."[90] However, the mentee is responsible for the consequences of discarding the pearls of wisdom. In private equity, for example, mentoring junior investment team members is an effective tactic for enhancing their leadership abilities in dealing with more seasoned C-level portfolio company personalities.

The toughest leadership call in private equity is determining when the business has outgrown its leadership. A version of the Peter Principle is the Poodle Principle: How much dog is underneath the fluffy hair? The deal teams must look ahead for triggers that warrant action. Poor leaders come in three forms. The first is affable, but risk averse. The second is Machiavellian. The third is narcissistic. Whatever leadership style adopted by the leader, there are mechanisms for confirming its effectiveness. One mechanism is skip-level management. Leaders should both sporadically and routinely bypass the normal chain of command to assure a clear read on conditions. Private equity deal teams execute skip-level by establishing direct lines of communication with the "owners" of key components of the portfolio company business model, for example, sales, manufacturing, and finance. Another mechanism is the town hall meeting that fosters two-way communication. Not only may the leader impart what he wants the followers to know, but she may encourage feedback and questions. Deal teams should plug into these mechanisms for insights.

One of the most effective applications of this I have observed in my consulting practice was a quarterly town hall in a manufacturing plant. The leader conducted the sessions on the factory floor. A large screen hung from the superstructure on which informational slides were projected. The leader reviewed the balanced scorecard results and analysis. Additionally, individual and team recognitions were celebrated. Finally, he entertained questions. It only took an hour, but the impact on morale was powerful. Essentially, this leader's communications style addressed one of converse corollaries to poor communications: he conducted an effective meeting. The approach included preparation, a script, punctuality, and process. He told them what he was going to tell them, told them, and then told them what he told them. It worked.

A simple set of principles may ultimately describe an effective leader-follower dynamic. Rotary International's "four-way test of things we think, say or do" provides such a framework:

- Do leaders and followers speak truthfully to each other?

- Are decisions equitable for those affected?

- Will the consequences of decisions build goodwill and better relationships?

- Are the consequences of decisions collectively beneficial?[91]

Leadership Challenges for Innovative Organizations

Innovation distinguishes between a leader and a follower.[92]

F. Scott Fitzgerald asserted that "the test of a first-rate intelligence is the ability to hold two opposed ideas in the mind at the same time, and still retain the ability to function."[93] (Perhaps Fitzgerald's opinion was influenced by Aristotle as his words were similar to a quote we deployed while examining worldviews in Chapter 4: The DNA of Packs.) Similarly, great teams sort through ambiguity with candor to identify rational choices. "It is not the strongest of the species that survives, nor the most intelligent that survives. It is the one that is the most adaptable to change."[94] "To prosper, companies need to do four things well:

- develop leaders of the future,

- improve productivity,

- execute strategy, and

- innovate.

Innovation is the glue that binds everything together. Without [promoting] the practice of innovation, no company can excel—or survive."[95] Like other global leaders, "leaders of innovation are made, not born ... . The four key building blocks of this process are:

- performance evaluation,

- early identification,

- developmental experiences, and

- rewards and recognition."[96]

Organizations that are "considered to have innovation as one of their core competencies utilize mentoring to facilitate and cultivate innovation."[97]

> *The single most important factor in a company's level of innovation competence is building an innovative culture that has total leadership commitment. In providing the right climate for innovation, leaders need to challenge and involve employees by committing to a big problem. Leaders also need to motivate, inspire and direct followers, overcome intra-organizational obstacles, and promote organizational innovation.*[98]

Leaders must manage across three overlapping realities of arguably escalating degree of difficulty:

- managing the core business,

- nurturing innovation in complement of the core business, and

- managing the change inherent in a dynamic operating environment.

Change-management is particularly problematic because organizations may be hostile to innovative change that threatens status quo. The leader's model for ushering in the necessity of innovative change includes the following topics:

- establishing a sense of urgency,

- creating a guiding coalition of change agents,

- developing a vision and strategy featuring the prominence of innovation,

- supporting the process with indefatigable communication,

- empowering employees to actions that make creativity marketable,

- creating and leveraging short-term accomplishments aligned with long-term aspirations,

- positioning the wins for more leverageable subsequent wins, and

- anchoring future state realities in the cultural norms.[99]

A leader's innovative options include deliberate and emergent strategies. Conducive conditions for deliberate strategies include:

- relevant, material details are known,

- responsibilities are understood and make sense to those responsible for their execution, and

- team focus on critical priorities without distraction.

Emergent strategies mutate and evolve dynamically relative to the ecosystem's conditions. Flexible tactics are required to address challenges and opportunities because of the high degree of uncertainty in the ecosystem.[100] Leaders must reconcile three types of innovation risk within an ecosystem:

- Execution risk: the challenges leaders face in bringing about innovation to the required specifications, within the required time.

- Co-innovation risk: the extent to which the successful commercialization of firm innovation depends on the successful commercialization of other innovators.

- Adoption chain risk: the extent to which partners will need to adopt the firm's innovation before end customers have a chance to assess the full value proposition.[101]

By example, electric vehicles portray the articulation of these three elements. First, engineering challenges exist for a vehicle whose reliability and performance must rival the internal combustion engine. Second, success relies on other factors such as battery life, battery cost, charging stations, charge time, power grid capacity—including peak demands, and repair centers. The combined probabilities of these covariant elements have significant bearing on first mover advantage.[102] In response, leaders may simultaneously mitigate risk and accentuate outcomes by manipulating these variables:

- determining what can be separated,

- identifying what can be combined,

- figuring out what can be relocated, and

- ascertaining what can be added.[103]

"There are in fact eight elements of any business that ultimately must be organized and led to drive innovation:"

1.   motivating purpose and values,

2.   stretch goals,

3.   choiceful (sic) strategies,

4.   unique core strengths,

5.   enabling structures,

6.   consistent and reliable systems,

7.   courageous and connected culture, and

8.   inspiring leadership.[104]

The leadership style that works for the rest of the company may be counterproductive to its innovative endeavors. In response, Peter Drucker advises leaders to engage:

- opportunity analysis,

- customer reaction validation,

- solutions aligned with needs,

- piloting that precedes implementation, and

- aspirations and actions toward market leadership.

Drucker further advises avoiding:

- cleverness instead of clarity,

- diluted execution focus, and

- innovation for the future instead of the present, i.e., exceeding your customers' comprehension of the product.

Drucker also offers four entrepreneurial leadership strategies—some colloquial—that are beneficial to innovation. These may be mixed and mingled for tailoring in response to unique situations:

- being the fustest (sic) with the mostest (sic);

- hit them where they ain't;

- establishing ecological niches, i.e., controlling one's domain; and

- changing values and characteristics, i.e., uniquely addressing the needs and wants of a target market.[105]

In *The Little Black Book of Innovation,* author Scott D. Anthony complements the argument by imparting the seven deadly leadership sins of innovation:

- pride, i.e., imposing the leader's or firm's worldview onto the market;

- sloth, i.e., sluggish execution;

- gluttony, i.e., allowing success to breed complacency;

- lust, i.e., over-extension instead of disciplined focus;

- envy, i.e., making the new the enemy of the existing;

- wrath, i.e., punishing risk-takers attempting to create new value; and

- greed, i.e., unreasonable impatience for growth to the detriment of innovation.[106]

Measures are an essential leadership tool, yet useful innovative measures are problematic. Indeed, few companies think they have it right.[107] Leaders should eschew vanity metrics that shed little useful light on the status of innovation. The non-negotiable metrics should be relevant and right. Such metrics may be framed as: (i) actionable, or useful to quick decision-making; (ii) accessible to those who need to make decisions, and (iii) auditable so that their integrity may withstand scrutiny.[108] Some possibilities include:

- The percentage of revenue comprised of new products, e.g., products in their first three years of use. Medical device manufacturers are among the industries using this type of measure. Of course, care must be taken to distinguish between a disruptively innovative offering and a product refresh.

- "Time-to-market" is an efficiency-oriented metric for tracking product conception to its initial delivery. For disruptive innovation, the minimally viable product is the unit of initial delivery.

- Return on inventory investment is calculated as the gross margin times the number of inventory turns.[109] Walmart, for example, is among the companies that use a similar computation called GMROI, or gross margin return on investment.

- Ratios offer additional possibilities: innovators to total employees, radical to incremental innovation projects, externally-to-internally sourced innovation, learning compiled over investment in projects, and commitments over key priorities.[110]

Although the toughest to manage, disruptive innovation holds the most potential. Disruptive budgets face comparatively higher scrutiny. The argument benefits by scenario analysis whose alternatives are threatening. Following funding approval, leaders wisely pivot emphasis to the potential of the initiative.[111] Mistakes along the disruptive path are certain. However, even as leaders must press for commercial viability that includes profitability, the early stages of development should emphasize growth over those very profits.[112] The economies of scale that accompany growth improve contribution margins to overcome sunk costs and absorb fixed overhead. Until the "Why?" is discredited by the learning process, the posture should be full steam ahead.

Organizational Design

I am the master of my fate: I am the captain of my soul.[113]

William Ernest Henley was wrong! "Control is an illusion."[114] Organizational design may effectively displace the belief that centralized control is necessary through "the unique ways in which each organization … motivates its people to achieve clearly articulated strategic objectives."[115]

> *Organization design is neither a science nor an art; it is an oxymoron. Organizational structures rarely result from systematic, methodical planning. Rather, they evolve over time, in fits and starts, shaped more by politics than by policies.*[116]

"Effective organizational design is a never-ending process."[117]

One of the challenges in applying organizational theory is differentiating it from leadership theory. To wit, people comprise the organizations. "Organization theory is a way to see and analyze organizations more accurately and deeply than one otherwise could… . [and is] based on patterns and regularities in organizational design and behavior."[118] The relationship between leadership theory and organizational theory may be depicted with a Venn diagram. (See Figure 8.4.) By picturing each theory as a circle, five options are possible:

- the circles have no overlap, inferring complete independence between leadership and organizational theory;

- partial overlap, inferring points of independence and convergence;

- the leadership circle within the organizational circle, inferring that leadership is a subset of organizational theory;

- the organizational circle within the leadership circle, inferring organizational is a subset of leadership theory; and

- absolute congruence of circles, inferring that leadership and organizational theory are the same thing.

Few humans possess, or have the ability to possess, all leadership options. Capitalizing on leadership strengths, as opposed to investing inordinate time in overcoming weaknesses, may be a wise course of action.[119] Organizational design is about putting the right people, with the right skills, in the right positions, with the right degree of autonomy, at the right time, with the right information at their disposal, and the right incentives, tied to the right results.[120]

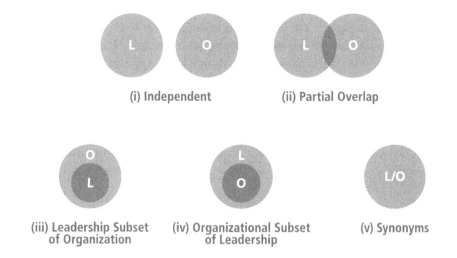

(i) Independent   (ii) Partial Overlap

(iii) Leadership Subset   (iv) Organizational Subset   (v) Synonyms
of Organization   of Leadership

Figure 8.4   Relational possibilities between leadership and organizational theories

The Social Quotient profile assists the process by calibrating a leader across eight descriptors:

1.   adaptor,

2.   architect,

3.   collaborator,

4.   connecter,

5.   creative thinker,

6.   transparent individual,

7.   risk taker, and

8.   visionary.[121]

With strengths identified, leaders may use organizational design in complement to leadership strengths. Thus, organizational design is an enabling tool for deriving competitively differentiable synergies among and across followers. The ecosystem influences contextual and dimensional leadership choices for organizational design.[122] There does, however, appear to be a bit of "chicken-and-egg" predicament between leadership and organizational theory. Were leadership to precede organizational design, one type of leadership style may be the obvious choice, for example, servant leadership. However, if new leadership encounters a staid organizational structure, another type of leadership may be rationalized, for example, transformational leadership.

Jay R. Galbraith popularized a star model for communicating the composition organizational design. The star model is comprised of five points:

1.   strategy,

2.   people,

3.   structure,

4.   rewards, and

5.   process.[123]

The articulation and emphasis among these design variables impact five organizational design options:

1.   function,

2.   product,

3.   market,

4.   geography, and

5.   process.

Among outcomes is governance, or the operating procedures of the business model that addresses the conflation of laws, regulations, purpose, vision, values, strategy, and goals.[124] In this section, we will emphasize process and structure. The other three points are addressed—even if not in Galbraith's nomenclature—in other areas. Structure should enable process. The discussion first benefits by reminding ourselves what the business model is supposed to do.

The organizational structure affects how the employee reacts to the work environment. The leader has a vested interest in reconciling the needs and wants of the firm with those of the employees. Appreciating these necessities may be understood through two behavioral models. Maslow's Hierarchy of Needs graduates through physiological, safety, love/belonging, self-esteem, and self-actualization.[125] (See Figure 8.5.) The last two hierarchies cannot be achieved until the company provides stability in the first three. Frederick Herzberg's two-factor theory of hygienic and motivating factors also provides insights.[126] Herzberg's hygienic and motivating factors are summarized below in Table 8.1. Hygienic factors do not motivate employees, but may be "demotivators" by their absence. Whereas hygienic factors constitute the minimum threshold, motivating factors lead to personal fulfillment.[127] Several design options are possible that reconcile to behavioral models. One design option is a front-back configuration.[128] "Front" is customer facing or touching, for example, sales and customers service. "Back" is the fulfillment engine.

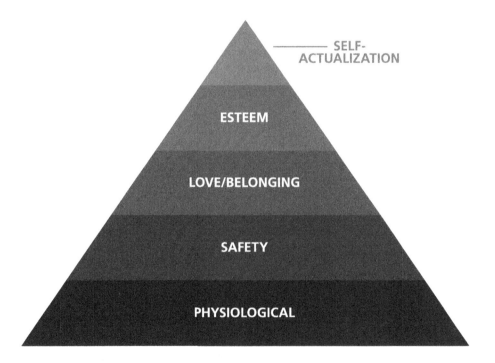

Figure 8.5   Maslow's hierarchy of needs

Source: Adapted from Maslow, A.H. (1943, July). A theory of human motivation. *Psychological Review, 50*(4). 370–96.

Table 8.1   Herzberg's hygienic and motivating factors

Hygienic Factors	Motivating Factors
Job span of control	Work context for the job
Compensation, incentives, and benefits	Opportunity for advancement
Job stability and security	Achievement, fulfillment, and intrinsic rewards
Working environment	Recognition within the organization
Supervisory and interpersonal relationships	Status within the organization
Policies, procedures, administrative practices, and communication	Responsibility

Open organizational design is particularly appealing to Gen Yers. The atmosphere lacks rigidity and fosters fluidity. Information flows freely in a boundaryless configuration. The "leader" may be hard to identify because the teammates dynamically defer to each other's expertise in pursuit of common goals.[129] The model is self-directional and has the poster children of Firefox, Linux, and Wikipedia in testament of its potential. There are similarities between open and team leadership. The team model is characterized by collectivism and collaboration, whereby self-directed groups are typical. Individuals are reconciled to team governance, skills, tasks, and the environment.

A parallel to leadership challenge reappears: that which got us here will not necessarily get us there. Scalable structure is one of the typical weaknesses of a private equity portfolio company. Scalability is sacrosanct to private equity investments, and rests upon economies of scale[130] and economies of scope.[131] The expected result is lower unit cost with growth. Indeed, manufacturing costs decrease by 20–30 percent each time the knowledge base doubles.[132] This aligns with the Lean manufacturing world in which speed is a relevant variable. Sometimes companies elect to achieve efficiency and approximate virtual fulfillment by outsourcing non-core competencies of their business models to cooperating, autonomous companies.[133]

The organization must create a quality product, and reliably provide the product to a receptive market, at a competitive price, and at a profit.[134] Weakness in any single attribute bodes poorly for the entire entity. Consider the metaphor of a river. Branches, streams and creeks eventually form rivers. Smaller rivers flow into larger rivers, for example, the Monongahela and Allegheny converge at Pittsburgh, Pennsylvania, to form the Ohio River, which converges with the Mississippi en route to the sea. Such is the flow of supply chains from the most elemental raw materials to the end user. This is a process—a very complex process.

Processes represent the "the unique ways in which each organization structures its work."[135] "Processes can directly alter patterns of activity, behavior, and performance."[136] "The role of design allows operational overlays. Within organizational knowledge markets, workers have networks among other knowledge markets that facilitate free exchange of information and collaboration among professionals."[137] Process design may "impact ... individuals, group relationships, and the political dynamics of the organization."[138]

My first encounter with hard core process evaluation occurred in the mid-90s. It was the era of Michael Hammer's and James Champy's "reengineering the corporation." At the time, America was hemorrhaging high labor content jobs to Asia. I was drafted into a process reengineering initiative that used Hammer's first two books as process bibles. Before receiving an explanation, I was dubbed a SME (pronounced with a long e). SME did not sound flattering. I later learned that it was an acronym that stood for "subject matter expert." I no longer felt insulted, but had not yet deciphered exactly over what subject matter I had been accorded expert status. The explanation was that I had impressed someone in authority that I understood how the place actually worked. My selection was also likely a byproduct of my outspoken criticism of how poorly the system worked on occasion. According to the "rules," one of the prices teammates paid for participating in process reengineering was leaving the company after the project was completed. The argument was that no teammate should be tempted to invent a soft landing for himself or herself, thus corrupting the process. I was comfortable with the idea, but it meant ending a 13 year run at the company. Interestingly, one of the unforeseen consequences of the experience was an introduction to process improvement. I learned I had a knack for it that has since served as the foundation for my career. I later punctuated my process reengineering credentials with Six Sigma Master Black Belt certification at GE. Additionally, I regularly work with Lean manufacturing professionals. Although I am not credentialed in Lean, I am very comfortable with the principles and use them regularly. I am not a purist beholden to any of the three disciplines and move among all three fluidly. Those who argue in favor of one to the exclusion of the others appear to miss the point. Indeed, their positions may be rooted in the insecurity of losing "flavor of the month" status. Basically, Lean is superior in designing a supply chain and Six Sigma is superior in isolating root cause to process defects and variation. Process reengineering principles are compatible with, and complementary to, both disciplines.

Process reengineering taught me that the overwhelming majority of business model processes are dead weight. The lexicon is "non-value added." Conversely, a process step is value-added if it meets one of three criteria:

- the step changes the form of the raw material, e.g., sheet metal is pressed;

- getting the step right the first time is important, e.g., scrap is waste that hurts profit margins; and

- the customer will pay for it, e.g., a painted appliance is more valuable than an unpainted appliance.[139]

The value-added argument applies to services the same as products.

The original process reengineering dogma assumed that all business processes were deficient—so, throw them out and start over. This did not make complete sense to me absent objective evaluation criteria. Practically, I suspected that some processes actually worked. The trick was figuring out what they were and keeping them. My skepticism was later vindicated as reengineering veterans reached similar conclusions. These lessons are highly relevant to the subject of organizational design. When engaged by a client to address organizational design, I always start with process. The reasons are deceptively simple. Organizational design should facilitate and undergird efficient processes.

The preferred tool for turning the workflow into a picture is a cross-functional process map.[140] (See Figure 8.6.) The map has these basic characteristics:

- Horizontal bands, or "swim lanes," denote primary stakeholders of the business model, e.g., the customer.

- Vertical siloes denoting a distinct business model step, e.g., manufacturing.

- Ovals represent process starts and stops.

- A task is box, or rectangle, is placed in the swim lane of responsible task owner.

- Diamonds mark options in a decision tree, i.e., there is more than one option for next steps. (This is not depicted in the simplified version of cross-function in Figure 8.6.)

- The male home plate and its female companion are off-page connectors. (This, too, is not depicted in Figure 8.6.)

- Circles are on-page connectors used to avoid flow lines confusingly crossing each other. (This is not depicted in Figure 8.6 either.)

- Rays connect the steps to portray flow.

The adage of a picture painting a thousand words was never so true as with a cross-functional process map. Reactions to, and outcomes of, the exercise are pretty consistent:

- The boss, typically several steps removed from the actual line work, remarks something tantamount to this question: "Is that how we actually do it?"

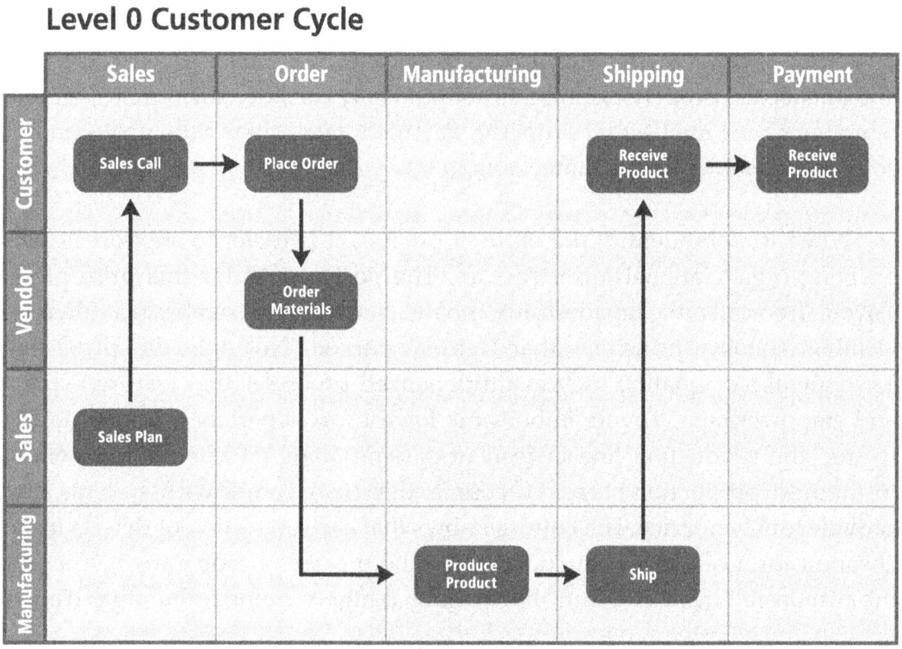

Level 0 Customer Cycle

Figure 8.6   A cross-functional process mapping example

- Non-value added steps are identified. For example, when we ask why inbound raw material is forked from freight doors that are on the opposite end of the building from raw materials storage, we might hear "We have done it that way for 15 years."

- Sometimes the order of the steps looks out of sync. For example, a COO once asked why credit checks were done before the customer confirmed the order. The conversion rate for this company was pretty low. By simply reversing the steps, capacity increased by 40 percent.

Process mapping epiphanies like these are common. However, more pressing conversations are often catalyzed. Consider areas with high FTE (fulltime equivalent employee) headcount. Why is the headcount so high? Is it because the process flow is inefficient? Is it because the company has skimped on automation for something rote and mundane? If this is the case, automation may reduce costs in a number of ways, including improved quality. An even bigger critical question might entail insourcing versus outsourcing. If high labor content is unavoidable, Asian manufacturing might be an alternative. Competitively, the choice is displacing some jobs near-term to assure company success long-term. Success fosters growth that may eventually regain domestic employment levels, but these jobs will likely require different skillsets. Even outsourcing is not a simple call. The bigger questions are core competencies and intellectual property. Companies should only consider outsourcing generic operations sans intellectual property. Patented items enjoy little protection in collectivist countries like China.

When leaders identify the optimal process, it is easier to support it with enabling organizational infrastructure. The poster child for this principle is Toyota. Ironically, the Japanese automobile manufacturers embraced Edwards Deming's quality principles that Detroit spurned. Not only did firms like Toyota embrace quality, they institutionalized processes that featured speed and empowerment. Toyota imbues the lowest level operator with the ability to stop the production line instead of passing along an inferior component to the next production stage. Of course, this rigor comes with systems that provide timely metrics. The culture knows that early detection of defects is the cheapest form of waste reduction. When the process is cooperative, efficient, the responsibilities clear, and the workforce highly trained, the organization may be much flatter in design.[141]

Since private equity portfolio companies have to be "lean and mean," process efficiency is a mechanism for turning this into reality. However, the argument thus far has implied a present state perspective. Thus, the argument is incomplete.

> *Organizational structures that may have worked well in the past are not suitable when an organization's goal is to be innovative and creative. Bureaucracy generally sets an upper limit to what employees are allowed to do in their work, which inhibits creativity and innovation. Organizations that have achieved innovation have changed their organizational design depending on the nature of the industry and their own goals.*[142]

Upon capturing the present state picture for juxtaposition, the follow-up question is "Can you run the company the same way if it were three times as large when you walked in the door tomorrow morning?" I have been asking this question since the mid-90s. The answer has never been "yes." Operating environments may be chaotic. Consequently teams must be nimble and flexible.

A future state process map facilitates a discussion that typically covers the following topics in some fashion:

- Workflow for a much larger business model becomes a picture.

- Technical skillsets required to support the new model are revealed.

- Systems requirements become more evident.

- Measures for management and incentives may be identified.

- Leadership skill requirements evolve.

In complement to the future state process map, the RACIX model is helpful for sorting workflow ownership:

- "R" stands for responsible,

- "A" denotes approval,

- "C" means consulted,

- "I" indicates informed, and

- "X" imparts no formal role.[143]

Anxiety commonly appears because leaders are confronted with technical skills and leadership deficiencies. However, this is a model to work toward—not one that has to instantaneously exist. Skill development is an easy investment for a leader willing to learn. Investors get nervous when false bravado attempts to discount the obvious need for development. Some common exercise epiphanies are worth mentioning, some of which tie into possible diligence discoveries.

- Smaller companies in highly regulated businesses realize the need for an autonomous compliance function.

- The role of human resource management becomes more prominent. This includes compliance, training, and performance management.

- The need for a technology strategy, replete with the ability to put real time information in the hands of decision makers, is imperative. Three criteria guide technology evaluation: (i) business model criticality; (ii) required performance; and (iii) cost to value.[144]

- The bifurcation of the CEO role into the strategic CEO function and a tactical COO function becomes self-evident.

- Similarly, the bifurcation of the sales and marketing functions into a strategic marking function in tandem with a tactical sales function is necessary to capture and keep market share.

Just as there is no single leadership style panacea, there is no singularly "correct" organizational design—even within an industry vertical. A plethora of guiding principles are available to leaders. Organizational design should "focus on the social, cultural, and political aspects of design to make it sustainable."[145] Three core elements define organizational architecture:

- span of control,

- information access, and

- performance management.[146]

The supervisory structure influences the three types of human relationships:

- cooperation,

- control, and

- autonomy.[147]

This does not mean running people into the ground, but rather designing a business model whose people, processes, and tools articulate to balance personal fulfillment with competitive efficiency. "If an individual believes he or she can implement an improved work method and has a strong reason to do so, he or she is likely to pursue proactive goals to improve organizational functioning."[148] Deft performance management enables this phenomenon. Performance management is "the process by which executives, managers, and supervisors work to align employee performance with the firm's [strategic] goals."[149]

Efficient processes incorporate the competitive advantage of speed.[150] Moreover, efficient processes drive economies of scope and scale. Economies of scope are realized by efficiencies of centralized functions that support multiple constituents, for example, finance, IT, and HR.[151] Economies of scale achieve the reduction of average cost per unit resulting from fixed cost absorption over increasing units, that is, a natural outcome of operating leverage.[152] A threshold of governance is required to manage the organization.[153] Vague and ambiguous structures threaten organizational vitality.[154] Several structural options are available to leaders:

- Functional hierarchies may be cluster specialties.[155]

- Product line outputs may rationalize autonomous divisional structures.[156]

- Homogenous customers may rationalize geographical structure.[157]

- Workflow may indicate linear structures.[158]

- Virtual options accommodate disparate geographical integration.[159]

- Matrix designs may be used for line and function articulation.[160]

All organizational design options should be evaluated in terms of size, particularly in deference to the highly social and networked Gen Y employees. Recall from the arguments in Chapter 4: The DNA of Packs that excessive size may lead to dysfunction.

Organizational design should empower ethical behavior. "Ethics is the process whereby we choose between competing moral and/or economic values."[161] Leaders face six areas of ethical challenges that must be considered for organizational design:

- employee rights,

- sexual harassment,

- romantic liaisons,

- organizational justice,

- whistle-blowing, and

- social responsibility.[162]

Whatever the design, leaders must approach structure with a keen eye toward employee fulfillment to accomplish optimal and efficient performance. In order to accomplish organizational chi, or flow, described in Chapter 4: The DNA of Packs, designers must avoid both the distress of overwhelming tasks and the boredom of underwhelming challenge.[163] Design homeostasis is accomplished through:

- clear goals,

- immediate feedback,

- task-skill balance,

- the ability to concentrate,

- focus on immediate obligations,

- autonomy,

- timing, and

- personal accomplishment.[164]

Alternatively, the organization faces the possibilities of entropy and atrophy.

Acquisition Integration

Acquisition integration is analogous to taking two individually complex jigsaw puzzles, dumping the pieces in a single pile, and then figuring out how to combine the aggregation of pieces into a single work of art.

We previously looked at the cultural challenges of acquisition integration in Chapter 4: The DNA of Packs. Indeed, the majority of acquisition integrations fail to realize their potential because the cultures do not jibe.[165] This implies that cultural integration trumps workflow integration. However, the integration of business models should not be discounted. Integration is also an organizational design challenge. In addition to the cultural alchemy, the organizational design resulting from the integration should be a better structure than either company before the integration. This is most certainly true if the rationale includes economies of scope and scale.

There are simple, effective acquisition integration best practices to consider. The first one is to start planning for integrations during diligence. This is worthwhile even if the transaction does not consummate. In short, it is better to have a plan that will not be executed than to be caught in need of an execution plan that does not exist. Besides, there is a likelihood that the plan will be a jump start to the next opportunity. In private equity, there is a high probability of next opportunities for defragmenting a market.

Since diligence precedes integration, we should revisit points made in Chapter 2: Primary Diligence Issues: The Trifecta of Oversight. Specifically, we want to reference the process map technique for understanding;

- workflow,

- "owners" of key workflow components, and

- tools at the disposal of those "owners."

Visual aids like process maps are quite useful, and may function as the outline for the memorialized integration plan. By comparing the map of the acquirer to the acquiree, the following picture emerges:

- gaps, i.e., a function neither company does but must exist in the future state organizational structure;

- redundancy, i.e., areas with duplicative functions that probably need reconciliation;

- complement, i.e., something unique to one of the companies that is beneficial to the integrated picture; and

- best practices which may be evident in the redundant and/or complementary discoveries.

In addition to the benefits enumerated above, these mapping exercise are most beneficial to the organizational structure considerations.

Communication is a hugely important aspect of acquisition integration. Let's start with internal communication. Employees' first official notice of the acquisition may be the "day one" announcement. Keep in mind, this may be true for the acquiring company employees, too. Irrespective of the value-creation rationale for the acquisition, three of the first things employees typically want to know is:

- "Do I have a job?",

- "Who is my boss?", and

- "What happened to my benefit package?"

Accordingly, it is wise to cover these points early to afford employees time to ameliorate the announcement shock in order to regain focus on other elements of the day one message.

Other internal communication integration best practices bear mention. One is the commitment and follow-through with deliberate, routine progress reports. Weekly updates to the employees are not too frequent. Second, more numerous town halls are advisable on the front end. For example, if the company normally does town halls at quarterly intervals, then monthly should be the cadence for at least three months. Third, creating and updating a frequently asked questions (FAQ) document serves as a transaction diary. A first draft should be distributed at the day one announcement and updated weekly.

Small companies tend to be challenged to communicate sufficiently amid rapid organic growth. Acquisitions are another dimension of complexity. Leaders should keep in mind despite the mammoth amounts of advisable communication, they will often be surprised by how little was actually absorbed. We will cover some of these change-management challenges in Chapter 9: Change-management Competencies: A Competitive Ace.

External communication is also on the critical short list. The stakeholders include, but are not limited to customers and vendors. At a minimum, these stakeholders want to walk away with a neutral reaction. The promise of upside will have to be proved. Especially with respect to major customers, face-to-face visits may be in order. For all customers, a compelling argument should be made to assuage any concerns about service deterioration during the integration. Leaders should keep in mind that most customers have choices, and customers should not be tempted to explore them because the company provided lousy service traceable to integration obsessions. A professional public relations firm should be considered for external communications.

Just as project management benefits the execution for the strategic plan (see Chapter 5: The Importance of Strategy), the same is true for acquisition integration. Project management governance for integrations, however, is unique. Let's build the argument from the bottom up. First, the functional areas that will be integrated need to be identified and named. For example, consider the finance function. The operational definition for "finance" may be different between companies. In one company, finance may include billing customers whereas in the other company this may be done in the customer service area.

Second, each functional area to be integrated should have a project manager. Generally speaking, this should not be the supervisor. Admittedly, this may seem counterproductive. However, bosses tend not to be good project managers because they need a little breathing room to think strategically. Moreover, they have to run the area despite the integration. The business still has customers to serve. Therefore, in most cases, someone on the functional leader's team is better suited for the project management role. Of course, they enjoy their boss's proxy for keeping things on track, and solicit the boss's assistance with impediment removal and resource needs. In some instances, one project manager may cover more than one function—but the idea should not be abused. These project management assignments are excellent developmental opportunities.

A similar proxy argument applies to the CEO. She needs a lieutenant who functions as her "super" project manager, or integration leader, across all individual projects. One of the reasons this role is so important regards critical path items. For example, whereas information technology (IT) is usually one of the functional areas requiring integration, most other projects will require some IT support. Someone needs to be looking across projects to anticipate and defuse critical path conflicts before they become execution threats. There is an inferred endorsement for project management software whose functionality can track critical path items. Such items may also be known as dependencies.

Project teams should meet weekly. Bosses of project managers should assure that they have sufficient bandwidth relief to do the job. Whereas the functional project managers may have a large portion of their bandwidth allocated to integration, the integration leader job is fulltime. Skimping on adequate resourcing is an overt threat to execution.

In wrapping up integration points, leaders should consider an external coach if they lack integration experience in the company. This is an investment — not an expense. The return will be self-evident upon successful integration completion. Finally, the company should officially celebrate integration completion. Successful integration is a big deal!

Organizational Design Challenges Unique to Innovation

> *In all chaos there is a cosmos, in all disorder a secret order.*[166]

Organizational design for innovative organizations is particularly perplexing — even more so for innovative units within established organizations.

> *Innovation has never been institutionalized. Systems have never been able to reproduce the synthesis created by the genius entrepreneur …*
> *and they likely never will.*[167]

Similar to leadership styles and general organizational design principles, there is no universally right answer for innovative organizational design.[168] Organizational design risks for innovative organizations are considerable.

- Only five percent of companies exceed their industry's average growth rate for an extended period of time.[169]

- An initiative failure casts a nearly insurmountable pall over future initiatives.[170] Perhaps one reason is the fear of loss more than cost—and the fear of both more than the reward of winning.[171] The ratio ranges from 2–4:1.[172]

- Risk aversion blocks line innovation from getting leadership visibility. The firewall is middle management.[173]

Three P's govern innovation organizational capabilities:

1. people,

2. process, and

3. philosophy.[174]

The gap between reality and necessity creates an organizational "valley of death."[175] Three options prevail when innovation necessities overtax the three P's:

1. acquisition,

2. alternative processes, and

3. a skunk works.[176]

Good organizational design encourages opportunity identification and exploitation.[177] Innovation organizational design benefits by the roles of champions, project managers, and implementers.[178] These roles are complementary, but typically performed by different people. Champions sponsor initiatives and remove obstacles. Champions should have the authority to engineer an environment conducive to the objective. Accordingly, they may draw upon six design guidance principles:

1. the relationship with existing firm core competencies—from collaboration to autonomy;

2. budgets;

3.   leveraging existing firm strengths, but the latitude to invent needed ones;

4.   expediting to assure time-to-market requirements;

5.   team composition, resource access, and governance; and

6.   changing course relative to the product life cycle, i.e., "ideation and prototyping, development, qualification, or commercialization."[179]

Champions intimately comprehend the mission. Project managers coordinate activities across diverse teammates, resources, and stakeholders—including the critical path of tasks that must occur in a certain order to assure the intended results. Finally, implementers make innovation commercially viable, and wield skills in marketing, sales, production, and delivery functions.

Endnotes

[1]   Famous leadership quotes: Gems of wisdom by the best leaders (Eleanor Roosevelt). *Self-improvement mentor*. Retrieved from http://www.self-improvement-mentor.com/famous-leadership-quotes.html

[2]   Frost, R. (1969). Stopping by woods on a snowy evening. In *The poetry of Robert Frost: The collected poems, complete and unabridged*. New York: Henry Holt and Company. p. 224.

[3]   Zweifel, T.D. (2003). *Culture clash: Managing the global high-performance team*. New York: SelectBooks. (ISBN: 1590790510). p. xxv.

[4]   Reddin, W.J. (1970). *Managerial effectiveness*. New York, NY: McGraw-Hill.

[5]   Covey, S.R. (2004). The 7 habits of highly effective people. New York, NY: Simon & Schuster. p. 47.

[6]   Kotter, J.P. (1982, November–December). What effective general managers really do. *Harvard Business Review, 60*(6),156–67.

[7]   DePree, M. and Malcolm, C. (Ed.). (1989). *Leadership is an art*. New York, NY: Doubleday.

[8]   Voltaire Quotes a/k/a François-Marie Arouet. (n.d.). *Goodreads*. Retrieved from http://www.goodreads.com/quotes/248-love-truth-but-pardon-error

[9] George Bernard Shaw quotes. (n.d.). *Thinkexist.com.* Retrieved from http://thinkexist.com/quotation/a_life_spent_making_mistakes_is_not_only_more/7710.html

[10] Stross, R.E. (2007). *The wizard of Menlo Park: How Thomas Alva Edison invented the modern world.* New York: Three Rivers Press.

[11] O'Toole, P. (Ed.). (2012). *In the words of Theodore Roosevelt: Quotation from the man in the arena.* Ithaca, NY: Cornell University Press. p. 122.

[12] Black, J.S., Morrison, A.J. and Gregersen, H.B. (1999). *Global explorers: The next generation of leaders.* New York: Routledge. (ISBN: 0415921481)

[13] Kurke, L.B. (2004). *The wisdom of Alexander the great: Enduring leadership lessons from the man who created an empire.* New York, NY: AMACOM. p. xi.

[14] Goffee, R. and Jones, G. (2000, September). Why should anyone be led by you? *Harvard Business Review, 78*(5), 67.

[15] Paglis, L. and Green, S. (2002). Leadership self-efficacy and managers' motivation for leading change. *Journal of Organizational Behavior, 23*(2), 217.

[16] Levine, A. and Heller, R. (2012). *Attached: The new science of adult attachment and how it can help you find and keep love.* New York: Tarcher/Penguin. (ISBN: 1585429139)

[17] Hughes, R.L. and Beatty, K.C. (2005). *Becoming a strategic leader: Your role in your organization's enduring success.* San Francisco, CA: Jossey-Bass. p. 28.

[18] Davenport, T.H. (2009). Make better decisions. *Harvard Business Review, 87*(11), 118.

[19] Argyris, C. (1977, September–October). Double loop learning in organizations. *Harvard Business Review, 55*(5), 115–25.

[20] Hughes and Beatty (2005). p. 160.

[21] McCall, M. and Hollenbeck, G. (2002). *Developing global executives.* Boston: Harvard Business School. (ISBN: 1578513367). p. 8.

[22] Ibid. pp. 42–7.

[23] Tichy, N.M. and Bennis, W.G. (2007). *Judgment: How winning leaders make great calls.* New York, NY: Penguin Group.

[24] Schruijer, S. and Vansina, L. (2002). Leader, leadership and leading: From individual characteristics to relating in context. *Journal of Organizational Behavior*, 23(7), 869–70.

[25] Chaleff, I. (2003). *The courageous follower: Standing up to and for our leaders*. San Francisco: Berrett-Koehler; Kelley, R.E. (1992). *The power of followership: How to create leaders people want to follow and followers who lead themselves*. New York: Doubleday Currency.

[26] Chaleff (2003).

[27] Kelley (1992). p. 27.

[28] Ibid. pp. 26–7.

[29] Chaleff (2003); Kelley (1992). pp. 7–8.

[30] Pfeffer, Jeffrey. (1998). *The human equation: Building profits by putting people first*. Boston, MA: Harvard Business School Press.

[31] Bell, C.R. (2002). Managers as mentors: Building partnerships for learning. New York: Berrett-Koehler.

[32] Covey, S.M.R. (2006). *The speed of trust: The one thing that changes everything*. New York: Free Press.

[33] Deming, E.W. (2000). *Out of the crisis*. Cambridge, MA: First MIT Press; Covey (2004); Drucker, P. (1985). *Innovation and entrepreneurship*. New York: HarperCollins. (ISBN: 9780060851132)

[34] Lencioni, P. (2002). *The five dysfunctions of a team: A leadership fable*. San Francisco, CA: Jossey-Bass.

[35] Covey, S.R., Whitman, B. and England, B. (2009). *Predictable results in unpredictable times*. Salt Lake City, UT: FranklinCovey.

[36] Bell (2002).

[37] Tichy and Bennis (2007).

[38] Ibid.

[39] DePree and Malcolm (1989).

40   Kahneman, D. (2011). *Thinking fast and slow*. New York, NY: Farrar, Straus, and Giroux.

41   Heath, C. and Heath, D. (2013). *Decisive: How to make better choices in life and work*. New York: Crown.

42   Strategic decisions: When can you trust your gut? (2010, March). *McKenzie Quarterly*. Retrieved from http://www.mckinsey.com/insights/strategy/strategic_decisions_when_can_you_trust_your_gut

43   Abraham Lincoln quotes. (n.d.). *Thinkexist.com*. Retrieved from http://thinkexist.com/quotation/nearly_all_men_can_stand_adversity-but_if_you/10078.html

44   James Lane Allen quotes. (n.d.). *IZ quotes*. Retrieved from http://izquotes.com/author/james-lane-allen/

45   Theodore Roosevelt quotes. (1901). *The free dictionary*. Retrieved from http://forum.thefreedictionary.com/postst29129_-Speak-Softly-and-Carry-a-Big-Stick---1901-.aspx

46   Mintzberg, H., Ahlstrand, B. and Lampel, J. (2005). *Strategy safari: A guided tour through the wilds of strategic management*. New York: The Free Press. pp. 234–61.

47   Northouse, P. (2006). *Leadership: Theory and practice* (4th ed.). Thousand Oaks, CA: Sage. p. 20.

48   Greer, M.E. (2002, February). Continuing the leadership quest: Character. *Professional Safety*, 47(2), 9.

49   Shakespeare, W., Mowat, B.A. (Ed.) and Werstine, P. (Ed.). (2012). *Hamlet*. New York: Simon & Schuster. Act 1, scene 3, line 85, p. 45.

50   Socrates quotes. (n.d.). *Goodreads*. Retrieved from http://www.goodreads.com/quotes/452128-to-know-thyself-is-the-beginning-of-wisdom

51   Northouse (2006). p. 342.

52   David, F.R. (2005). *Strategic management concepts and cases* (10th ed.). Upper Saddle River, NJ: Pearson Education, Inc./Prentice Hall. p. 20.

53   Northouse (2006). pp. 350–6.

54   Hoy, W.K. (2010). *Quantitative research in education: A primer*. Thousand Oaks, CA: Sage. p. 10.

55 Black, et al. (1999). p. 28.

56 Black, et al. (1999). p. xi.

57 Rosen, R., Digh, P., Singer, M. and Philips, C. (2000). *Global literacies: Lessons on business leadership and national cultures.* New York: Simon and Schuster. (ISBN: 0684859025). p. 29.

58 Ibid.

59 Black, et al. (1999). pp. 23, 26.

60 Marquardt, M. and Berger, N. (2000). *Global leaders for the 21st century.* Albany, NY: State University of New York. (ISBN: 0791446611). p. 176.

61 Lanier, J.A. (2010). Leadership style motivators. *Regent University School of Business & Leadership.* Virginia Beach, VA: Regent University.

62 Tichy and Bennis (2007).

63 Winston, B. (2002). *Be a leader for God's sake.* Virginia Beach, VA: School of Leadership Studies, Regent University.

64 Northouse (2006).

65 Daft, R.L. (2007). *Organizational theory and design* (9th ed.). Mason, OH: Thomson South-Western.

66 Blake, R.R. and McCanse, A.A. (1991). *Leadership dilemmas-grid® solutions: a visionary new look at a classic tool for defining and attaining leadership and management excellence.* Houston, TX: Gulf Publishing Company; Blake, R.R. and Mouton, J.S. (1964). *The managerial grid.* Houston, TX: Gulf Publishing Company.

67 Kuhnert, K.W. (1994). Transforming leadership: Developing people through delegation. In B.M. Bass and B.J. Avolio (Eds.), *Improving organizational effectiveness through transformational leadership.* Thousand Oaks, CA: Sage. pp. 10–25.

68 Northouse (2006). p. 181.

69 Brickley, J.A., Smith, Jr., C.W. and Zimmerman, J.L. (2007). *Managerial economics and organizational architecture.* (4th ed.) New York: McGraw-Hill Irwin. p. 290.

70 Northouse (2006).

[71]   Blake and McCanse (1991); Blake and Mouton (1964).

[72]   Northouse (2006).

[73]   Blanchard, K., Zigarmi, P. and Zigarmi, D. (2013). *Leadership and the one minute manager: Increasing effectiveness through situational leadership®*. New York: HarperCollins.

[74]   Yun, S., Cox, J. and Sims, H.P. (2006). The forgotten follower: A contingency model of leadership and follower self-leadership. *Journal of Managerial Psychology, 21*(4), 374–88. doi:http://dx.doi.org/10.1108/02683940610663141

[75]   Avolio, B.J. (1999). *Full leadership development: Building the vital forces in organizations*. Thousand Oaks, CA: Sage; Bass, B.M. and Avolio, B.J. (1990). The implications of transactional and transformation leadership for individual, team, and organizational development. *Research in Organizational Change and Development, 4*, 231–72.

[76]   Northouse (2006). p. 348.

[77]   Winston (2002). p. 5.

[78]   Northouse (2006).

[79]   Ziegert, J.C. (2005). *Does more than one cook spoil the broth? An examination of shared team leadership.* (Order No. 3175238, University of Maryland, College Park). *ProQuest Dissertations and Theses*, p. 123. Retrieved from http://0-search.proquest.com.library.regent.edu/docview/304995886?accountid=13479. (304995886).

[80]   Sanders, T.O. (2006). *Collectivity and influence: The nature of shared leadership and its relationship with team learning orientation, vertical leadership and team effectiveness.* (Order No. 3237041, The George Washington University). *ProQuest Dissertations and Theses*, p. 181. Retrieved from http://0-search.proquest.com.library.regent.edu/docview/305335398?accountid=13479. (305335398).

[81]   Carson, J.B. (2006). *Internal team leadership: An examination of leadership roles, role structure, and member outcomes.* (Order No. 3222618, University of Maryland, College Park). ProQuest Dissertations and Theses, p. 165. Retrieved from http://0-search.proquest.com.library.regent.edu/docview/305299992?accountid=13479. (305299992).

[82]   Northouse (2006). p. 186.

[83]   Nelson, D. and Quick, J.C. (2006). *Organizational behavior: Foundations, realities and challenges*. (5th ed.). Mason, Ohio: South-Western. p. 390.

[84]   Nelson and Quick (2006).

[85]   Ivancevich, J.M. (2007). *Human resource management* (10th ed.). New York, NY: McGraw-Hill Irwin. p. 11.

[86]   Welch, J. (2005). *Winning*. New York: HarperCollins.

[87]   Buddhist proverb. (n.d.). *Thinkexist.com*. Retrieved from http://thinkexist.com/quotation/when_the_student_is_ready-the_teacher_will/181633.html

[88]   Black, et al. (1999). p. xvi.

[89]   Bell (2002).

[90]   John C. Crosby. (n.d.). *BrainyQuote.com* Retrieved from http://www.brainyquote.com/quotes/quotes/j/johnccros137546.html

[91]   The four-way test. (1981). *Rotary Club*. Retrieved from http://www.rotaryfirst100.org/history/headings/4-way_ethics.htm

[92]   Steve Jobs quotes. (n.d.). *BrainyQuote.com*. Retrieved from http://www.brainyquote.com/quotes/keywords/innovation.html

[93]   Fitzgerald, F.S. and Wilson, E. (Ed.). (2009). *The crack-up*. New York: New Directions. p. 57.

[94]   Charles Darwin quotes. (n.d.). *BrainyQuote.com* Retrieved from http://www.brainyquote.com/quotes/authors/c/charles_darwin.html#l3T3wJdjytCqkYj6.99

[95]   Lafley, A.G. and Charan, R. (2008). *The game-changer: How you can drive revenue and profit growth with innovation*. New York: Random House. p. 28.

[96]   Ibid. p. 272.

[97]   Amat, S.W. (2008, June). *Cultivating innovation: The role of mentoring in the innovation process* (Doctoral dissertation, University of Miami, Coral Gables, FL). Retrieved from http://scholarlyrepository.miami.edu/oa_dissertations/308/

[98]   Maughan, C. (2012). Organisational innovation: A review of the literature. *CRC-REP Working Paper CW001*. Ninti One Limited, Australia: Alice Springs, 7. p. iii.

[99]   Kotter, J.P. (1996). *Leading change* (1st ed.). Boston, MA: Harvard Business School Press.

[100] Christensen, C.M. and Raynor, M.E. (2003). *The innovator's solution: Creating and sustaining successful growth*. Boston, MA: Harvard Business School Publishing. pp. 214–6.

[101] Adner, R. (2012). *The wide lens: A new strategy for innovation*. New York: Portfolio Hardcover. (ISBN: 1591844606). pp. 33–4.

[102] Ibid.

[103] Ibid. p. 177.

[104] Lafley and Charan (2008). pp. 10–1.

[105] Drucker (1985). pp. 207–52.

[106] Anthony, S.D. (2012). *The little black book of innovation*. Boston: Harvard Business Press. p. 72.

[107] Innovation frustration: Lacking management and metrics. (2005). *Strategic Direction, 21*(11), 36.

[108] Ries, E. (2011). *Lean startup: How today's entrepreneurs use continuous innovation to create radically successful businesses*. New York: Crown Business. pp. 143–8.

[109] Christensen, C.M. (1997). *The innovator's dilemma: When new technologies cause great firms to fail*. Boston, MA: Harvard Business School Press. p. 112.

[110] Mascarenhas, O. (2009, May 12). Strategic innovation management. *University of Detroit-Mercy*. p. 19. Retrieved from www.udmercy.edu

[111] Christensen and Raynor (2003). pp. 112–3

[112] Ibid. p. 236.

[113] Henley, W.E. (n.d.). Invictus. *PoemHunter.com*. Retrieved from http://www.poemhunter.com/poem/invictus/

[114] McGrath, P.B. (2011, April 11). Don't try harder, try different! Control is an illusion part 1. *Psychology Today*. Retrieved from http://www.psychologytoday.com/blog/dont-try-harder-try-different/201104/control-is-illusion-part-1

[115] Nadler, D. and Tushman, M. (1997). *Competing by design: The power of organizational architecture*. New York: Oxford University Press. p. 5.

[116] Goold, M. and Campbell, A. (2002). Do you have a well-designed organization?. *Harvard Business Review, 80*(3), 117.

[117] Nadler and Tushman (1997). p. 6.

[118] Daft (2007). p. 25.

[119] Buckingham, M. and Clifton, D.O. (2001). *Now, discover your strengths*. New York, NY: Free Press.

[120] Collins, J. (2001). *Good to great: Why some companies make the leap and others don't*. New York, NY: HarperCollins.; Brickley et al. (2007). p. 5.

[121] Libert, B. (2010). *Social nation: How to harness the power of social media to attract customers, motivate employees, and grow your business*. Hoboken, NY: John Wiley & Sons. p. 49.

[122] Daft (2007). pp. 17–20.

[123] Galbraith, J. (2002). *Designing organizations: An executive guide to strategy, structure, and process*. San Francisco: Jossey-Bass. p. 10.

[124] Troiani, T.C. (2004). *Vision to reality: Making governance work for you* (2nd ed.). Redondo Beach, CA: Craft Publishing.

[125] Nelson and Quick (2006). p. 153; Maslow, A.H. (1943). A theory of human motivation. *Psychology Review, 50,* 370–96.

[126] Herzberg, F., Mausner, B and Snyderman, B.B. (2010). *The motivation to work* (12th ed.). New Brunswick, NJ: Transaction Publishers.; Miner, J.B. (2007). *Organizational behavior: From theory to practice* (4th ed.). New York: M.E. Sharpe. p. 48; Nelson and Quick (2006). pp. 158–9.; Herzberg, F., Mausner, B. and Snyderman, B. (1959). *The motivation to work*. New York: John Wiley & Sons; Herzberg, F. (1966). *Work and the nature of man*. Cleveland, OH: World.

[127] Nelson and Quick (2006). pp. 158–9. Herzberg et al. (1959); Herzberg (1966).

[128] Galbraith (2002).

[129] Northouse (2006); Foster, P. (2013). Organization 3.0: The evolution of leadership and organizational theories toward an open system for the 21st century. *Regent University School of Business & Leadership*. Virginia Beach, VA: Regent University.

[130] Brickley et al. (2007). p. 148.

[131] Ibid. p. 149.

[132] Henderson, B.D. (1974). The experience curve: Price stability. In Stern, C.W. and Deimler, M.S. (Eds.). (2006). *The Boston Consulting Group on Strategy: Classic concepts and new perspectives* (2nd ed.). Hoboken, NJ: John Wiley & Sons. p.19.

[133] Bryne J., Brandt. R. and Port, O., (1993, February 8). The virtual corporation. *Business Week,* 98–102.

[134] Kaufman, K. (2012). *The personal MBA: Master the art of business.* New York: Penguin. p. 38.

[135] Hoffman, P. (n.d.).The role of organizational design in 21st century organizations. *Ezine @rticles.* Retrieved from http://ezinearticles.com/?The-Role-of-Organizational-Design-in-21st-Century-Organizations&id=502071. p. 5.

[136] Nadler and Tushman (1997). p. 46.

[137] Hoffman (n.d.).

[138] Ibid. p. 15.

[139] Hammer, M. and Stanton, S.A. (1995). *The reengineering revolution.* New York: HarperBusiness; Hammer, M. and Champey, J. (1993). *Reengineering the corporation: A manifesto for business revolution.* New York, NY: HarperCollins; Pande, Neuman, & Cavanagh (2002). pp. 225–6.

[140] Pande et al. (2002). pp. 263–4.; Kano, N., Seraku, N., Takahashi, F. and Tsuji, S. (1984). Attractive quality and must be quality. *Quality, 14*(2), 39–48.

[141] Keidel, R. (1995). *Seeing organizational patterns.* San Francisco: Berrett-Koehler Publishers. pp. 67–8.

[142] Maughan (2012). p. 7.

[143] Galbraith (2002).

[144] Merrifield, R., Calhoun, J. and Stevens, D. (2008). The next revolution in productivity. *Harvard Business Review, 86*(6), 77.

[145] Nadler and Tushman (1997). p. 13.

[146] Brickley et al. (2007). p. 5.

[147] Keidel (1995). p. 6.

[148] Parker, S., Bindl, U. and Strauss, K. (2010). Making things happen: A model of proactive motivation. *Journal of Management*, *36*(4), 848.

[149] Ivancevich (2007). p. 251.

[150] Jennings, J. and Haughton, L. (2000). *It's not the big that eat the small … it's the fast that eat the slow: How to use speed as a competitive tool in business.* New York, NY: HarperBusiness.

[151] Brickley et al. (2007). p. 149.

[152] Ibid. p. 148.

[153] Troiani (2004).

[154] Goold and Campbell (2002). p. 117.

[155] Daft (2007). pp. 102–4.

[156] Ibid. pp. 104–7.

[157] Ibid. pp. 107–8.

[158] Ibid. pp. 113–7.

[159] Ibid. pp. 117–20.

[160] Ibid. pp. 108–10.

[161] Troiani (2004).

[162] Nelson and Quick (2006).

[163] Csikszentmihaly, M. (2003).*Good business: Leadership, flow, and the making of meaning.* New York, NY: Penguin.

[164] Ibid.

[165] Eisenstaedt, L.H. and Montgomery, J.L. (2010). M&A integration challenges: The process doesn't stop at closing. *CPA Practice Management Forum*, 6(10), 12–5.

[166] Carl Jung quotes. (n.d.). *BrainyQuote.com*. Retrieved from http://www.brainyquote.com/quotes/keywords/chaos.html

[167] Mintzberg, H. (1994, January–February). The fall and rise of strategic planning. *Harvard Business Review*, 72(1), 110.

[168] Lafley and Charan (2008). p. 151.

[169] Christensen and Raynor (2003). p. 21.

[170] Ibid. p. 7.

[171] Kahneman (2011).

[172] Heath and Heath (2013).

[173] Christensen and Raynor (2003). pp. 10, 11, 13, 217, 220, 270.

[174] Dyer, J., Gregersen, H. and Christensen, C.M. (2011). *The innovator's DNA: Mastering the five skills of disruptive innovators*. Boston, MA: Harvard Business School Publishing. (ISBN: 9781422134818)

[175] Griffin, A., Price, R. and Vojak, B. (2012). *Serial innovators: How individuals create and deliver breakthrough innovations in mature firms*. Stanford, CA: Stanford Business Books. p. 21; Markham, S.K. (2002). Product champions: Crossing the valley of death. In P. Belliveay, A. Griffin and S. Somermeyer (Eds.). *The PDMA toolbook for new product development*. New York: John Wiley & Sons. pp. 119–40.

[176] Christensen (1997). p. 172.

[177] Griffin et al. (2012). p. 27; Leifer, R., McDermott, C.M., O'Connor, G.C., Peters, L.S., Rice, M. and Veryzer, R.W. (2000). *Radical innovation: How mature companies can outsmart upstarts. Boston*, MS: Harvard Business School Press; O'Connor, G.D., Leifer, R., Paulson, A.S. and Peters, L.S. (2008). *Grabbing lightning*. San Francisco, CA: Jossey-Bass.

[178] Griffin et al. (2012). pp. 24–5.

[179] Lafley and Charan (2008). pp. 120–1.

Chapter 9

Change-management Competencies: A Competitive Ace

I could not help myself. It is my nature.[1]

Henry Ford declared, "If you think you can do a thing or think you can't do a thing, you're right." You can lead a horse to water, but you cannot make him drink. However, you may engineer conditions conducive to thirst, for example, a salt block or a long ride. One of the most valuable career skills an individual may assimilate is change-management. Peter Senge explains why: "People don't resist change. They resist being changed."[2] Of course, change agents need to focus on the "can" of change and turn it into a self-fulfilling prophecy. Frogs do not become princes, but untrained kids with potential can train hard enough to win more Olympic medals than any swimmer in history. Just ask Michael Phelps. Effective change agents, like good sales professionals, wield tailored applications of IQ, EQ, and PQ to rally their teams around the necessity of change.

Everett Rogers helps us understand Senge's point statistically. Roger's Diffusion of Innovations curve parses the population on a bell curve[3] (see Figure 9.1). Innovators constitute 2.5 percent of the population. These people bore easily with the status quo. They are the first people in one's social network to try something new. Firms who introduce disruptive innovation love these people because they are hardwired to be guinea pigs for gadgets. They do so even before the product is normatively functional or cost-effective. Being a customer innovator is an expensive habit.

Moving from the innovator left tail of Roger's bell curve toward the right enters the early adopter zone. This portion of the population is 13.5 percent. Whereas innovators may be the spark in the internal combustion cylinder, early adopters are the compressed, fuel-rich mixture who ignite for the power stroke. Early adopters quickly grasp the utility of the change embraced by the innovators. When the early adopters are satisfied that assimilation risk has migrated past the 50–50 toward the 80–20, they make their move. Early adopters legitimize change.

The next segment in Roger's curve is the early majority. These people comprise 34 percent of the population. They do not want to be first, but they also do not want to be last. The change-management tipping point is reached when this segment buys into change. Because these people push the aggregate audience over the halfway point of the target market for change, they make the momentum of change inevitable.

An equally large portion of the population, 34 percent, is the next segment of the bell curve. They are called late majority. They certainly are not comfortable leading, but they do not mind following a sure thing. They elected to finally get smart phones primarily because they were more conspicuous in not having them. However, they are two models behind because they are content with what they have. If these people ever buy in, they are not likely to change. Late adopters keep bad companies in business because they will indulge all manner of incompetence and poor service before reluctantly making a switch—never mind that they can get the same functionality from a better vendor at a cheaper price.

Roger's right tail on the Diffusion of Innovations curve is reserved for laggards. A whopping 16 percent of the population falls into this category. These people could disparage a gold strike in their back yard. Their glass is always half-empty. Zig Ziglar explained the attitude tantamount to enjoying one's misery.[4] Laggards enjoy doing the backstroke in the victim pool of life. If laggards were responsible for developing pharmaceuticals, medicine would still practice bloodletting.

Getting back to Senge's line, change is always better for the other guy, that is, "You should ... ." "I will" comes much later for most of us." Why? The answer may be rooted in an acronym called WIIFM, which stands for "What's in it for me?"[5] The point reconciles with the Parable of the Blind Men and the Elephant introduced in Chapter 7: Marketing versus Selling: absent context, "reality" depends on the boundaries of our perspective.[6] The two primary variables are effectiveness, that is, buy in, and efficiency, that is, task productivity.

Leaders know that change is inevitable. However, getting people to embrace that necessity is hard. The Jack Welch era at GE tackled this issue head on. One of its inventions was its Change Acceleration Process, or CAP model.[7] The model

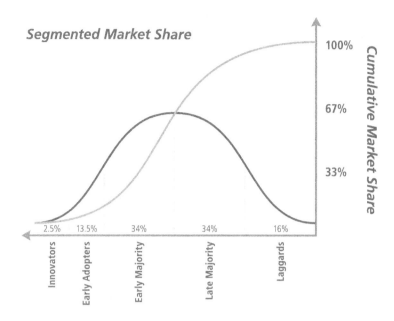

Figure 9.1   Roger's Diffusion of Innovations categories and accumulation

Source: Reprinted with the permission of Simon & Schuster Publishing Group from the Free Press edition of *Diffusion of Innovations*, 5th Edition by Everett M. Rogers. Copyright 1962, 1971, 1983 by The Free Press. All rights reserved.

draws from some of the best minds in behavioral research, including Everett Rogers. GE still uses it, and continues to update it based on their commitment to continuous learning and improvement. Change-management is such an integral part of GE's vaunted Six Sigma culture that it is required curriculum for Master Black Belt certification. As an alumnus of the program, I attest to the value of the tools and know them by heart. Welch's human resources leader, Bill Conaty, recently collaborated with the prolific management guru, Ram Charan, on a book called *Talent Masters: Why Smart People Put People Before Numbers*, whereby the differentiable leadership labs of superlative companies were profiled. CAP is among the featured differentiators. The outline will be borrowed here. The components of the model are:

- leading change,

- creating a shared need,

- shaping a vision,

- mobilizing commitment,

- making change last,

- monitoring progress, and

- changing systems and structures.[8]

GE's seven part CAP model compares with John P. Kotter's eight-stage process:

- establishing a sense of urgency,

- creating the guiding coalition,

- developing a vision and strategy,

- communicating the change vision,

- empowering employees for broad-based action,

- generating short-term wins,

- consolidating gains and producing more change, and

- anchoring new approaches in the culture.[9]

Amid my academic research in pursuit of a terminal degree, I encountered considerable luminary writings for which GE (during the Jack Welch era) was a subject. Accordingly, it is reasonable to hypothesize that the influence was bisynchronous.

Stock homework assignments for Middle Market Methods™'s Value-creation Roadmap™ engagements included a battery of blind surveys. Unless these small company employees came from Fortune 1000s, this may be the first such outlet they have ever been afforded. In homage to GE, one regards change-management. The objective is to benchmark the leadership change-management personality. (See Figure 9.2.) Attendees are asked to rate each category on a scale of 100, zero being decrepit and 100 being perfect. The results are always enlightening and sometimes controversial. The data are graphically presented two ways: averages and standard deviations.

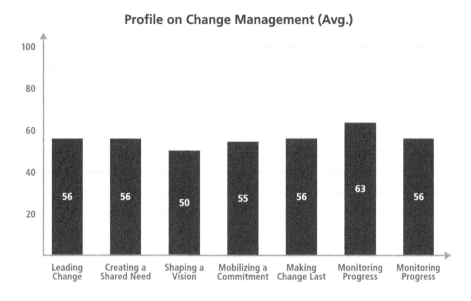

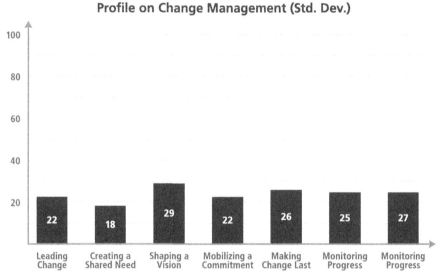

Figure 9.2   Change-management survey results example

Three themes are consistent. First, the patterns are as unique to each company as fingerprints are to individuals. Second, the average scores are seldom in the upper quartile. Moreover, the average scores for at least one of the questions are commonly in the lower quartile. The take-away is clear: room for improvement. Third, material variation is common across all question responses. This take-away is also clear: teammates do not see things similarly.

Even in higher average scores, variation can be extreme. As I learned in statistics and later revisited at GE, averages are misleading because they hide variation. One of the stellar GE instructors explained averages thusly: Suppose you had one bare foot in hot ashes and the other bare foot in a block of ice. On average, you would be comfortable. Edwards Deming more potently equated variation with something tantamount to evil.[10] The moral of the story is twofold. First, change agents should strive for the organization to view change similarly, or at least rooted in the same factual data. Second, change agents are seldom as superlative as they may think, so we should be careful about reading our own press.

Leading Change (Aligning the Head and the Heart)

You must be the change you wish to see in the world.[11]

Alexander the Great amassed an unrivaled Macedonian empire in the fourth century BCE. The warrior king led from the front, even at great peril to himself. He walked the talk. Battle for ancient cavalrymen was not too different for infantry. Wounds were common. Alexander experienced his share. His lore includes that even upon sustaining severe wounds, Alexander insisted upon his men first being treated for their injuries.

In the 18th century, the American colonies officially declared independence from England in 1776 after years of unrest that included armed episodes like the Boston Massacre in 1770. General George Washington led a ragtag and inferior military machine from 1775 to 1783. His services were volunteered. He lost most of his battles. Military victory was secured in the decisive battle of Yorktown in 1781. When peace was secured, he resigned his commission, compelling an incredulous King George to remark, "If [Washington] does that, he will be the greatest man in the world."[12] The new nation called upon Washington again as its first President in 1789 following ratification of the US Constitution.

In the 19th century, the infant United States suffered a Civil War whose casualties exceeded any armed conflict in the country's history. The Confederacy had a tenth the industry and manpower of the Union, yet the South intrepidly waged a campaign lasting four years. One reason was superior leadership. Robert E. Lee was not only a brilliant strategist and tactician, he was a superlative leader. He ate and slept among his troops to share their hardships and privations.

In the 20th century, amid a devastating economic depression, President Franklin Roosevelt declared to Americans in his first inaugural speech that "the only thing we have to fear is fear itself."[13] Roosevelt's administration implemented numerous programs beginning in 1933 attempting economic recovery before entry into World War II in 1941 awakened the industrial revival of the country. Throughout the ordeal, FDR comforted a weary nation with his ebullient charisma through his radio fireside chats.

Leading change is summed up in the breakfast principle. Chickens are involved by providing the eggs. Pigs are committed by providing the bacon. Leaders have to be committed with their own bacon. They cannot lead from the rear. They have to be out front modeling leadership behavior. Sometimes change agents do well to reflect on four guiding principles:

- separate the people from the problem,

- focus on interests instead of positions,

- create options for mutual benefit, and

- use objective decision criteria.[14]

Cultural change agents should pursue balance across goals, praise, and reprimands in support of change.[15] Charisma may be a useful change agent attribute. Charismatic leaders:

- "are strong role models for the beliefs and values [that] they want their followers to adopt;"

- "appear competent to followers;"

- "articulate ideological goals that have moral overtones;"

- exhibit confidence in their expectations of high follower performance; and

- "arouse task-relevant motives in followers that may include affiliation, power, or esteem."[16]

Creating a Shared Need (Shared Purpose)

To improve is to change; to be perfect is to change often.[17]

Status quo enjoys considerable inertia. What catalyzes change? Charles
Darwin argued that environmental factors affected the adaptation of species.[18]
Changing direction requires injecting new information into the pool of
knowledge. When the change agent frames the initiative, will the incumbents'
response be fight, flight, or follow? Sometimes leaders resort to the creation of
a "burning platform." For example, when the Spanish conquistador, Hernán
Cortés, landed in the New World (modern Mexico), he scuttled his ships to
block any notion of mutiny or capitulation. Cortés proceeded to conquer the
Aztecs.

The SWOT tool's opportunities and threats components offer some utility
for change agent preparation. Is an exploitable opportunity more enticing than
standing pat? Alternatively, is danger driven from inaction, that is, a threat?
Returning to the foresight principles, horizon scanning sheds light on both.
Additionally, data establishes a baseline or benchmark for both opportunities
and threats. Moreover, the best seller shelves are full of biographies of success
stories awaiting discovery for potential analogous applications. The caveat is
that the failures do not get as much press, but may be more valuable learning
opportunities.

A cute story encapsulates perspective that is borrowed from Rosamund
Stone Zander and Benjamin Zander's *The Art of Possibility: Transforming
Professional and Personal Life.*[19] It seems two shoe salesmen went to a primitive
corner of a continent and encountered multitudes of barefoot inhabitants. One
salesman was distraught. He reported back to his leadership that the situation
was hopeless because no one wore shoes. The other relayed a similar scenario,
but with delight. He saw attractive potential in putting his shoes on all the bare
feet. The story classically depicts the glass half empty versus glass half full.
Change agents need to often reflect on the adage: "Can't never could and won't
never will." Leaders create a shared need for teams to motivate migration from
status quo.

Shaping a Vision (Where is "There?")

The only thing worse than being blind is having sight but no vision.[20]

Max DePree imparted that the first objective of leadership is to explain reality.[21] Sometimes reality is ugly. Indeed, it may be ugly enough to catalyze action. The value of a vision was discussed in Chapter 4: The DNA of Packs. The point here is that whereas a vision may be necessary to guide the organization in a macro sense, a vision also has utility for change agency for initiatives in support of strategy. Process improvement is an apt example. People are unlikely to support the change until they are comfortable with its personal impact. Behavioral change is essential to institutionalizing change. This entails two categories of behaviors: (i) those that must cease; and (ii) those that must be assimilated. This should not repeat the lessons of the process reengineering saga, that is, all resident behaviors are not bad. Rather, it is incumbent upon change agents to identify behaviors that should be preserved. This actually serves as a foundation for persuasion.

Mobilizing Commitment (Rallying Constituents)

Commitment is an act, not a word.[22]

Abraham Maslow observed, "If the only tool you have is a hammer, you tend to see every problem as a nail."[23] Change agents need a toolbox full of options for tailoring the response to the situation. Mark Twain presented an excellent case study in *The Adventures of Tom Sawyer*.[24] To prime protagonist Tom Sawyer's chagrin, Aunt Polly charged him with whitewashing (painting) the backyard fence at her Missouri home. Of course, Tom had other designs on the usage of his time. Even so, Tom feigned enjoyment to his friends who, at first, derided him as saddled with an abominable chore. However, Tom shrugged it off and kept his wits. Curiosity got the best of his friends who wanted to try their hand. An amateur would have immediately pivoted. Not Tom. He was a marketing genius and change agent extraordinaire ahead of his time. Tom applied the Diffusion of Innovations principles. By the time Tom allowed his chums to touch his paintbrush, he had persuaded them that it was worth their paying for the privilege. The story imparts the essence of change-management. It does not count until people voluntarily change for reasons clear to their unique motivational code, that is, their WIIFM.

Deciphering the code unique to organizational culture requires the identification of resistance root causes. Conflict may be triggered by goal incompatibility, differentiation, task interdependence, and resource constraints.[25] Categories of change resistance include skill deficiencies, turf, cultural inertia, and personal baggage—or some combination thereof. (See

Figure 9.3.) Each will be summarized. Skill deficiencies create resistance when leaders ask followers to do something for which they are not trained. Leaders have a responsibility to provide skills training; otherwise, they are setting followers up to fail.

Turf and power are synonyms. "The power to do good is also the power to do harm."[26] Transitioning to flatter organizations may entail fewer direct reports—or no direct reports, that is, individual contribution. Incumbents may like a new role, but dislike how the new role is perceived by others in the organization.

Cultural inertia regards confronting institutionalized processes that feel normal despite the possibility that they have become non-value add. "But we have always done it that way" is symptomatic for this obstacle. One of the most amusing manifestations of the phenomenon is "That won't work in this industry." While there may be occasional merit to the assertion, the protest is more commonly a red herring. The ruse is typically revealed when the change agent acknowledges the point as a matter of courtesy before asking for specific examples to investigate. The 80/20 is that there are few examples.

Finally, constituents bring personal baggage to work in measures often beyond the awareness of leadership. Examples can include family issues such as illness, marital discord, and financial stress. Even though the company

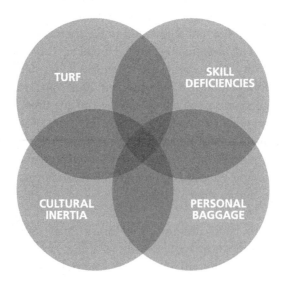

Figure 9.3   Resistance to change root causes model

did not cause the problem, it remains impacted by the constituent's inability to leave it out of the work environment. I must confess having held initial unfavorable opinions for some people before discovering the employee's condition that was beyond my line of sight. After enlightenment, I came to respect them for their character in dealing great personal challenges. Of course, the change-management strategy appropriately morphed to accommodate these epiphanies. The real problem with personal baggage is that there are limitations to how a leader may discover these data points that are rooted in privacy laws. Leaders should lean on the expertise of their human resource professionals in these situations.

Resistance to change may be in a single category, or a combination across categories. The recipe is unique to the individual. However, once the prime sources of resistance are identified, a change-management strategy may be implemented. Change agents should recognize that the constituency need not universally brandish wild enthusiasm for the change. Rather the degree of support may be relative to the function the incumbent holds in the organizational design. For example, leaders might desire the sales function to be effusively excited about a change. However, the risk management function need only be neutral, that is, their compliance and risk mitigation concerns have been addressed.

There is another way to evaluate resistance to change: situation, stamina, and clarity.[27] The situation may be impossible to modify. What does the parent of a kidnapped child do when the kidnappers threaten the life of the kid if the parents contact the police? Stamina is a finite quantity. Change should be engaged with charged personal batteries. Incumbents are ill-equipped to defy gravity if exhausted.[28] Finally, change agents should be aware that apparent resistance may actually regard ambiguity. This is why multifaceted and frequent communication is warranted amid change.

Making Change Last (Institutionalizing New Behaviors)

If you do not change direction, you may end up where you were heading.[29]

Having identified the quit, keep, and add behaviors required of the future state aspirations, the change agent should examine reasons for incumbents to resist versus support the new paradigm. Kurt Lewin created an ideal tool for his unfreeze, change, refreeze model: force field analysis. The tool was also used in the foresight roadmap in Chapter 5: The Importance of Strategy (see Figure 5.4 in Chapter 5). It is the same tool, just with a different application. The change agent's mission is to support the enabling behaviors and remove the resisting behaviors. Of course, this is easier said than done. However, an identified enemy is more easily challenged than a ghost.

In their book, *Switch: How to Change Things When Change is Hard*, Chip and Dan Heath describe change-management in terms of the elephant and its rider. The elephant symbolizes emotion and the rider symbolizes reason. Their message is straight forward. Emotion is more powerful than reason. "People choose to commit to a decision based on emotion, feelings, intuition, trust, [and] hope."[30] Therefore, behaviors are changed by the articulation of three actions: directing the rider (change agent), motivating the elephant, and shaping the options path.

Fear is not a good long-term motivator.[31] Moreover, complex change is hard to implement. Incumbents may fear radical change that breaks "the frame of reference for the organization, often transforming the entire organization."[32] The best formula is manufacturing a leverageable, small win. Returning to Chip and Dan Heath's elephant, we are reminded that grandiose change should be incrementally executed the same as digesting a pachyderm: one bite at a time.[33]

"Between stimulus and response there is a space. In that space is our power to choose our response. In our response lies our growth and our freedom."[34] About 40 percent of our behaviors are rooted in habit. The challenge is to displace old habits with new ones. (We touched on this principle in Chapter 7: Marketing versus Selling.) This involves identifying a cue for a Pavlovian response, or routine. Rewards—extrinsic and/or intrinsic—reinforce the routine. Sufficiently anchored, incumbents develop a craving for doing things the new way.[35]

The commentary above is a contemporary version of mature topic: behavioral modification, or "individual learning through reinforcement," that is, "anything that both increases the strength of response and induces repetition of the behavior that preceded the reinforcements."[36] Positive reinforcement may be extrinsic in the form of compensation and incentives. Positive reinforcement may also be in the form of intrinsic fulfillment as described in the higher echelons of Maslow's need hierarchy, that is, self-actualization.[37] Reinforcement is negative "if its removal after a response increases the performance of that response."[38] "Extinction" is associated with both positive and negative reinforcement. Extinction occurs when undesirable behavior is not rewarded.[39]

Punishment is the "stick" approach, that is, the "uncomfortable consequence of a particular behavioral response."[40] Figuring out rewards is more beneficial than administering punishments.

Monitoring Progress (Measuring to Manage)

In God we trust; all others bring data.[41]

Peter Drucker explained something to the effect that if something gets measured, it gets managed. Indeed, correct measures are a chronic deficiency in the middle market. This is especially true for dynamic behavioral change metrics. In this case, the measures pursued are those unique to gauging the transition to future state stability. "Not everything that can be counted counts, and not everything that counts can be counted."[42] This may be actually harder than the input, process, and output metrics of the generic business model. The culprit is timing absent context. For example, how would a leader measure the success of a process improvement initiative aimed at prompt product delivery? First, change agents should embark on their odyssey knowing that productivity during transition is likely to deteriorate before improving. This is sometimes referred to as a J-curve. Indeed, leaders should prepare for this and disarm its potential for subverting the change. In response, leaders may need to adjust productivity incentives during some change implementations.

Let's ponder an example in each of the people, process, and tools categories. In the people category, the leader might contrast a baseline, pre-change, employee version of the Net Promoter® score with a stable, post-change version. More specifically, the leader should identify key influencers and role models among the affected stakeholders. These people should be clearly understood for concerns about the proposed change. Moreover, their inputs should be sought for change-management design and implementation. As contributors or co-authors, these influencers and role models have invested their personal capital in the credibility of the process. Accordingly, change agents should utilize them as a barometer for the effectiveness of the transition.

What about a process measure? Customers hate delivery variation because it disrupts their supply chain. Variation changes order habits and warehousing requirements. The measure of average on time delivery hides variation for both early and late deliveries. Moreover, the discrete yes–no measure of delivery before the deadline hides early shipment variation. In response to these issues, "span" was a measure adopted by GE to demonstrate the range of days early versus days late for deliveries. Depending on the sample size, the fifth and 95th percentiles were compared to depict what the customer "felt." One of the most extreme client examples I ever encountered was a span of over 180 days. The data demonstrated to the client that the only reason his customers tolerated them as a vendor was price. Moreover, absent quick resolution, the customers would replace them with a more reliable vendor. Indeed, we later confirmed that the customers were already pursuing alternatives. Had the problem not been addressed, sales were surely the imminent casualty.

Finally, what about tools? Technology adoption typically faces resistance in the form of skill deficiencies. If training is provided, then how might tool adoption be measured? What about error rates tied to incentives? The only way to measure errors might be with usage of the tool. Eschewing tool adoption forgoes incentive participation.

Change measures are likely unique to the situation. The challenge is to think. Such thinking should be collaborative. Change agents should ask constituents what measure they think will confirm the company's progress along the change-management path.

Changing Systems and Structures (Organizational Architecture)

The achievements of an organization are the results of the combined effort of each individual.[43]

The previous chapter (Chapter 8: Leadership Choices and Organizational Design) covered organizational design. The purpose here is to calibrate it to change-management endeavors. One of the Six Sigma tools is potential problem analysis (PPA). This requires change agents to scrutinize the unintended consequences of "the new thing." Basically, "What if?" is applied to a decision tree format. Applying PPA could have forewarned of looming icons of disaster like Fannie, Freddie, rogue traders, etc. However, poor leaders rarely own their mistakes. Even worse, cowards deflect responsibility to someone else. One way to approach PPA is with a decision tree that resembles the strategic foresight tool (see Figure 5.3 in Chapter 5: The Importance of Strategy).

By example, PPA will be applied to a kid's first car. What if a 16-year-old boy is given a 500 horsepower automobile? Assuming the (responsible?) parent concludes that a speeding ticket is likely, the question becomes preventable, or error-proofed, design. Of course, one of the first decisions should have probably

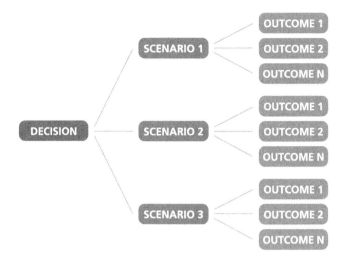

Figure 9.4   Decision tree tool

been an underpowered clunker instead of a muscle car. However, for the sake of argument, suppose the die is cast and junior has his hotrod. How about his paying for the gas, maintenance, and insurance? Consider these individually. A muscle car tends to get poor gas mileage, exacerbated by a lead foot. This also correlates with more expensive maintenance. Peeling rubber means more frequent new tires. Speeding also increases tire wear. The kicker is probably the insurance. First, hotrod insurance for a 16-year-old kid will be painfully expensive. Second, a speeding ticket is the gift that keeps on giving. Begin with the fine. Add to this the accumulated points that threaten license suspension and revocation. However, getting rated by the insurance carrier increases the premium for years. Does the kid understand this on the front end of the first car process? A minimum wage part-time job to pay for this does not leave much room for dating money.

Two additional systems and structures issues should be emphasized: (i) compensation mechanisms; and (ii) communication. Compensation is one of the toughest leadership challenges. While human resource professionals benchmark compensation across industry sectors, the sad fact is that no panacea awaits practitioners. Additionally, what works at Company A may not work at Company B. The first thing leaders must recognize is that rewarded behaviors strengthen. However, the method of reward is nearly unique to the individual. The transition from Baby Boomers through Generation X to Generation Y only makes the rewards Gordian Knot more difficult to solve because intrinsic and extrinsic motivations are materially different. We can only offer guiding principles.

First, compensation should be "enough" to keep it from being a "de-motivator." Motivating factors are more elusive. Agency theory is compatible with motivators, that is, sufficient monetary incentives will predictably influence behavior. Unfortunately, financial incentives have asymptotic impact, that is, compensation eventually exhausts its motivating potential. Another wrinkle is the time delay between behavior and reward. In order for financial incentives to be most effective, they need to be proximal to desired results, for example, weekly or monthly. This was a rationalization of Frederick Taylor's piece rate compensation.

Financial incentives have to be part of the performance management equation. Two components are proffered here. First, a portion of the incentives have to be tied to the overall performance of the company. This is partly due to alignment, that is, the employee's efforts should contribute to the overall improvement of company performance. Second, a portion should be tied to metrics within the employee's direct control. For example, a production employee might be rewarded for units of production. However, a better system entails virgin yield production, that is, error free units. This focuses the operator on controllable quality issues. Inevitably, money begs a question that Jack Welch addresses in his book, *Winning*. What happens to exceptional individual performance in a struggling situation, that is, turning around a losing division—before it is in the black. Welch reserved the leadership prerogative to bonus the employee.[44]

One of the firm's primary objectives to perpetuate itself is making money. Contrary to popular opinion, companies cannot make too much money. Free markets are sufficiently self-governing in this respect. When companies appear to be making too much money, they invite interloping competition. A similar phenomenon is in play for CEO compensation. The more visibility a CEO garners for compensation relative to company performance—and that leader's compensation distance from the employee population—he or she invites trouble. This is a judgment call. Small business founders/leaders may leverage themselves to the hilt. They deserve equitable compensation when the company performs. However, they should avoid the excesses demonstrated in behemoth, multinational corporations. Max DePree set a good example at Herman Miller by limiting CEO compensation to a multiple of the lowest entry level position.[45] Deferred gratification in the capital gains category is fine. Brandishing ostentation, however, breeds contemptible demotivation. Socrates offered a simple behavioral formula: "The way to gain a good reputation is to endeavor to be what you desire to appear."[46]

Communication is an underappreciated management tool, much less an underutilized change-management tool. It is impossible to over-communicate.[47] Unfortunately, communication tends to be among the first casualties of crisis. On the contrary, it should actually be among the preferred tools. Leaders should never be too busy to communicate. People may not hear leaders, despite how many times those leaders repeat the message. Consequently, a communication plan (see Figure 9.5) helps sort through the audiences, objectives, messages, owners, media, and frequency.

The private equity transaction is among the most disruptive changes a portfolio company will encounter. Both the investment team and the portfolio company leadership have a vested interest in change-management best practices for positioning the company for its next phase of growth. The stakeholders of private equity relationships should be vigilantly reminded of pre-Socratic Greek philosopher Heraclitus' admonition that "nothing endures but change."[48]

Target Audience	Owner	Message	Owner	Medium	Frequency
Customers					
Vendors					
Employees					
Creditors					
Investors					
Communities					

Figure 9.5   Communications plan framework tool

Endnotes

[1]   The scorpion and the frog. *Aesop's fables*. Retrieved from http://www.aesopfables.com/cgi/aesop1.cgi?4&TheScorpionandtheFrog

[2]   Senge, P.M. (1990). *The fifth discipline: The art and practice of the learning organization*. New York, NY: Doubleday. p. 142.

[3]   Rogers, E.M. (2003). *Diffusion of innovations* (5th ed.). New York: Free Press. pp. 279–85.

[4]   Zig Ziglar articles. (n.d.). *PlanetMotivation.com*. Retrieved from http://www.planetmotivation.com/zigziglararticles.html

[5]   Finlay-Robinson, D. (2009). Practitioner comment: What's in it for me? The fundamental importance of stakeholder evaluation. *Journal of Management Development, 28*(4), 380–8.

[6]   Elephant and the blind men. (n.d.). *Jainworld.com*. Retrieved from http://www.jainworld.com/education/stories25.asp

[7]   Von Der Linn, B. (2009, January 25). Overview of GE's change acceleration process (CAP). Bob Von Der Linn's HPT Blog: *Change Management and Human Performance Technology*. Retrieved from   http://bvonderlinn.wordpress.com/2009/01/25/overview-of-ges-change-acceleration-process-cap/; Change acceleration process. (n.d). In *GE Capital's website*. Retrieved from http://gecapsol.com/cms/servlet/cmsview/GE_Capital_Solutions/prod/en/acfc_efficiency/efficiency/cap.html; Conaty and Charan (2010).

[8]   Driving change and continuous process improvement. (2012). *General Electric Capital Corporation*. Retrieved from http://www.gecapital.eu/en/docs/GE_Capital_HowTo_Driving_Change_and_Continuous_Process_Improvement.pdf. pp. 19–21.

[9]   Kotter, J.P. (1996). *Leading change* (1st ed.). Boston, MA: Harvard Business School Press.

[10] Deming, W.E. (1986). *Out of the crisis*. Cambridge, MA: MIT Center for Advanced Engineering Study.

[11] Mahatma Ghandi quotes. (n.d.). *BrainyQuotes.com*. Retrieved from http://www.brainyquote.com/quotes/topics/topic_change.html

[12] Johnson, P. (2009). *George Washington: The founding father (eminent lives)*. New York: Harper Perennial. p. 78.

[13] Franklin D. Roosevelt quotes. (n.d.). *BrainyQuote.com* Retrieved from http://www.brainyquote. com/quotes/authors/f/franklin_d_roosevelt.html

[14] Fisher, R. and Ury. W. (1991). *Getting to yes* (2nd ed.). New York: Penguin.

[15] Blanchard, K. (1985). *One minute manager.* New York, NY: William Merrom and Company.

[16] Northouse, P. (2006). *Leadership: Theory and practice* (4th ed.). Thousand Oaks, CA: Sage. p. 179.

[17] Winston Churchill quotes. (n.d.). *BrainyQuote.com.* Retrieved from http://www.brainyquote. com/quotes/topics/topic_change.html

[18] Darwin, C. (1859). *On the origin of species by means of natural selection* (1st ed.). London: John Murray.

[19] Zander, R.M. and Zander, E. (2000). *The art of possibility. Transforming professional and personal life.* Cambridge, MA: Harvard Business School Press. p. 9.

[20] Helen Keller quotes. (n.d.). *BrainyQuote.com.* Retrieved from http://www.brainyquote.com/ quotes/keywords/vision.html

[21] DePree, M. and Malcolm, C. (Ed.). (1989). *Leadership is an art.* New York, NY: Doubleday.

[22] Jean-Paul Sarte quotes. (n.d.). *BrainyQuote.com.* Retrieved from http://www.brainyquote.com/ quotes/keywords/commitment.html

[23] Abraham Maslow quotes. (n.d.). *ThinkExist.com.* Retrieved from http://thinkexist.com/ quotation/if_the_only_tool_you_have_is_a_hammer-you_tend_to/221060.html

[24] Twain, M. (1917). *The adventures of Tom Sawyer.* New York: Harper & Brothers.

[25] Daft, R.L. (2007). *Organizational theory and design* (9th ed.). Mason, OH: Thomson South-Western. pp. 484–7.

[26] Friedman, M. (2002). *Capitalism and freedom* (fortieth anniversary ed.). Chicago: University of Chicago Press.

[27] Heath, D. and Heath, C. (2010). *Switch: How to change things when change is hard.* New York: Crown Business. (ISBN: 0385528752)

[28] Ibid.

[29]   Lao Tzu quotes. (n.d.). *BrainyQuote.com*. Retrieved from http://www.brainyquote.com/quotes/topics/topic_change.html

[30]   Block, P. (2000). *Flawless consulting: A guide to getting your expertise used* (2nd ed.). San Francisco: Jossey-Bass/Pfeiffer. p 263.

[31]   Heath and Heath (2010).

[32]   Daft (2007). p. 401.

[33]   Hogan, B. (2004). *How do you eat an elephant?: One bite at a time*. Coral Springs, FL: Llumina Press.

[34]   Viktor E. Frankl quotes. (n.d.). *BrainyQuote.com*. Retrieved from http://www.brainyquote.com/quotes/quotes/v/viktorefr160380.html

[35]   Duhigg, C. (2012). *The power of habit: Why we do what we do in life and business*. New York: Random House.

[36]   Ivancevich, J.M. (2007). *Human resource management* (10th ed.). New York, NY: McGraw-Hill Irwin. p. 422.

[37]   Nelson, D. and Quick, J.C. (2006). *Organizational behavior: Foundations, realities and challenges*. (5th Ed.). Mason, Ohio: South-Western. p. 153.

[38]   Ivancevich (2007). p. 422.

[39]   Ibid. p. 423.

[40]   Ibid. p. 422.

[41]   William Edwards Deming quote. (1990–93). In Hastie, T., Tibshirani, R and Friedman, J. (2009). *The elements of statistical learning: Data mining, inference, and prediction*. New York: Springer Science+Business Media. p. vii.

[42]   Albert Einstein quotes. (n.d.). *The Quotations Page*. Retrieved from http://www.quotationspage.com/quote/26950.html

[43]   Vince Lombardi quotes. (n.d.). *BrainyQuote.com*. Retrieved from http://www.brainyquote.com/quotes/keywords/organization.html

[44]   Welch, J. (2005). *Winning*. New York: HarperCollins.

[45] DePree and Malcolm (1989).

[46] 7 pieces of wisdom from Socrates. (n.d.). *Dumb little man tips for life*. Retrieved from http://www. dumblittleman.com/2010/06/7-pieces-of-wisdom-from-socrates.html

[47] Covey, S.R., Whitman, B. and England, B. (2009). *Predictable results in unpredictable times*. Salt Lake City, UT: FranklinCovey.; Covey, S.M.R. (2006). *The speed of trust: The one thing that changes everything*. New York: Free Press; Covey, S.R. (2004). *The 7 habits of highly effective people*. New York, NY: Simon & Schuster; Kotter, J.P. and Cohen, D.S. (2002). *The heart of change*. Boston, MA: Harvard Business School Press; Porter, M.E. (1980). *Competitive strategy: Techniques for analyzing industries and competitors*. New York, NY: Free Press.

[48] Heraclitus. (n.d.). *The quotations page*. Retrieved from http://www.quotationspage.com/search. php3?Author=Heraclitus&file=other

Chapter 10
The Legacy Effect

Produce great persons, the rest follows.[1]

Simple Things, Big Impact

"There are no easy answers, but there are simple answers. We must have the courage to do what we know is morally right."[2]

The global workforce is increasingly diverse. In the West, this means higher proportions of women and lower proportions of Caucasians.[3] Tomorrow's winners will harness these supertrends for competitive edge. By casting a wider talent net, leaders are more likely to identify top performers and performance potential.[4] Employees have fun building a dynamic organization. However, they might not learn as much absent a little adversarial seasoning. Indeed, at least one operational speed bump likely awaits all companies. Some will tempt disaster. One of the tenets of good leadership is to prepare the organization to make the most of smooth seas but prepare for the hurricane even if it never happens. Machiavelli summed the point this way:

> *When things are quiet, everyone dances attendance, everyone makes promises, and everybody would die for him [the prince] as long as death is far off. But in times of adversity, when the state has need of its citizens, there are few to be found.*[5]

Preparing a company to make the most of its opportunities is serious business.

> *The primary goal of any organization is to perpetuate itself, but the individual, human needs of its leaders and managers are far more complex than mere survival ... . [S]taying on one path must lead eventually to a dead end. If you are not breaking new ground, gaining new knowledge, you are risking being trapped in your success.*[6]

The greatest epitaph a leader could enjoy is that the place runs at least as well without him or her.

> An organization that is not capable of perpetuating itself has failed. An organization therefore has to provide today the [professionals] who can run it tomorrow ... . An organization which just perpetuates today's level ... has lost the capacity to adapt. And since the one and only thing certain in human affairs is change, it will not be capable of survival in a changed tomorrow.[7]

Successful organizations, by necessity, continually reinvent themselves for competitive differentiation. This is tantamount to playing offense. There is also a defensive argument: reinvention is necessary for survival. This axiom follows Charles Darwin's evolution of species arguments. This analogy should not be discounted as far-fetched. While an organization may be a legalistic entity, it remains an organism by virtue of its reliance on humans to perform its processes. Thus, institutionalizing the organization's ability to reinvent in perpetuity is the best imprint a leader may leave on his or her organization. Such foresighted human engineering brands the organization as a talent magnet for the best and brightest—a place where talent may demonstrate that they have "the right stuff."

Succession planning is integral to perpetuating the business. "Before you are a leader, success is all about growing yourself. When you become a leader, success is all about growing others."[8] Succession planning is

> a means of identifying critical management positions [throughout the organization]. Succession planning also describes management positions to provide maximum flexibility in lateral management moves and to ensure that as individuals achieve greater seniority, their management skills will broaden and become more generalized in relation to total organizational objectives rather than to purely departmental objectives.[9]

Succession may sometimes be confused with replacement planning. However, replacement planning is actually a subset of succession planning.[10] Succession, therefore should be viewed in more holistic terms. Indeed, this holistic perspective is presented by William J. Rothwell in *Effective Succession Planning: Ensuring Leadership Continuity and Building Talent from Within* (4th edition). In both instances, replacement and succession, organizations often resort to external recruitment, an action that may indicate a talent management deficiency.[11] In contrast, internally cultivated talent has inherent advantages that outside candidates struggle to overcome—at least in the short run. Such advantages include tacit knowledge ("based on personal experience, rules of thumb, intuition, and judgment"[12]), explicit knowledge ("formal, systematic knowledge that can be codified, written down, and passed on to others in documents or general instructions"[13]), and cultural norms. Indeed, organizational context may be more important than the intelligence of the person in it.[14] Deficiencies in these areas contribute to the two out of five failure rate specific to executive recruiting.[15] Cultural onboarding alone may consume up to 26 weeks![16] These phenomena also contribute to materially high failure rates among subordinate recruitment.

Middle Market Methods™ created a legacy axes tool to guide managers in proactive thinking about human asset needs relative growth defined by the corporate strategy. (See Figure 10.1.) The concept was inspired by Christensen et al.'s disruptive innovation arguments.[17] One axis regards skill complexity and the other work rules. Recruitment channels are germane to all quadrants. However, the recruitment lead time may be longer for the complex roles.

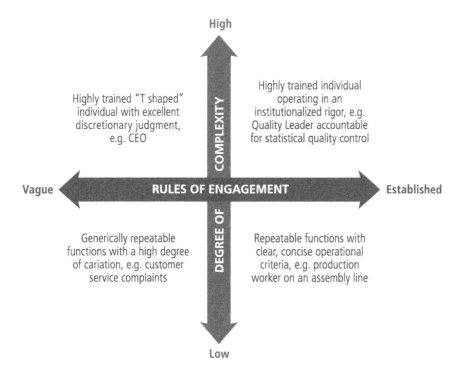

Figure 10.1   Legacy axes example

Legacy is particularly relevant to private equity investments for two reasons. First, value is more easily built if the seasoned and skilled team is already in place. Second, and even if the private equity firm encourages the portfolio company's leadership to improve its ranks, a potent team is more appealing to the buyers constituting the investment exit. This is even more important for financial buyers, that is to say other private equity investors. Financial buyers are more likely to rely on the existing C-level team than strategic buyers that are more likely to eliminate duplicative positions in integration. The legacy argument may also be aimed at the private equity firm. Unless the firm founders think about succession, they only train their subordinates to become their competitors, as the best and brightest often eject to start their own firms. Whereas broad and deep T-shaped people[18] were featured in the innovative comments in Chapter 6: Innovation and Value-creation, their utility is also self-evident here: broad and deep makes for good succession leadership potential.

Portfolio companies tend to have underdeveloped competencies relative to legacy:

- Decision-making tends to be excessively hierarchical and centralized.

- Performance management is more of a popularity contest than a meritocracy.

- The recruitment and onboarding process is reactive—not proactive.

- Training and development are more likely associated with compliance than competitive differentiation.

Each point will be probed.

At business inception, organizational ranks are thin and employees must multitask—despite the inherent multitasking inefficiencies.[19] As the company grows, new members join the team. While tasks may be delegated, authority might not. This is the unsavory "responsibility without authority" scenario. Some entrepreneurial governance models retain centralized control because of the leader's discomfort zone. This is a control issue, perhaps rooted in insecurity associated with the absence of leverageable delegation expertise and experience. This might also be a commentary on the inadequacy of systems undergirding governance. While this dictatorship may be benevolent, its scalability is limited. Eventually, the leader runs out of bandwidth. Even if this happens after the private equity firm controls the board, transitions may be messy. While the autocrat may concede the need for leadership assistance, this does not guarantee smooth transition. Power is sometimes only begrudgingly relinquished. Sadly and in worst case scenarios when CEOs fail to engineer sufficient legacy talent processes, new, externally recruited leadership is recruited of necessity to resolve the problem. The new leaders are faced with the challenges of personal assimilation, change-management inertia, identifying the proper response, and successfully implementing appropriate policies.[20]

The business model commonly reflects the leader's personality, that is, a sales culture. If writing the order or closing the deal trumps all other decisions in isolation, the imminent "brick wall" collision is the fulfillment engine's inability to keep up. In response, the board may authorize a "corporate savior"[21] in the form of a COO intended to build scalable infrastructure commensurate to complement the sales engine. However practical this action may appear, the CEO may feel threatened. The resistance becomes evident upon the reluctance of the CEO to authentically embrace the requisite behavioral modifications. Stated more bluntly, the CEO may not want to let go.

Performance management is an elusive discipline. First consider that unless the managerial ranks came to the organization trained by another company, unconscious ignorance may prevail. Even if the leaders were exposed to performance management, the experience may have been poor. Thus, the temptation may be overwhelming to eschew performance management in the new environment. This scenario is exacerbated by the reality that giving subordinates negative feedback is not fun. Procrastination is also a powerful temptation. "You can grade someone's performance only if you know their performance."[22] This leans on process and tool adequacy.

Effective leaders embrace talent development responsibilities and challenge other leaders to do so.[23] Leaders responsible for developing talent within their organizations should be wary of the "stereotype threat."[24] By pigeon-holing people into profiles that assume the disinterest or inability to perform certain jobs, the company may be robbing itself and the incumbent. Leaders should consciously avoid the Peter Principle[25] infection in the organization in favor of promoting the Pygmalion effect.[26] The gist is thus: avoid imposing limitations on followers, or allowing followers to impose limitations on themselves, because they belong to a certain group—irrespective of how that group may be defined. Encouragement to be one's best may surprise all parties to the scenario. Wilma Rudolph overcame polio to win track and field Olympic gold. One of the best gifts a leader can develop in a follower is critical thinking and good habits. Both may preclude the crisis paralysis of panicking and choking. "Panic is about thinking too little. Choking is about loss of instinct."[27]

Confucius counseled, "Choose a job you love, and you will never have to work a day in your life."[28] The challenge for leaders is first to build an organization in which people would love to work, then develop channels to pursue those talented candidates most likely to find the organization alluring. Busy leaders sometimes find themselves faced with the dilemma of growth that eclipses human resource capacity. This may be exacerbated by key personnel turnover among those who opted out of the stressful situation that appeared to have no reprieve in sight. Proactive recruitment is not an option at this point. Managers become reactive and may succumb to pressure to settle. This can lead to expensive mistakes. The opportunity cost of a poor hire tends to be in multiples of fully loaded compensation—irrespective of length of time in the position. The multiple increases with seniority of the position.

Leaders should resolve to establish an anticipatory talent pipeline to avoid the pitfalls of reactionary responses under duress.

> *Most organizations rely on a fairly conservative selection process that focuses on narrow abilities and gives short shrift to broader or unusual potential, excluding some of the most promising candidates.... The real challenge may not be so much identifying talent as getting serious about seeking it. Most employers worry far more about the devastating effects of making a bad hire than about selecting someone who is competent but not exceptional—good, not great.*[29]

The talent pipeline brands the organization among recruitment channels as a great place to invest personal passions while refining existing skills and developing new ones. IQ and success have a low correlation—less than 0.2.[30] Therefore, the leader's job is to find bright people who will fit in the culture and perform in the assignment. A good process includes projecting future talent requirements for the business strategy relative to growth. Proactive recruitment should commence in advance of open positions to develop interest among qualified candidates. When positions are posted, the company may avoid settling under duress, and instead select among viable options. In complement, a robust onboarding process should support the new hires' cultural and position assimilation. Career paths should be punctuated with coaching and development opportunities to improve skills.[31]

Proactive recruitment should be approached much like marketing channels for customers. One of my favorite examples regards a PhD-caliber technical role at a metallurgical manufacturer. Relative a long vacant position, the head of operations lamented that there were only five people in the world who knew how to do the work. He knew all five and none of them wanted the job. We resolved the problem by identifying recruitment channels: research universities, think tanks, trade organizations, and the like. The result was a list of highly qualified people never before encountered. The position was promptly filled by someone at least as qualified as the "fab five."

The organization should develop contingency plans in anticipation of voluntary or involuntary separation. Good performance management systems give consistent and continual feedback such that reviews are never a surprise. Rewards should be at least partially tied to measures within the employee's control. If these bases are covered, the leader may be hit by a truck without inducing duress on the daily activities of the organization.[32]

Training and development may be another sink or swim proposition. The lucky are mentored by the veterans in execution of best practices. Alternatively, the new hire may be greeted with skepticism. Moreover, information may be scarce and/or hoarded as a power scepter. Feedback may be more negative than positive or constructive. The routine may be more akin to hazing than onboarding.

Seasoned leaders counter these missteps by rolling back the clock at inception and posing some critical thinking and corresponding options. This begins with revisiting strategy, that is, what the company purports it is trying to accomplish in a relative time range. "A firm's strategy must be aligned with employees' competencies and performance if profitability, growth, effectiveness, and valuation are to be achieved."[33] Among the best all-around CEOs I have ever had the pleasure of serving is Bill Scheller, former CEO of ORS Nasco. Scheller knew that his organic growth was outpacing his ability to recruit support personnel. Moreover, his hiring managers needed training to include pivoting from a reactive to proactive posture. Not only was the training provided, but its institutionalization was a non-negotiable governance attribute. The results of his leadership were game-changing.

Corporate myopia kills organizations. The best leaders who architect the best cultures are not afraid of challenging all aspects of their business model. Assumptions being the mother of all disaster, the "Why?" question should be inexhaustibly applied until the adopted attributes are clearly understood to be sound, based upon reality and plausible scenarios.

Consider that neither the CEO nor any of the indispensable C-levels—along with their key employees—is immortal. Borrowing from Charles Dickens' *Christmas Carol*, suppose the ghost of "your company future" transports us to a point where this army of talent is no more. First question: What are the dumbest things we did as leaders to make a mess of things for our successors? Second question: Even worse, what did we do to worsen the positions of those who depended on our stewardship for their estates?

Paraphrasing Benjamin Franklin, leaders typically do not plan to fail, but they may fail to plan.[34] Even though planning is important, it falls prey to daily urgencies. Moreover, the word "planning" may connote something other than people planning. If the strategy is solid, but the team is shaky, then the options are skill development or top-grading. Ten suggestions outline effective employee development:

- test for ability, focus, and ambition;

- stress futuristic skills;

- top-grade the ranks;

- deliberately assign challenging assignments;

- place aspirants in demanding roles;

- individualize development plans;

- annually assess the talent pool;

- leverage compensation;

- hold talent town hall communication events; and

- personalize and reconcile individual career paths with the strategic vision.[35]

Interestingly, even planning is the wrong first step. Going forward amid prosecuting the strategy through the business model, the culture should return to the strategic thinking and foresight principle of horizon scanning to look for ecosystem signals warranting change (see Chapter 5: The Importance of Strategy). The analogous question starts with "What type of talent are we likely to need a decade out?" While precise answers are error prone, the directional answers are sufficient. The "right" people should have foundational skills, complemented by the aptitude and attitude to learn. GE developed its Session C process in response to this challenge. Proctor & Gamble uses a similar methodology to evaluate an incumbent's potential to be two levels higher in the organization. Session C is a talent evaluation tool, yet it is done in the context of strategy—not an isolated and disconnected human resources exercise. GE's vitality matrix (see Figure 10.2) compels leaders to profile their teams relative to two axes: performance and potential. This is a forced distribution. Generally, leaders should go out of their way to retain and further challenge their top performers who possess promising potential. Similarly, leaders should immediately address poor performance with apparent low potential. The root cause may be improper positioning or poor corporate fit. An unforgivable sin is force ranking absent a performance management process. Indeed, only about half of companies use an evaluation tool.[36] Since managers tend to loath doing this, especially if untrained, some simple steps are offered to head in the right direction:

- Share the corporate goals with the incumbent.

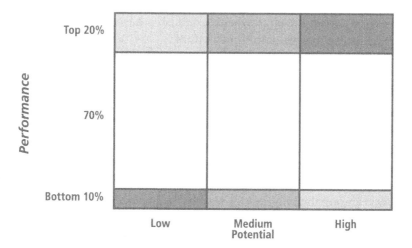

Figure 10.2   Vitality matrix tool

- Ask the incumbent to identify three personal goals that increase the likelihood that the corporate goals will be met. Then, reconcile any alignment issues.

- ALWAYS complement the three with a fourth: living the values.

- Ask the incumbent to identify a measure within their control that substantiates accomplishment for each of the personal goals. As with the goals, the manager should attune the measures to the goals.

- Provide continual feedback through the year, especially if: (i) performance does not meet expectations; and (ii) values are ignored. No year-end performance review should be a surprise to the incumbent. If it is, shame on the manager.

- Engage the incumbent quarterly for a high level feedback session that includes three bullet points of affirmation and three bullet points of particular improvement focus. Improvement focus does not mean the employee is failing, but rather may have potential to exceed expectations as a step toward advancement.

- Formally conduct annual reviews. Require the employee to first evaluate himself (or herself). This benefits novice evaluators by requiring the employee to establish a baseline while concurrently giving the evaluator time to think.

Leaders who will not terminate an employee over values are strongly signaling that the company has no real values. Jack Welch's position on values is highly publicized, including in his book, *Winning*. He asserts the necessity of terminating a producer who does not live the values. His reasoning is analogous to eschewing treatment upon diagnosing cancer: if you do not treat the problem and indulge metastasis, the corporate outcome may be terminal. Even so, the otherwise decisive and brash Welch lamented that firing these people was among the toughest leadership calls he ever made.[37]

Returning to the vitality matrix, the question the leader should ask is what happens when key positions vacate—irrespective of the catalyst. The second question is what the leader should do to develop existing talent toward the strategic vision. This is where the rationale for the pipeline begins. Indeed, the best organizations tend to hire entry-level positions who are promoted based upon ability and performance.[38] The new hire's previous job might not be a good predictor due to variation upon comparison with new job. That's why the "test job" of an entry level hire works. Of course, training is a part of the equation. Training is tailored to the technical and behavioral requirements of the strategy. This process bypasses the traditional issues of middle management and senior level hiring. Indeed the whole talent pipeline process is a perpetual performance review. Moreover, those who aspire to and achieve senior leadership positions have both a perspective on the business model and its culture that averts assimilation challenges of new hires. The downside of blowing this off is corporate myopia.

Larger competitors spend billions annually on training. Middle market companies cannot ignore this, but they may resolve to innovatively approach training by bootstrapping principles. First, they may conduct situational post mortems for lessons learned. Second, they may identify suggested reading that is periodically discussed over brown bag lunches. Third, they may identify gratis videos. For example, TED.com is a content-rich website with topical presentations. Fourth, they can attend seminars and panels concurrent with trade show activity. Fifth, they may download podcasts covering points of interest. Where there is a will, there is a way. Teams must resolve that the way should be found. Carthaginian Hannibal's thoughts are apropos: "We will either find a way or make one."[39]

The aspirational training model for the middle market should be the "university" concept for which the North Star is corporate strategy. Training must align with what the business intends to do. Two generic buckets of skills emerge: technical and behavioral. Technical skills undergird the delivery of value-creating products and services for customers. An example might be CAD/CAM (computer-aided design/computer-aided manufacturing) tools. Behavioral skills regard the leadership competencies for attracting, motivating, and retaining the talent with the technical skills. An example might be managing difficult people. Indeed, a material portion of those "technical" people may require new behavioral skills. Gap analysis is the next step, that is to say, the training available in the company versus that needed. Next, the gaps are prioritized. Finally, leadership must resolve to insource or outsource the prioritized training modules.

Sometimes, external hiring beyond entry level positions is unavoidable. When this is the scenario for rapidly growing companies, leaders should over-hire talent because the organization will grow into them. The point may be more easily understood from a simple economic opportunity cost perspective.

Suppose the purported cost to the organization was an extra $25 thousand in base salary for replacing an incumbent. (The focus of this example is economics, not the root cause for the position vacancy.) Over three years, the incremental compensation cost in our example is $75 thousand. Further suppose that the candidate had the technical and leadership skills to improve profitability—and with a technique that inspired her subordinates. Additionally, suppose the profitability improvement began in the second year--the first year being consumed with assimilation, analysis, and implementation. If after tax profitability attributable to the new hire improved a modest five times the incremental salary, or $125 thousand in years two and three, the internal rate of return for the decision is 383 percent! The moral of the story is "do the math" to avoid shortsightedness. Moreover, tying compensation to targets like this might be a good negotiation tactic. Getting portfolio company leadership teams to "do the math" is one of the toughest talent pipeline leadership challenges faced by private equity professionals.

Professional recruiters are common. However, like marque consultants, big name recruiters tend to be poor fits for the middle market. Boutique firms specializing in verticals tend to be better choices. A well-constructed job description is a prerequisite for engaging a recruiter. Additionally, Middle Market Methods™ advised its clients to select a discrete subset thereof as the firewall for resumes that will be considered. "Discrete" means the candidate either does, or does not, have the skill relative to the position the company seeks to fill. For example, acquisition integration may be on the short list for a Chief Human Resources Leader, just as installing an ERP system may be on the short list for a Chief Information Officer. Since the recruiter's motivation is quick success to earn their contingency fee, they also benefit from this best practice.

Middle Market Methods™ observed only about a one in ten chance that portfolio company hiring managers have been trained in hiring best practices. Thus, it comes as no surprise that they interview poorly. Besides, interviews tend to be lousy indicators of performance.[40] Among the reasons are that even similar work experiences may not be entirely applicable to the position for which the candidate is interviewing. Additionally, hiring manager attribution error, confirmation bias, and psychological projection may be at work in response to cognitive dissonance. Even so, structured interviews across all interviewers are the correct approach.[41] The structure should pose relevant, open-ended, hypothetical questions rooted in likely scenarios, enabling the candidate to respond with analogous examples from past experience. The interviewers should actively listen for cues about directing versus collaborative traits relative to context and time pressure.

When going outside of the talent pipeline to hire, candidate vetting looms paramount. Certain interviewing principles offer utility:

- Train the hiring managers to focus on open-ended questions. Avoid discrete questions that telescope the "correct" answer, e.g., "You don't criticize your employees to their peers, do you?"

- Structure the questions with a hint of TORC (threat of reference check), e.g., "What would your best ally cite as a bad fit for this position?"

- Probing relevant past results are useful—yet not infallible—indicators of future performance.[42]

- Interview questions should be challenging—even tough. Better to scare a candidate away who is uncertain about the fit than experience costly turnover later. This principle is called "vaccination."[43] If the interviewers are blunt, the candidate cannot feign surprise by subsequent reality.

- Interview questions should follow a similar outline. This assures that all interviewers are focused on the same topics.

- Partner with another interviewer to create a tag team. While one asks questions, the other observes. The pair may not hear responses the same way. Moreover, non-verbal cues should be observed.

- Interviewers should use a scoring tool immediately upon concluding the interview to capture impressions while they remain in short-term memory.

- Interviewers should conduct a debriefing to reconcile variations in perspective. This may lead to pursuit of clarifications. This may also influence reference check questions.

Even though reference checks are increasingly difficult to obtain, they should be pursued. Again, a tool is advisable to guide consistency across all references. Finally, a mix of past subordinates, peers, and bosses should be included for three-dimensional perspective. This approach facilitates the vetting process by detecting traits like "managing up" to superiors better than "managing down" to subordinates.

Even if hiring managers land a good person, there may only be a sink or swim onboarding process awaiting the new hire. Onboarding should not be confused with orientation. Whereas orientation covers things like benefits enrollment, policy, and documentation, onboarding acclimates the new hire to the company culture and how the job is done. Unfortunately, this is one of the Achilles' Heals of the middle market that is easily exacerbated by relatively weak human resource leadership. New hire onboarding should be compared to the kid who moved cross-country encountering the first day in a new school. The perspective for developing good onboarding should be that of empathy. A sample of performing veterans should be pinged for their insights rooted in a basic question: Given what you know as a veteran, what do you wish someone had told you upon joining the company. In complement, pairing the new hire with a "buddy" outside of the new hire's chain of command will afford the new hire a safe haven for questions. "Buddies" should be carefully chosen, that is, it should be a point of pride to be a new hire "buddy."

No talent management system is complete without measures. Indeed, human resource measures should be part of the balanced scorecard. Consequently, surveys are a handy tool.[44] Similar to the Net Promoter® score principles employed in other chapters of this book, leaders should want to know that their most talented people would readily recommend the company as a great place to work. This aspirational atmosphere is sometimes called "employer of choice." If this is the case, recruitment channel development is easier. Indeed, happy employees may already be spreading the word throughout their networks using social media tools. If this is not the case, two problems prevail. First, the condition will surely hinder recruitment. Second, the talented people become flight risks.

About Generation Y, The Millennials

> *"Forward, the Light Brigade!"*
> *Was there a man dismay'd ?*
> *Not tho' the soldier knew*
> *Someone had blunder'd:*
> *Theirs not to make reply,*
> *Theirs not to reason why,*

Theirs but to do & die,
Into the valley of Death
Rode the six hundred.[45]

Tennyson was not writing about Generation Y. Whereas "the world runs on individuals pursuing their self-interests,"[46] Gen Yers have their own formulation of the axiom. In 1965, the rock band, The Who, released a song called "My Generation" that *Rolling Stone* magazine named among its 500 Greatest Songs of All Time.[47] The lyrics were among the anthems of Baby Boomers celebrating their difference from their parents: the Greatest Generation. The Boomers are entering retirement. By necessity, they are handing the reins to Generations X and Y. The generation gaps are just as omnipresent between Boomers and their successors as was the case between Greatest and Boomers. The only "revenge" that Boomers may "enjoy" is that the cycle will likely be repeated between Generations Y and Z. The transition mirrors hazing: one does not get even, but he or she may enjoy knowing that their successors "felt their pain."

The Greatest Generation survived a Depression and World War II. They taught faith, frugality, and work ethic to their Boomers (born 1946–1964). However, the Vietnam War undermined the value system. Even so, agency theory inspired Boomers to overcome stagflation and build empires. Along the way, some unexpectedly experienced disillusionment and displacement with the advent of the global economy. Process reengineering, downsizing, and outsourcing inflicted the collateral damage of unemployment. The fact that these actions may have been necessary to save the company was irrelevant. Boomers' kids and grandkids, Generations X (born 1965–1980) and Y's (born 1981–2000), have not experienced economic calamity or the draft—despite numerous limited wars and recessions. However, they reject the lifestyle of their parents and grandparents as enslaved to "the man," only to be RIFed (reduction in force—a euphemism for termination without cause) in a seemingly coldly calculating corporate culture. The X and Y's seek work-life balance and purpose. They do not mind hard work, but they eschew mindless, disconnected hard work on things for which they have no emotional attachment. X and Y's may not be as concerned about downside risk because the entitlement society provides them an unprecedented safety net. However, the deficit spending and accumulating national debt awaiting their payment may place them in the same peril as their grandparents and great grandparents (The Greatest Generation). Until then, there are leadership challenges germane to the corporate legacy.

Before considering how to manage Generations X and Y, it is first helpful to understand the difference in their realities from Boomers at their ages. Keep in mind the points are even more profoundly contrasting between Boomers and Y's than comparison with X's by either:

- The workforce is more gender balanced.

- The workforce is more ethnically diverse—not just in black and white terms, but also in Latino, Asian, and African terms.

- Religious orientation is less pronounced, i.e., more secular.

- Values are different.

- Alternate lifestyles and sexual orientation are more open.

- Office romances are less taboo.

- Parental roles are less traditional and enjoy stronger legal protections, e.g., the Family Leave Act.

- The apex of Maslow's Hierarch of Needs is different, i.e., the operational definition of self-actualization may be more altruistic.

- College degrees are more commonplace, including advanced degrees.

- "The office" may have a virtual definition, enabling telecommuting and flexible hours.

- Jobs change frequently within and across companies, i.e., nomadic mobility.

- Supply chains tend to be at least partially global.

- Expatriate assignments are more commonplace.

- Position authority is challenged by an ability mindset, i.e., title infallibility is non sequitur.

- Independent problem-solving is more pronounced.

- Technology is omnipresent and changes very rapidly.

- Information, i.e., intangibles, is a more common ecosystem variable than widgets, i.e., tangibles.

- Achievement, collaboration, cooperation, recognition, nature of the assignments, responsibility, advancement, and personal growth are emphasized.[48]

Gen Yers may find open organizational design particularly appealing. "An open system is one that interacts with its environment: it draws input from external sources and transforms it into some form of output."[49] Gen Yers are the antithesis of the "organizational man."[50] Accordingly, leaders should consciously make leadership choices to avoid common Generation Y supervisory mistakes:[51]

- Do not take them for granted. [52]

- Avoid extrapolating their past to stereotype their future. They tend to bore easily and enjoy variety.

- Emphasize personal development through assignments, coaching, and mentoring. Consciously develop their strengths. [53]

- Challenge them with stretch assignments. Approach policies as guidelines instead of directives. Exceptions are warranted for high-potential incumbents.[54]

- Do not expect martyrdom for a greater good. Remember, it did not do their parents any good.

In order to attract, inspire, and retain Gen Y talent, effective leaders may, of necessity, resemble chameleons who change color relative to the ecosystem requirements. This is one of the prices paid for accomplishing the legacy effect. Not only is this leadership dexterity necessary for the "present state" organization, but it is also necessary to model the chameleon qualities to the next generation of leadership. Who knows what they will encounter?

One possible way to bridge the gap is mentoring and reverse mentoring. Indeed, this technique addresses a Gen Y blind spot: wisdom. Whereas Gen Ys often come with impeccable skills-based credentials, they may simply lack certain life experiences that correlate more strongly with age. Although Gen Ys may not experience the exact scenario shared by a Boomer, they may draw upon useful leadership principles in analogous encounters. Mentoring and reverse mentoring plays on the leader-follower dynamics discussed in Chapter 4: The DNA of Packs.

Whereas Gen Y's may have an interest in the tacit knowledge accumulated in a Boomer's experiences, the Boomer may have reciprocal interest in the Y's explicit technology expertise, for example, social media. This is a synergistic form of win-win. The point is that good leaders must make the first move, even if vulnerability is demonstrated in the process. The legacy effect is teaching the emerging leadership generation a methodology for analysis, implementation, and monitoring toward their personalized strategic configurations of people, processes, and tools.

Endnotes

1   Whitman, W. (1855). Poem of many in one. In Waldrip, M.C. (Gen. Ed.) and Pine, J.T. (Ed.). (2007). *Leaves of Grass: The original 1855 edition*. (Dover Thrifts ed.). Mineola, NY: Dover Publications. Retrieved from http://www.whitmanarchive.org/published/LG/1856/poems/8. p. 181.

2   Ronald Reagan quotes. (n.d.). BrainyQuotes.com. Retrieved from http://www.brainyquote. com/quotes/quotes/r/ronaldreag183976.html#7g5E3FxOOtxS5xSU.99

3   Canton, J. (2007) *The extreme future: The top trends that will reshape the world for the next 5, 10, and 20 years*. New York, NY: Plume.

4   Fernández-Aráoz, C., Groysberg, B. and Nohria, N. (2011). How to hang on to your high potentials. *Harvard Business Review, 89*(10), 78–9.

5   Machiavelli, N. (1994). *The prince*. New York: Barnes & Noble. p. 71.

6   O'Neil, J.R. (1993). *The paradox of success: A book of renewal for leaders*. New York: Penguin Putnam Books. (ISBN0–87477–772–0). pp. 14–5.

7   Drucker, P. (1985). *Innovation and entrepreneurship*. New York: HarperCollins. (ISBN: 9780060851132). pp. 55–6.

8   100 best quotes on leadership (Jack Welch). *Forbes*. Retrieved from http://www.forbes.com/sites/ kevinkruse/2012/10/16/quotes-on-leadership/

9   Bennis, W. and Nanus, B. (1985). *Leaders: The strategies for taking charge*. New York: Harper & Row. p. 2.

[10] Rothwell, W. (2010). *Effective succession planning: Ensuring leadership continuity and building talent from within* (4th ed.). New York: Amacom. (ISBN: 9780814414163). p. 12.

[11] Tichy, N.M. and Bennis, W.G. (2007). *Judgment: How winning leaders make great calls.* New York, NY: Penguin Group.

[12] Daft, R.L. (2007). *Organization theory and design* (9th ed.). Mason, OH: Thomson South-Western. p. 301.

[13] Ibid.

[14] Gladwell. M. (2009). *What the dog saw and other adventures.* New York: Little, Brown, and Company.

[15] Watkins, M.D. (2007, June). Help newly hired executives adapt quickly. *Harvard Business Review, 85*(6), 26–30.

[16] Byham, W.C. (n.d.). Strong start to job success. *Development Dimensions International.* Retrieved from http://www.ddiworld.com/pdf/strongstarttojobsuccess_wp_ddi.pdf

[17] Christensen, C.M., Roth, E.A. and Anthony, S.D. (2004). *Seeing what's next: Using theories of innovation to predict industry change.* Boston: Harvard Business School Press.

[18] Kelly, T. and Littman, J. (2000). *The art of innovation: Success through innovation the IDEO way.* New York: Currency.

[19] Dyer, J., Gregersen, H. and Christensen, C.M. (2011). *The innovator's DNA: Mastering the five skills of disruptive innovators.* Boston, MA: Harvard Business School Publishing. (ISBN: 9781422134818); Kahneman, D. (2011). *Thinking fast and slow.* New York, NY: Farrar, Straus, and Giroux.

[20] Khurana, R. (2002) *Searching for a corporate savior: The irrational quest for charismatic CEOs.* Princeton, NJ: Princeton Press. (ISBN0: 691074372)

[21] Ibid.

[22] Gladwell (2009). p. 362

[23] Garvin, D.A. and Levesque, L.C. (2008). The multiunit enterprise. *Harvard Business Review, 86*(6), 117.; Conaty & Charan (2010).

[24] Gladwell (2009). p. 275.

[25] Peter, L. and Hull, R. (1969). *The Peter principle: Why things always go wrong*. New York: William Morrow & Company.

[26] Livingston, J.S. (2009). *Pygmalion in management*. Boston, MA: Harvard Business School Press.

[27] Gladwell (2009). p. 269.

[28] Confucius quotes. (n.d.). *BrainyQuote.com* Retrieved from http://www.brainyquote.com/quotes/quotes/c/confucius134717.html

[29] Shawitz, D.A. (2011, October 19). Desperately seeking talent. *The Wall Street Journal: Life and Culture.* Retrieved from http://online.wsj.com/article/SB1000142405311190426550457656515311 6078830.html?mod=opinion_newsreel

[30] Gladwell (2009). p. 363.

[31] Rothwell (2010).

[32] Ibid.

[33] Ivancevich, J.M. (2007). *Human resource management* (10th ed.). New York, NY: McGraw-Hill Irwin. p. 253.

[34] Quotes about planning: Benjamin Franklin. (n.d.). *Goodreads.com*. Retrieved from http://www.goodreads.com/quotes/tag/planning

[35] Martin, J. and Schmidt, C. (2010). How to keep your top talent. *Harvard Business Review, 88*(5), 54–61.

[36] Rothwell (2010). p. 237.

[37] Welch, J. (2005). *Winning*. New York: HarperCollins.

[38] Heath, C. and Heath, D. (2013). *Decisive: How to make better choices in life and work*. New York: Crown.

[39] Hannibal quotes. (n.d.). *Goodreads*. Retrieved from http://www.goodreads.com/quotes/65178-we-will-either-find-a-way-or-make-one

40 Heath and Heath (2013); Sullivan, J. (2011, March 25). 20 reasons why weak managers never hire A-talent. *Ere.net*. Retrieved from http://www.ere.net/2011/03/25/20-reasons-why-weak-managers-never-hire-a-level-talent/

41 Gladwell (2009). pp. 390–1; Duhigg, C. (2012). *The power of habit: Why we do what we do in life and business*. New York: Random House.

42 Smart, B.A. (1999). *Topgrading: How leading companies win by hiring, coaching, and keeping the best people*. Paramus, NJ: Prentice Hall.

43 Heath and Heath (2013).

44 SHRM research spotlight: Workplace flexibility in the 21st century. (n.d.). *Society for Human Resource Management*. Retrieved from http://www.shrm.org/Research/SurveyFindings/Documents/10-WorkFlexFlier_FINAL_Spotlight.pdf

45 Tennyson, A. (1854). *The charge of the light brigade*. Retrieved from http://www.nationalcenter.org/ChargeoftheLightBrigade.html

46 Milton Friedman quotes. (n.d.). *BrainyQuote.com* Retrieved from http://www.brainyquote.com/quotes/quotes/m/miltonfrie412621.html

47 Townshend, P. (1965). *My Generation*. [Recorded by The Who]. On *My Generation* [LP]. New York: Decca.

48 What Gen Y women want: Autonomy and self-direction. (2011, April 26). *Society for Human Resource Management*. Retrieved from http://www.shrm.org/hrdisciplines/benefits/articles/pages/genywomen.aspx; Libert (2010); Gurchiek, K. (2009, November 10). Gen Y poses unique management challenges. *Society for Human Resource Management*. Retrieved from http://www.shrm.org/hrdisciplines/employeerelations/articles/pages/genychallenges.aspx; Ivancevich (2007). p. 443; Kehrli, S. and Sopp, T. (2006, May 1). HR magazine: Managing generationY. *Society for Human Resource Management*. Retrieved from http://www.shrm.org/publications/hrmagazine/editorialcontent/pages/0506managementtools.aspx; Harris, P. (2005, May). Boomer vs. echo booker: The work war. *T+D*, *59*(5)44–49; Wallace, J. (2001, April). After X comes Y. *HR Magazine*, *46*(4), 192.

49 Nadler, D. and Tushman, M. (1997). *Competing by design: The power of organizational architecture*. New York: Oxford University Press. p. 26.

50 Whyte, W. (1956). *The organization man*. Simon & Schuster: New York, NY.

[51]   Martin and Schmidt (2010). p. 57.

[52]   Ibid.

[53]   Burkus, D. (2011). Building the strong organization: Exploring the role of organizational design in strengths-based leadership. *Journal of Strategic Leadership*, 3(1), 54–66.

[54]   Lawler III, E.E., Pringle, A., Branham, F., Cornelius, J. and Martin, J. (2008). Why are we losing all our good people? *Harvard Business Review*, 86(6), 45.

Chapter 11
Wrapping It Up

*… Somewhere ages and ages hence: Two roads diverged in a wood, and
I, I took the one less traveled by, And that has made all the difference.*[1]

Winston Churchill observed that "success is not final, failure is not fatal; it is the courage to continue that counts."[2] During the worst of the blitz during World War II, Churchill rallied his countrymen with "never, never, never give up!"[3] Zig Ziglar offers three complementary points:

- "Remember that failure is an event, not a person."

- "If you learn from defeat, you haven't really lost."

- "Your attitude, not your aptitude, will determine your altitude."[4]

This does not mean attempting the impossible by trying to please everyone. Aesop chided "Please all and you will please none."[5] Indeed, organizations cannot please all prospects and turn them into customers. Nor can leaders please all prospective or existing employees. While highly fulfilling, leadership may be lonely amid tough decisions. The principles of this book are offered to assist leaders in finding a sweet spot whereby people, processes, and tools are configured to satisfy a growing target market of profitable customers with a motivated pack of inspired professionals.

Jeff Bezos, CEO of Amazon.com, makes a compelling argument to approach customer relations from the perspective that it is always a day one proposition, that is, loyalty is earned daily.[6] This is a good thing. However, "customer" should be interpreted more broadly, and perhaps reframed as stakeholders. In this regard, followers are included as a leader's customers with whom he or she should desire mutually fulfilling relationships. Today provides the opportunity to learn from our past experiences and acquired knowledge in order to improve subsequent execution toward something competitively differentiable.

Leaders are not reckless. Neither are they timid. Plato taught, "Courage is knowing what not to fear."[7] Shakespeare put his spin on the point in *Julius Caesar*: "Cowards die many times before their deaths. The valiant never taste of death but once."[8] Why end such a good book with seeming downers? Reality! People learn more from setbacks than successes. The celebrities of success made plenty of mistakes. Their mistakes just do not tend to get as much coverage. Press coverage of stumbles tends to be reserved for those of cataclysmic proportions, for example, Enron. Revisiting Charles Handy's depiction of the business cycle as a sigmoid curve is a useful prop. (See Figure 6.4 in Chapter 6: Innovation and Value-creation.) Handy admonishes leaders to plot their organizations on the curve for perspective. The position along the curve should compel leaders to react and address any inherent threats to the organization.[9] Decisions resulting from this examination might include markets, products, organizational design, and employee behaviors.[10]

> So that the record of history is absolutely crystal clear, there is no alternative way, so far discovered, of improving the lot of the ordinary people that can hold a candle to the productive activities that are unleashed by a free enterprise system.[11]

In this regard, the private equity industry and its portfolio companies are standard bearers for demonstrating the value-creating potential of middle market companies whose leaders are scaling efficient, innovative, profitable business models. Private equity firms have fiduciary responsibilities to create value for the limited partners of their funds. C-level leaders have the same obligations for their shareholders; however, the dynamic changes once the private equity firm controls the board. Each party has leadership challenges in isolation, as well as interactively. Since no two investment experiences are identical, each investment scenario adds to the pool of knowledge. Professionals in both camps should embrace this perspective.

Everything the private equity firm does brands the firm to its limited partners, lenders, vendors, prospects, portfolio companies, investment bankers, intermediaries, and potential buyers. Similarly, everything the portfolio company does brands the organization to its supply chain stakeholders. When both parties espouse leadership excellence, they are laying a foundation for a good return on investment. Both parties should resolve to brand themselves with the leadership excellence commitment, seasoned by the odyssey of continual improvement. This quest always entails the alchemy of people, process, and tools relative to growth, efficiency, and culture. Along the way, decisions and actions should be tempered with the serenity prayer: "God, grant me the serenity to accept the things I cannot change, courage to change the things I can, and wisdom to know the difference."[12]

Let's revisit the major points of this book to recognize where private equity investment teams and their portfolio companies can make an even bigger difference to the economy than they already do. During diligence, complement the existing rigor in three additional areas:

- Scrutinize IT systems for their ability to meet the needs of a much larger company. Think in terms of three times the size of the company you are buying.

- Develop a perspective on how activity-based costing would challenge standard costing for customer and SKU profitability.

- Observe governance in terms of key business model processes and their "owners" for clues about the way the place runs when visitors go home.

The point was earlier made that private equity abides by more consistent diligence discipline than it does in post-cost value creation best practices. This fact begs corrective action. The opportunities are deceptively simple. Think of them as the "Value-creation 10 Commandments."

- Approach the post-close actions analogous to acquisition integration best practices, i.e., start planning before the close. The effort is worth the risk even if the deal does not close.

- Within 30 days of closing the deal, take the C-levels and the "owners" of the major business model processes through a strategic planning rigor—in an off-site setting. The investment team should participate. The objective is transferring ownership of the investment thesis from the firm to the company. Use tools in the planning exercise that challenge all conventional wisdom of diligence. Be prepared to confirm some diligence, complement some diligence, clarify some diligence, refute some diligence, and identify absolute misses of diligence.

- Codify the purpose, vision, and values that will be anchored in the performance management system and institutionalized in all company activities.

- Identify no more than three strategic initiatives for concurrent execution. If more than three are identified in the planning off-site, prioritize them and execute them iteratively. Spread the initiatives across growth, efficiency, and cultural categories. Support them with project management rigor. Anchor them in the performance management system. Include progress reports in the quarterly board packages.

- Rethink marketing and sales as complementary peers in strategic and tactical terms, respectively. Figure out how Net Promoter® philosophy applies to the business model. Train the sales professionals in a methodology—not to be confused with product training.

- Resolve to measure the right stuff. Put it in the hands of people who can use those measures to create value through growth, efficiency, and culture. Make it part of the dashboard metrics and performance management system.

- Adopt an organizational design that encourages innovation. Protect innovation from the corporate antibodies. Assure that the measurements make sense to innovative objectives. Such "sense" is as unique to a business model as fingerprints are to individuals.

- Assure that employees are regarded as assets instead of expenses. Commit to developing a talent magnet business model that can sustain attrition without disruption. This is the essence of leadership, i.e., creating a place than runs smoothly without the boss.

- Promote a culture that does not punish reasonable mistakes, but rather learns from them. Take time to celebrate success.

- Prioritize communication so that the organization is informed. Adopt a communications plan to optimize the messaging configuration.

This book ends with specific reference to values. Middle Market Methods™ routinely included them as one of the foundational elements of its Value-creation Roadmap™. Values, or philosophy, determine how organizations approach value-creation. This is particularly relevant as businesses expand around the globe and beyond the line of sight of the home office. Organizations simply must know how their employees will behave. Similarly, employees must know the consequences of violating ethical principles.

Values espousal may be more complicated than it may seem. First, individuals have a personal set of values. So do companies. The values of the individual need not be identical to the organization; however, they must be compatible. In all likelihood, they at least partially overlap. Keep in mind that "organization" includes both the private equity firm and the portfolio company. Just as the respective employees and organizations must jibe, so to must the two organizations (the private equity firm and the portfolio company).

Private equity professionals and prospective portfolio companies apply considerable resources toward transaction consummation that becomes a sunk cost if the deal does not close. A single portfolio company has limited influence over changing a private equity firm's values. Going the other way, the private equity firm does have such leverage—at least partially. Since it controls the board, the private equity firm could replace leadership. However, this oversimplifies the difficulty of rewiring the portfolio company's organizational culture. Realistically, this is a protracted challenge. Disengagement is the wise call should either party detect values conflict with improbable resolution. Indeed, it is the ethical thing to do. When value-creation philosophies are aligned, the private equity firm and its portfolio company may engage all strategic challenges the same as two ballroom dancers gliding across the floor. Each anticipates the other's moves and trusts the outcome of the dance. This is when value-creation is fun.

"Paying attention to simple little things that most [people] neglect makes a few [people] rich."[13] In my observations (which cannot be more specific due to non-disclosure agreements), those who have embraced the principles discussed in this book tend to be rewarded with higher relative exit multiples. Again, this is because the firm and the portfolio company resolved to identify and execute accretive initiatives. Relative to scalability, the buyer derives some comfort that value-creation impediments were addressed, thus mitigating investment risk. Consider the math. Suppose a portfolio company tripled its EBITDA during the hold period from $10 million to $30 million. Assuming a modest six times exit, the enterprise value on would be $180 million (six times $30 million). An extra half turn to a 6.5 times multiple is a bonus of $15 million. Is it worth the investment in best practices? Let's take the converse position of eschewing value-creation best practices. Do you think it coincidental that the book ends with Chapter 11? Borrowing from Fox News, "We report. You decide."

"Whenever you see a successful business, someone once made a courageous decision."[14] Good hunting!

Endnotes

1   Frost, R. (1920). *Mountain interval*. New York, NY: Henry Holt and Company.

2   Winston Churchill quotes. (n.d.). *BrainyQuote.com* Retrieved from http://www.brainyquote.com/quotes/authors/w/winston_churchill.html

3   Ibid.

4   Zig Ziglar quotes. (n.d.). *BrainyQuote.com* Retrieved from http://www.brainyquote.com/quotes/authors/z/zig_ziglar.html

5   Aesop quotes. (n.d.). *BrainyQuote.com* Retrieved from http://www.brainyquote.com/quotes/authors/a/aesop.html

6   Brandt, R.L. (2012). *One click: Jeff Bezos and the rise of Amazon.com*. New York: Penguin.

7   Plato quotes. (n.d.). *BrainyQuote.com* Retrieved from http://www.brainyquote.com/quotes/quotes/p/plato104744.html

8   Shakespeare, W. (2012). *Julius Caesar*. New York: Empire. Act 2, scene 2, p. 33.

9   Handy, C. (1995). *The age of paradox*. Boston, MA: The Harvard Business School Press. pp. 50–6.

10   Ibid.

11   Donohue. T. (2012, August 6). Free enterprise: The life and legacy of Milton Friedman. *Free Enterprise*. Retrieved from http://www.freeenterprise.com/free-enterprise-life-and-legacy-milton-friedman

12   Serenity prayer. (n.d.). *Beliefnet*. Retrieved from http://www.beliefnet.com/Prayers/Protestant/Addiction/Serenity-Prayer.aspx

13   Henry Ford quotes. (n.d.). *Thinkexist.com*. Retrieved from http://thinkexist.com/quotation/paying-attention-to-simple-little-things-that/1022900.html

14   Peter Drucker quotes. (n.d.). *The quotations page*. Retrieved from http://www.quotationspage.com/quotes/Peter_Drucker/

Index